[*In Beyond the Obvious: Doorways to Understanding the New Testament,*] Dale Walker has written an engaging, insightful collection of essays that offers a fresh way to introduce the historical study of the New Testament to students of the Bible. With clarity and brevity, each essay explores a critical observation to open up historical analysis of the New Testament for the reader. Each essay is accessible to the nonspecialist and offers an ideal prompt for classroom discussion. This book is an excellent guide through the historical complexity of the production of the texts that came to be included in the New Testament.

—Christopher Mount
DePaul University

Dale Walker's new book, *Beyond the Obvious: Doorways to Understanding the New Testament*, represents an introduction to the New Testament unlike any other. Rather than outlining and analyzing each New Testament text, Walker begins each of the seven chapters of the work with an observation about the New Testament. Walker then goes "beyond the obvious" to explore the ramifications of the observation. . . . Walker's book meets students where they are intellectually, and it sensitively leads them to a point where they can begin their own exploration of the New Testament texts. . . .

—Paul B. Duff
George Washington University

Beyond the Obvious: Doorways to Understanding the New Testament provides reliable, incisive treatments of classic problems of scholarship. But it does this while also modeling the sort of creative, sustained development of basic premises that professors want to see. . . . [This book] should be ideal not only for generating classroom discussion but for anyone looking for an accessible guide to what the historical study of the New T̲—̲ all about.

̲n-McCabe
University

Author Acknowledgments

I would like to thank a number of people who helped in the creation of this book, beginning with the talented people at Anselm Academic: Jerry Ruff, Bradley Harmon, Maura Hagarty, Penny Koehler, Paul Peterson, and Beth Erickson. I appreciate the interest in this project shown by the editorial staff and the countless, helpful suggestions they made. I am also grateful for the commitment of Anselm Academic to promote effective teaching and communication about the Bible.

The book would never have come about without conversation partners. Thank you to Paul Flesher-McCracken (University of Wyoming) for his encouragement when the project was just an idea, and for his insights and comments along the way. Thanks also are due to James C. Hanges (Miami University of Ohio), Matt Jackson-McCabe (Cleveland State University), and Christopher N. Mount (DePaul University) for comments directly related to this book and the years of conversations that inform it. Friends Joel Newton and Margo Schwartz-Newton kindly read the manuscript and provided insightful feedback. The book's shortcomings remain my own, but I am grateful for the many contributions colleagues and friends have made to improve it.

Lastly, I wish to thank my wife Eileen Ielmini for her unstinting support and encouragement in my undertaking of this project and seeing it through to completion. The library books will now be returned, eliminating the clutter around the house.

Publisher Acknowledgments

Thank you to the following individuals who reviewed this work in progress:

Jenny L. DeVivo,
Loyola University, Chicago, Illinois

James Riley Strange,
Samford University, Birmingham, Alabama

BEYOND THE OBVIOUS

DOORWAYS TO UNDERSTANDING THE NEW TESTAMENT

DONALD DALE WALKER

Created by the publishing team of Anselm Academic.

Cover image royalty free from *www.shutterstock.com*

The scriptural quotations contained herein are from the New Revised Standard Version of the Bible (unless otherwise noted). Copyright © 1993 and 1989 by the Division of Christian Education of the National Council of the Churches of Christ in the United States of America. All rights reserved.

Printed in the United States of America

7061

ISBN 978-1-59982-271-6

CONTENTS

CONVENTIONS AND ABBREVIATIONS

The essays in this volume quote the New Revised Standard Version of the English Bible (NRSV), unless indicated otherwise.

Style note from the author: In these essays, *gospel* is spelled with an uppercase letter when it indicates one or more of the canonical Gospels, that is, Matthew, Mark, Luke, or John, whereas *gospel* is used in these three instances: to reference the noncanonical gospels (except when part of the title), the written genre of gospel, or a spoken message of salvation. Thus, Matthew wrote a Gospel, the *Gospel of Mary* is a noncanonical gospel, gospels are sometimes referred to as a type of biography, and Paul preached the gospel. This differentiation of *Gospel* and *gospel* is standard style, and although it aligns with the historical trend, it is prejudicial with respect to the canonical and noncanonical gospels. From the perspective of canon, the canonical Gospels are more special. But, from the point of view of the historian, this approach to capitalization skews how things unfolded and the importance of the noncanonical gospels.

KJV   King James Version
LXX   Septuagint
NRSV   New Revised Standard Version
REB   Revised English Bible

Introduction

As best that I can tell, I have never met anyone who has not heard of the Bible. No student in any of the classes I have taught was discovering it for the first time. When standing before a room of undergraduates to introduce them to the New Testament, the challenge has always been to figure out what level of knowledge they have in order to target instruction appropriately.

To help with this, I administer a simple quiz on the first day of class. (No, it is not a factor in a student's grade.) I emphasize that it is simple, yet less than 1 percent of students ace it. The questions, I think, are transparent, assuming one knows anything about the Bible. For example, name a modern country in which events recorded in the New Testament occurred. Or, in what century did the events in the New Testament take place? Or, how many Gospels are there in the New Testament? It turns out the answers are not as obvious as I thought.

After asking how many Gospels there are, I ask students to name them. This has become my favorite question. Some students rattle them right off: Matthew, Mark, Luke, and John. At some point in childhood, they may have earned a candy bar for memorizing that. Others, without this training, stare blankly; but a few think for a moment and then write. These are the ones I call on to answer. These students think of a couple of names, while some come up with all four: John, Matthew, Luke, and Mark—or some other random order. I love that the information is there but is not as neatly organized as it is for those of us who memorized the canonical list. These students have a familiarity that comes from experience, not memorization.

The first time I heard all four Gospels named but not in "correct" order, I was dumbfounded. The student knew them, but not as a preprogrammed sequence. The student evidenced an interaction with

Christian scripture wholly different from mine. I suspect a further difference existed between us. I think of Matthew, Mark, Luke, and John as texts, growing up as I did in unadorned, "Bible-believing" churches. What if I had grown up with statues, stained-glass windows, and other religious art? Might I instead think of the Evangelists as people? People who exist in no prescribed order?

I give this quiz on the first day of class simply to orient myself to the students whom I am about to teach, and it turns into a teachable moment for all of us. The questions, we discover, are not as simple as they seem at first blush.

Take the question about the century in which New Testament events take place. The expected answer is the first century CE. Thinking it was so easy, I was embarrassed even to put that question on the quiz. I was wrong. Few undergraduates recognize the calendar as a cultural and historical artifact. The question, however, is not as straightforward as it might seem, because Jesus was born during the reign of Herod the Great who died in 4 BCE. At the other end of the time line, many scholars date some of the documents in the New Testament to the second century CE, so the New Testament reflects three centuries. The point is, the answers to some seemingly simple questions prove complex, not as obvious as they first appear, providing an opportunity for deeper consideration.

Simple questions are often the most consequential. For example, how many Gospels are there? The lion's share of New Testament scholarship in the twentieth century, and especially after World War II, devoted itself to answering this question. Well, let me qualify that. Scholars expended their energy on investigating the implications of the question, as will I in chapters four and six. *This book demonstrates that what seems so obvious and straightforward is, upon reflection, a way of entering into some of the most important questions about the New Testament*—and consequently the early church and Christianity.

A Word to Readers

There are different ways to introduce the New Testament. One kind of book surveys its content, providing summaries of each of its twenty-seven books with interpretive comments. Another focuses on the issues of each text's origin: authorship, date, location, and other questions. Typically these volumes are analytical, breaking down each question into a distinct item for discussion, while some weave the many questions into a larger narrative about Christian origins. Most run to many hundreds of pages.

This book takes a different direction and adopts the essay form to discuss multiple texts in the New Testament in an integrated manner. Individual matters of biblical interpretation do not stand as isolated points of analysis but add up to something larger, as expressed by the titles of every chapter. The titles are not clever enticements or simple topics but actual theses—that is, they make a case for something—such as chapter 6, "There Are More Than Four Gospels." Each title is a propositional sentence, stating a premise or argument that the corresponding essay attempts to expand on and make meaningful.

The desired outcome for the reader is to learn seven basic propositions about the New Testament. The thesis of each essay points the reader to something important. I want the reader to get more than a list of names and dates. I want the reader to gain ideas that link many documents in the New Testament. Together, the essays will help orient the reader to the academic reading of the New Testament and provide a foundation for examining other issues, such as the historical Jesus or the development of Christian morality.

These essays, like most academic writing on the Bible, may surprise the reader. They do not provide advice about how to live, do not offer life-affirming encouragement, do not provide guidance on how to approach the New Testament devotionally or for worship. Instead, they reflect the academic discourse about the Christian scriptures, particularly as this conversation has evolved in the last two centuries.

The academic enterprise is ecumenical. People from many branches of Christianity participate in it, certainly from Catholicism and mainline Protestants. Students may be surprised to listen in on these conversations. What they will find are not the confident answers they may have expected but many more questions and options. With every good question scholars ask, multiple competing answers emerge.

The essays in this book reflect a conversation between scholarship and the author. I try to represent the broad stream of scholarship as much as possible and not idiosyncratic views, yet at times, I side with a minority point of view. For example:

1. I think the Gospel according to Luke and the Acts of the Apostles were written in the second century, a later date than the vast majority of scholars. I tried to avoid making this opinion the linchpin of any arguments in these essays.

2. I agree with the majority of scholars that the same person wrote Luke and Acts. However, scholars have been challenging this, arguing that different people wrote them. I do not think they have won the day—yet—but even this once seemingly safe view now encounters dissent.

3. As I read the Gospel of John, I detect allusions to the traditions associated with the other three Gospels. This is probably a minority point of view, but the tides of scholarship have gone back and forth on the question of the influence on John's Gospel by the other three, with a range of options between yes and no.

4. I think that the Gospel of John was written earlier than Luke. This is certainly an idiosyncratic view. Nothing in the essays to follow depends on that, so it will just be an eccentricity.

5. I do reflect the consensus in scholarship that there was an early document (called Q) that contained sayings of Jesus, a document used in the writing of the Gospels of Matthew and Luke. I admit, however, that I have moments when I question whether this hypothesis is one of the brilliant gains of scholarship or just an amazing house of cards, ready to collapse with one incisive insight. Though I fear that attempts to identify the stages of Q's evolution involve skating on thin ice, I have presented this, for it represents the current state of the scholarly conversation about Q. Meanwhile, on the other end of the spectrum, a number of scholars, though still a minority, think the author of Luke knew and used Matthew's Gospel, which makes Q irrelevant.

6. It may surprise readers to learn that most scholars harbor suspicions about surface claims made by the New Testament, especially where authorship is concerned. In my opinion, a minority

of letters in the New Testament were written by the alleged authors. While I have lots of good company in my suspicions, many scholars are less skeptical. These are questions that make an enormous impact on one's views of early Christian history. One cannot really paper over the differences in responses.

7. Chapter 5 presents an argument that the "beloved disciple" mentioned in John's Gospel is Lazarus. This is a decidedly minority position but is presented because of the problem it introduces for the traditional view of John's authorship.

8. Most problematic, the theory that "the Gospels are anonymous" is neither obvious nor easily or widely accepted. So, I have provided one thesis that the reader will have to think about with caution.

These issues could easily have made for sidebars and lengthy footnotes, but such would undermine the goal of focusing on larger themes and examining them from a variety of angles in a reasonable amount of time. I hope that, as this text is read in classes, readers raise questions and discover that their teachers have still other views.

My advice while reading is simple: keep moving, and try to see the whole. The reader should also understand that the essays are indeed idiosyncratic in their organization. There is no rigidly right or wrong way to elaborate on any of the themes in this volume. Their composition is entirely an act of rhetorical invention, and that very enterprise created moments of discovery and insight for me. If the reader starts rearranging the parts and adjusting points of emphasis, additional learning might take place. All the better.

If after finishing this book, the reader can recite seven basic observations about the New Testament (things one should recognize from the start) and understand their consequences, then I will consider this book a success. But it is only a beginning. Interest in the New Testament likely arises from curiosity about what Jesus taught, the nature of Christian faith, or the origins of Christianity. These essays will not resolve those questions, which can easily consume a lifetime of investigation but will provide information and perspectives to inform their discussion. The seven theses will help anchor and guide further reflection.

A Word to Teachers

This book represents five challenges to me as a teacher. These include (1) making knowledge meaningful, while (2) making the effort to learn manageable, and (3) striving for brevity. At the same time, I want to contribute to students' general education, helping them (4) to improve their written communication and (5) become more creative. Though the content will necessarily focus on early Christianity, I want students (and readers) to become better thinkers, writers, and innovators.

As to the first challenge, dates and lists are easy things to put on a test and easy things to grade. But do they matter? I can ask students, "In what language was the New Testament written?" But (1) do I have any *meaningful* reason for doing so? The essays in this volume attempt to elevate simple observations into meaningful ones, turning rote, fill-in-the-blank questions into clues that lead to synthetic knowledge and consequential insights, so that knowing obvious and basic facts about the New Testament leads to broader understanding.

Beyond this main objective of making the basic meaningful, this book addresses additional pedagogical concerns. Introducing the New Testament creates a struggle between an analytical approach that breaks everything down into individual, isolated questions of dates, authors, locations, etc., and a broader sweep that creates a narrative thread. These essays reflect a compromise. Each focuses on a single, very specific observation but then attempts to weave together many interpretive judgments to create a broader, more integrated perspective. I like to think of these (2) as *manageable* bites that help organize information so it can build into larger, more complex questions. The reader will not finish this book with a comprehensive view of the origin and content of the New Testament but will know seven crucial observations that apply to these narratives.

In addition to trying to make a sea of data digestible, this book (3) strives for *brevity*. It will be brief, so individuals can finish it quickly, and groups can read and discuss it in seven or fewer weeks. This, too, reflects my experiences teaching. A brilliant book that goes unread serves no purpose. Seven manageable bites, chewed and digested, can lead to real learning. To be sure, more than seven simple, fundamental observations could be made. Others come to mind, and readers may wonder why their favorite is missing. But brevity here will permit readers to move on to other things, especially the actual reading of the biblical books.

Another objective I have as a teacher in this volume is to contribute to students' general education. For this reason, (4) I have written *essays*. Apart from discussions in class, essays are a fundamental way students communicate with teachers. Putting these essays in front of students provides an opportunity to talk about the writing of essays, a contribution, I hope, to general education as well as the particular course.

These essays will also contribute to students' general education by noting (5) examples of *creativity* within the New Testament and among those who interpret it. One way of becoming more creative is to recognize how others have done it and build a vocabulary for talking about it. The creative arts do this. Designers, for example, habitually talk about ideating, reframing, iterating, and prototyping. Books such as Vijay Kumar's *101 Design Methods* and *The Ten Types of Innovation* by Lawrence Keeley wonderfully open one's eyes to possible ways of approaching creative action. These essays will point to examples of creativity on the part of biblical authors and critics to add to students' ideas about innovation.

The essays also reflect my own exercise in creative thinking. In the first, I consciously use an analogy as a creative device and, in the book's concluding remarks, explicitly reflect on how Christians—ancient and modern—exercised creativity in the production and interpretation of the New Testament. In between, each essay is an exercise in rhetorical invention. Each could follow a different path than it does and, in fact, did during the course of writing and revising. The final result reflects a persistent dissatisfaction that kept me asking, "So what?" Anyone can memorize the names of the four canonical Gospels and repeat that information on a test. This remains a nearly mindless task unless someone asks a question. By asking, "So what?" over and over, I was able to see where the answers led and where I might take them.

The New Testament
Is a Library

Centuries of history have made it easy to refer to the Bible as a single book or to the New Testament as a single entity that may be printed independently of the Bible. But there was a time when none of this was possible, for the Christian scriptures are comprised of many independent documents written at different times by different people. For centuries, this was recognized by calling the church's collection of sacred writings *bibliotheca*, Latin for library. The English language extends this habit, labeling its sacred texts as the Bible, which derives ultimately from the Greek word for books, *biblia*. Our reflections on the New Testament, then, begin with a general observation about its construction: The New Testament is a library, both literally and figuratively. Recognizing this points to its origin, structure, and content, while hinting at its use.

The New Testament Is a Library

Imagine a shelf with a number of rolls of paper towels lying on it. Now, imagine that these rolls of paper towels have stories written on them, from beginning to end. If we step back in time two thousand years, this is similar to what a household library would look like—not a shelf with books lined up along it, but rather, a shelf with a collection of scrolls stacked two or three deep. Whatever is put on that shelf becomes part of one's library.

If we could step inside the home of a wealthy, early Christian, we might find such a shelf or perhaps a basket with a dozen scrolls, maybe even a book. This tiny collection represents a step toward what would become the New Testament. Yet, if we could look closer at this imaginary shelf, we might also find a scroll containing the writings of the prophet Isaiah or the Psalms. Maybe a copy of Homer and a play by Euripides would be there as well. Perhaps the earliest collectors differentiated Christian texts from others, or perhaps they intermingled Christian, Jewish, and other writings. The possibility that Christian texts could grow into a distinct collection would not have been clear.

Before reaching a point where one can speak of a New Testament, a corpus of Christian writings had to exist, which one could collect and begin to differentiate. Once distinctions were made, these early collections could be considered libraries, albeit tiny ones. The individual writings collected were not a series of texts composed to create a multipart whole. Though many relationships exist among early Christian writings, by and large, each of the twenty-seven books that came to comprise the New Testament could stand on its own.

In fact, many of the documents did just that. When Paul wrote the first letter to the Christians in Thessalonica, the letter arrived alone. The church in Thessalonica did not have other letters by Paul to compare or read along with it. They had the one and only letter, which they read only with their sense of the circumstances surrounding it.

Christians in the city of Corinth, similarly, had only the first letter when it arrived. Oddly, this first letter was not what is known today as 1 Corinthians. When they received subsequent letters from Paul, they could then have made comparisons between the two, then three, then four, and so on—and did so. Even visiting preachers read them. The Corinthians might also have had quick access to letters Paul wrote to other churches, specifically his letter to Christians in Rome. A collection of Paul's letters occurred early, likely in the first century. Still, the Corinthians were limited in what they received at first and had to understand Paul's letters in light of the circumstances of their relationship with Paul.

As editors and audiences interacted with early Christian texts, they added to the library. Paul's letters to Corinth have a complicated history. What is read today is not exactly what Paul wrote, because the letters are not encountered in their original form. Up to half a dozen shorter letters were edited and woven together to become the one longer letter that is known today as 2 Corinthians. These various letters likely never have stood on their own among Christian readers at large and have only ever been known beyond Corinth as 2 Corinthians. This literary activity became possible only because at least one person kept copies of Paul's writings. Whether acting individually or on behalf of a community, this unknown person was one of the earliest collectors of Christian writings. The corpus of early Christian literature was just beginning.

The author of Luke and Acts would be surprised at what happened to his books. Luke and Acts were meant to stand on their own as a pair, two parts of a single whole. What happened? For centuries, scribes bundled Acts with the General Epistles, using it as an introduction for the letters bearing the names of Peter, James, John, and Jude. Eventually it was placed between the Gospels and Epistles, as a bridge between Jesus and the apostles, an introduction to all the Epistles. Thus, for most of church history the two volumes, Luke and Acts, were read independently of each other, despite being a two-part unit. The second odd twist of fate was that the Gospel of Mark was retained and linked to the Gospel of Luke. Luke's Gospel was meant to stand on its own as a reliable presentation of correct teaching by and about Jesus. The author of Luke saw his Gospel as an improvement over the texts written previously, including Mark. The New Testament ignored this by forever placing Luke in a series with Matthew and Mark. Why keep Mark's Gospel once one has Luke's superior revision? This is a question the author of Luke would likely ask.

Over time, many of the so-called books in the New Testament were written with an eye on others, as was the case with the Synoptic Gospels (i.e., Matthew, Mark, and Luke), or the imitation of 1 Thessalonians by the author of 2 Thessalonians. Even so, the books stood on their own physically, each written on sheets or rolls of paper or, to be more precise, sheets of papyrus in books and scrolls or on parchment, which is animal skin. In general, each Gospel would have fit nicely on a single scroll. As a result, the four Gospels and Acts would have resulted in a collection of five scrolls, if one could get them. Paul's letters might have fit onto a larger scroll; which letters were included varied. So, as these different texts became available, those who could get access to and afford a copy might have obtained one, thereby building a collection of scrolls.

At the same time the individual books of the New Testament were composed, early Christians were busy writing other texts as well. This might have caused confusion in building a Christian library. How many books would one collect? Would one collect Gospels and Acts other than the five now in the New Testament? Letters other than Paul's? Apocalypses other than John's? Writings from Christians other than apostles and bishops? Each document collected would have been a scroll or notebook placed on a shelf or in a basket with the others. Was any scroll or notebook more special than another? The answer would not have been obvious.

The choice about which early Christian texts to read and collect was a dilemma that emerged in the second century. As Christian writings multiplied over the course of the second century, a fair-sized body of writings came into existence. As their distribution expanded, so did collections. Choices became necessary. What were the most foundational documents? Which offered reliable stories or ideas? Which were beneficial and edifying for Christians to read? Christians also had different motives for reading these texts. They might read in public worship or private devotion, for moral edification or for intellectual progress, reasons that affected what they chose to read.

By the end of the second century, discussions about which texts to honor and which to avoid had begun. General agreement took shape around the four Gospels, Acts, and Paul's letters, with a fuzzy boundary that contained other respected writings. By the year 200, then, a recognizable core collection emerged. Lingering questions focused on what else to include. Revelation? The *Teaching of the Twelve Apostles* (aka, the *Didache*)? The *Shepherd of Hermas*? Christians vacillated back and forth on these.

If one listens only to leading bishops, one focuses only on the uncertainties around the edges of the New Testament (e.g., *Didache* and *Hermas*). If one pauses to hear other voices, the situation is more raucous. The collection of writings discovered in Egypt at Nag Hammadi reveals little resemblance to the New Testament and shows how differently Christians could think about their religion. For example, the gospels in this corpus do not provide a narrative focused on Jesus' ministry; furthermore, one encounters exploration into the meaning of life and the cosmos that goes beyond the New Testament. Writings by early Christians had warned that many texts other than those in the New Testament existed and that so-called "heretics" used them to understand and explain Christian teaching. Rediscovering those texts in the twentieth century reinforces how consequential early Christians' choices about what to read had proven. Agreement about appropriate reading became a bulwark for orthodoxy, while the move toward orthodox doctrine provided a litmus test for what to read.

The New Testament is not simply *like* a library, but is one very literally, as it presents a collection of different writings. Unlike the libraries of today, with thousands and often millions of books, the New Testament library is tiny. Even if it were expanded to include all early Christian literature for two centuries, the library would remain small. Of course, the likelihood that anyone at that time could successfully get a copy of everything Christians wrote was even smaller. By recognizing that the New Testament is a library, one gains a fundamental insight into its origin and content.

And then the insight fades. Just as the technology of the scroll clarifies the nature of the New Testament as a library, the technology of the book helps fix the content of the library and then obscure its origins. At the same time as the church took root, people began to sew sheets of papyrus or parchment together to create a series of pages placed between two wooden panels. Thus was born the book, or to use the Latin word, *codex*. These were less formal than the scroll and appear to have been used, at first, for more casual records, not literature.

The fact of sewing many pages together in a codex created the possibility of linking multiple writings. From an early date, Christian texts were written in books, not scrolls. This is remarkable, because the codex evolved during the Roman Empire, beginning in the first century and reaching dominance in the fourth. In fact, a reference by a Roman poet to the codex in about 85 CE makes clear the novelty of the form. Yet, based on the evidence of surviving manuscripts, Paul's letters typically circulated together as a collection in codex form. A small fragment of a manuscript of John's Gospel dating to about 125 CE also survives from a codex. Christians apparently were among the early adopters; some scholars argue that Christians adopted this new technology more aggressively than the broader world. Regardless, Christians were taking advantage of the new form, and it provided the capability to combine texts. This changed how texts were acquired and curated and, in turn, how they were viewed. A codex privileged the selected documents and, over the centuries, helped create the impression of a unified work, not a varied collection of writings, i.e., a library.

The New Testament Is *Like* a Library

Calling the New Testament a library reveals its essential composition. If one expands the analogy of a library to encompass it as a physical space and organization, one learns even more. Common activities in a library involve (1) acquisition, the purchase of books and other materials; (2) cataloging, in which the library's materials are classified, described, labeled, and tracked; (3) providing access, which expresses the library's goal of making materials available to users; (4) reading and research, the activity of the library's users; and (5) curation, the careful decisions a librarian makes about what materials to add to the collection. Each of these activities provides a lens for looking at the New Testament, as does (6) the actor, i.e., the librarian.

Acquisition. The opening section of this chapter pointed to a number of the problems encountered by early Christians in obtaining writings for their collections. At first, very little was written. Once works were written, publication became a problem. In antiquity, texts were not produced and reproduced the way books are today. No editors reviewed and advised. No copyright was assigned. No formal distribution channels existed. There was no Amazon.com nor any catalogs or bookstores from which to order. Every copy was handwritten. To obtain a book required that someone copy it from someone else's copy. Acquiring Christian writings, or any kind of writing for that matter, required access to a previous copy and a literate person, as well as the equipment and leisure to write out something by hand—including, perhaps, ten, twenty, or even more pages. It seems likely that wealthy Christians and their slaves were key actors in this.

Cataloging. As with a library, the documents that make up the New Testament are not arranged randomly but are organized. The first level of classification is genre, which reflects the historical process. The earliest collection was of Paul's letters. Next, Gospels were brought together. Acts did not reflect any other text and typically was placed with the General Epistles, forming a third corpus comprised of history and letters. Finally, the collection is rounded out by the Apocalypse of St. John, also known as Revelation, which reflects a fourth genre, apocalyptic, a heavenly revelation full of symbolism and concerned with God's justice. Though Acts and Revelation are the only examples of their genre in the New Testament, many other acts and apocalypses were written in the early church, none of which made the cut.

After texts were grouped together by genre, other principles of organization were followed. One seems to have been a tendency to put together similar works in the front. Thus, in the Gospels, John, which is least like the others, was placed last. Among the epistles, Paul's were placed first, and those by others were placed after his. Paul's letters were further organized into two groups: those written to churches and those addressed to individuals. Within these two categories, the letters were arranged, generally according to length, from longest to shortest.

Recognizing how the writings in the New Testament are organized warns people against false assumptions. For example, the order of the writings tells nothing about when they were written. Romans, which stands at the head of Paul's letters, was likely the last he wrote. Was 1 Timothy written before 2 Timothy? The numbers in the titles do not answer the question. Moreover, one should not forget the fact that the titles of the different writings were invented long after each document was written. As part of the process of cataloging its library, the early church labeled the Gospels, giving them what now appear to be titles. The labels, or titles, became necessary only when the individual texts came together, creating a situation in which some designation was needed to distinguish each.

Access. Among the many wonderful aspects of libraries is the service they offer readers by providing access to books and manuscripts. Even in the digital age, librarians are the helpful people who make electronic journals and databases available to the public.

An outcome of gathering early Christian writings into a corpus of Christian scriptures was that they became accessible for use across centuries. Early Christians wrote countless things; many were lost for centuries, and many remain lost. Were it not that Mark's Gospel or one of Paul's letters was collected into the New Testament, they might be lost, too. For example, it is known that Paul wrote another letter to the church in Corinth that did not survive. Consider all the other early Christian texts that disappeared or languished in obscurity precisely because they were not part of the New Testament, such as the *Acts of Paul and Thecla*, the *Acts of Peter*, the *Acts of Andrew*, or the *Acts of Thomas*. An important consequence of the New Testament being a library is that people have access to the writings that it contains. Precisely because twenty-seven early Christian texts were collected into a special group, they have remained available throughout the centuries.

Reading and research. If there had been no audience for what Christians wrote, there would have been no reason for the New Testament to be created. Readership drove copying and recopying. Use drove the process of identifying favorite and preferred texts, a process that built up a special collection that became the New Testament. In turn, the very fact of the New Testament guaranteed that people would read the books it enshrined. But being part of a collection also created a context for their reading that forever affected how they were read. Just as the contents of a library determine the research that can be done in it, so the twenty-seven books of the New Testament provided the material to be used in the church's reflection and teaching.

The debates about who Jesus was illustrate this. Each of the Gospels presents a unique take on Jesus, drawing on shared ideas, fleshing them out, and adding its own unique perspective. Other writers added more ideas to the mix. Centuries later, when official summits of bishops convened to settle debates about Jesus, the Gospels and Paul's letters played a central role in their deliberations, providing the evidence that the bishops' creedal statements had to take into account. Philosophy, semantics, and politics played critical roles, but the discussions remained connected to what the bishops read in the New Testament.

In a library, each book has a relationship to the other books on the shelves, whether direct and explicit or accidental and implicit. On a shelf of books about Abraham Lincoln, it is likely that the author of the most recent book read the others that rest on the shelf next to his own. Well, maybe not all, but certainly a few, probably many, ideally most. In some books, the author will make it very clear what other books are saying; while in others, readers will have to discern this on their own. This situation exists in the New Testament. Its books sometimes quote directly from others and sometimes paraphrase. Some books inspire others; some correct others. For example, 2 Peter borrowed much of Jude, and Matthew drew upon Mark. As the documents inform each other, we must watch very closely to see the notes being passed. *Intertextuality* refers to the conversations that take place among texts.

Books not only talk to each other directly but also converse indirectly and implicitly. No biographer reads every biography ever written, but the writer of a person's life steps into a network of ideas and methods created by other biographies and will interact with these traditions, both consciously and unconsciously. The resulting biography will be a product of a conversation with these cultural and literary traditions. The biographer will be aware of some of this give and take but not likely all of it.

This is equally true of early Christians, who were influenced by the literary forms of the world in which they lived, often knowingly, sometimes not. The individual stories in Mark's Gospel look like the same kinds of stories told by pagan and Jewish authors. The stories of Jesus' miracles and the arguments he had with people resemble those told about others and gods in the ancient world. In general, early Christians told stories in the way their culture taught them. Sometimes, these conventions caused one author to correct another. At a broad level, the author of Luke appears to reshape Mark's Gospel to create a better example of a biography. Sometimes, the conventions hide in plain sight. The book of Revelation, also known as the Apocalypse of St. John, presents itself as the written record of what a man saw in a heavenly vision. The careful reader, however, will recognize in the text frequent interaction with older scriptures. These countless scriptural allusions in Revelation reveal a very literate enterprise, which suggests the writer participated in a specific textual tradition—one that rummages through scripture. The existence of many earlier apocalypses adds further proof that the author of St. John's Apocalypse worked in a literary tradition. Despite the way Revelation presents itself, the origin of the text is more complicated and grounded in tradition. Like the hushed, implicit conversations between books in a library, so also the documents collected into the New Testament contain myriad hidden footnotes.

Not all the footnotes are obscure. Later Christians obviously, even explicitly, imitated earlier Christian writers. Paul wrote letters, and others followed his example. The Gospel of Mark provided a narrative account of Jesus that others then followed. Likewise, the Acts of the Apostles was followed by other writers. Christians would turn to other genres, but the genres of widespread, respected writings inspired other Christians to continue writing in those literary forms.

Continuing to think about biography, once a new one joins the others on a library's shelf, it starts a fresh, book-to-book conversation. The new biography may be conventional, in which case the conversation affirms past practices, or it might be innovative, upsetting the satisfied conversation that preceded. The author may or may not be aware of this. Instead, it may await discovery by later readers. In the New Testament, amazing conversations that were barely audible for centuries take place among the four Gospels. Each Gospel provides implicit and explicit commentary on previous ones. The volume on these conversations will be turned up in chapter 4.

The conversations among the books of the New Testament took place not only in their composition but also in their interpretation, which continue today. An important method for centuries in biblical interpretation was that scripture interprets scripture. When one is unsure what the Bible is saying, one should look to the rest of the Bible for clarity. Not sure what a word means? See how it is used elsewhere in the Bible and that will provide the clue. Not sure about an idea or its details? Again, look elsewhere in the Bible for the answer.

While there is nothing wrong with using the rest of the Bible for evidence, considering such data superior may be misleading and using it exclusively skews everything. For example, when attempting to decode symbols in the Bible, comparing different passages makes sense. When looking beyond the literal meaning of a text for an allegorical or spiritual meaning, scripture-interprets-scripture again proves an important tool: It not only opens paths to interpretation but also holds in check wild flights of fancy. It also makes it possible to stretch a false veneer of theological unity across the Bible. For example, John's Gospel says that God is a spirit, a statement commonly taken by many readers as a fundamental proposition relevant to every other statement in the Bible. Even if God created Adam in God's own image, and then walked with Adam in the Garden of Eden, God did not have a body like humans, so the argument goes, because John's Gospel says so. This leveling obscures the novelty of John's theology and the mythic quality of Genesis. Similarly, some take "I permit no woman to teach or have authority over a man" (1 Tim 2:12) as the clear statement that informs the reading of other biblical passages, even examples in which women do, in fact, teach and hold authority. Such imposed unity deprives women of the roles they played in the early church.

Many practitioners of scripture-interprets-scripture assume that the hand of God provides a unity to all writings of the Old and New Testaments, such that ambiguities or difficulties in one part can be resolved by information provided elsewhere. This theological method of interpretation makes the Bible a self-contained collection that can be understood on its own and smooths away the interesting diversity of views the Bible contains. To return to our analogy, this view treats the Bible less as a library and more as a single, multi-chapter work.

A more robust, theological method of interpretation has even deeper roots in the early church, namely, the rule of faith. This approach assumes that the church's writings support what the church teaches. The gospel message has priority in the church's teaching, and the Bible reinforces it. The correct way to read the Bible, then, is through the lens of the preached gospel. This may sound circular, but early Christians had to figure out which writings to trust. Those that aligned with what was preached were more reliable.

The early church also had to find a way to interpret Jewish scriptures as its own. The most obvious position was that Jewish scriptures belonged to Jews and not the Gentile church, but the church developed along a path that would not permit this outcome. Ingenuity was required by Christians to claim Jewish scriptures for themselves. Starting with the gospel and then reading Jewish scriptures in light of Christ allowed Gentile Christians to claim the alien writings as their own. Layering figurative methods of reading over Jewish scriptures further helped Christians in this enterprise. In this process, biblical interpretation was a conversation between biblical texts and among the community of faith.

To return to the analogy of a library, the church decided and limited, over time, which materials were allowed on the library's shelves, who was allowed to enter the library and use its materials, and how the materials were to be used. Conversations indeed took place among the books on the shelves, but the ones that were valued and amplified were those that interacted reliably with the gospel message. In great part, biblical interpretation since the Enlightenment can be described as a move away from theological interpretation and its allegorical mind-set. The books were freed to say what they wanted and readers to work without constraints on method. Readers again began to listen for all the conversations taking place within and among the texts, not just those some preferred to hear.

Curation. A good collection of books represents the work of thoughtful guidance, not the result of random purchases and gifts. This judicious process of selecting individual pieces to bring together for the purpose of creating a better whole is called curation.

Think for a moment about the following example. To a collection of one thousand books in English, someone adds one hundred written in Chinese. What does that say? It could say many different things. It might be a complete accident, resulting from what was found in someone's basement or what was on sale at the used bookstore. Neither case would be thoughtful curation. However, the Chinese volumes might say something about the intellectual path of the collector or about the historical development of the topics covered in those books. A professional architect who has expanded his practice into China might reasonably add Chinese books on architecture to his collection. Their addition would then represent the collection's reasoned, coherent growth.

The New Testament calls for similar consideration. Since not every piece of early Christian writing made it into the New Testament, selection took place. How did this happen? Why collect gospels and letters? Why are Paul's letters combined with letters written by other people? The very fact of putting things together initiates conversations between the materials and raises questions. For those who take the New Testament for granted as a single entity, these questions may not come to mind, but they exist and are worth asking.

When the early church debated which texts to read and follow in worship, three basic arguments emerged to defend choices: apostolicity, catholicity, and orthodoxy. *Apostolicity* represents the belief that a text was written by an apostle or someone closely associated with an apostle. Proximity to Jesus and the very origin of the church gave authors credibility either as eyewitnesses or, second-best, students of eyewitnesses.

This rule was not hard and fast. For example, the Gospels of Mark and Luke take their names from people who did not know Jesus. This troubled some people, like the great Egyptian theologian, Clement of Alexandria, and required an explanation. Apostolicity therefore expanded to include associates of apostles. Mark's Gospel was believed to be written by one of Peter's associates, and Luke's by one of Paul's. Paul's lack of connection to Jesus troubled some, but the larger church soon marginalized such critics.

The value of apostolicity was complicated, because many of the writings that failed to make it into the New Testament bore the names of actual apostles in their titles. Perhaps the best-known example is the *Gospel of Thomas*. The *Gospel of Philip*, likewise, failed to make the cut, though also named for an apostle. The *Gospel of Mary* may not bear the name of a traditional apostle, but certainly Mary stands closer to Jesus than any link to Paul. But the church did not adopt these as official and sanctioned texts. The presence of texts named for apostles but not included in the approved list leads to the next two lines of argument, catholicity and orthodoxy.

The most important factor that led to the inclusion of certain writings in the New Testament was their widespread use. The word for this is *catholicity*, which means general or common, like the Greek word from which it is derived. In this context, catholicity does not mean the Catholic Church, but refers to many churches, enough to establish a broadly shared practice, perhaps even a majority. Christian writings read by many churches across the Roman Empire gained more status than texts with limited circulation and use. This provided an advantage to texts written in Greek. Widespread readership also raised the odds of survival.

Some of the noncanonical gospels are esoteric texts, presenting teachings that not just any reader could be expected to understand. Their teachings are purposefully veiled, meant only to be understood by those inside the small circle of people to whom this privileged information belonged. These texts, though proud of their complexity and obscurity, were thereby doomed to limited readership. Though even the Gospels of Mark and, particularly, John have esoteric elements, they nevertheless received a wide enough readership to survive.

As a test, catholicity focused on established facts. Texts were not passed around to be read and voted on to determine popularity. Rather, catholicity recognized what had already taken place in the church. Certain texts had received wide distribution and were read by many Christians, particularly for teaching and worship. Catholicity represents a backward glance at what had already happened, making widespread readership a precedent for continuing to use and advocate for those texts.

Widespread, general use also reflects a third characteristic, namely, widespread, generally-agreed-upon teaching. Although commonly called *orthodoxy*, this label is a misleading anachronism. What today is called orthodox Christian teaching stands on six centuries of debates about God and Christ, as well as the creeds these generated. When Christians debated which of their writings to recommend for general use and privileged status, the Christological arguments were ongoing. Still, Christians shared many practices and ideas and thought they enjoyed more in common than they did. The things generally assumed to be shared in common by Christians around the Mediterranean Sea are what are referred to here as orthodoxy, the final test for whether a text would make it into the Christian scriptures.

The books that made it into the New Testament taught what many Christians thought all Christians should think and do. This is what made fraud easy to detect: If a text did not teach what every good bishop knew to be correct, then it was not really written by an apostle. For example, if a text taught that Jesus did not have a real flesh-and-blood body, but only seemed human, that was evidence an apostle did not write it, so it was fraudulent and rejected. What a text taught validated its claim to authorship and sanctioned its use.

Thus, the three criteria interact with one another. A text claiming apostolic origin could be a candidate for widespread use among churches. If it received widespread use, then it was likely to find reception among still other churches and become a text shared by nearly all Christians. But if it taught anything offensive to church leaders, it would not be recommended nor used. Moreover, obviously incorrect teaching furnished clear proof that the text lacked apostolic origin, eliminating its candidacy for general acceptance and use by churches.

No one person determined what books made it into the New Testament. The three arguments appear more clearly as criteria from hindsight. The New Testament emerged from a centuries-long process of consensus, while rejected texts appear to have fallen from contention in a much shorter span of time. Still, when explicit reasons were called for, apostolicity, catholicity, and orthodoxy played their roles. These three criteria provided guidance to Christians as they curated their growing libraries.

Librarian. In thinking about the New Testament as a library, the analogy also suggests we ask, "Who was the librarian?" I just said, "No one person" established the content of the New Testament, which suggests there was no librarian; yet curation requires intelligence and discretion. Was there a librarian or librarians? In answering this question, we run into two distinct ways of viewing the New Testament, a theological and a historical, the former seeing a divinely guided plan and the latter an outcome of converging and diverging circumstances that played out over time. To consider this element of the analogy, we need to think descriptively about the New Testament.

Here are two possible ways of describing the New Testament:

Theological. The New Testament presents the writings of the apostles and their companions, which the divine spirit inspired to preserve true teaching. Divine providence also guided the church to recognize the New Testament as authoritative and preserve it for use by Christians of all times.

Historical. The New Testament is a collection of some early Christian writings from the first and second centuries that many Christians decided are beneficial, convey appropriate Christian teaching, possess significant historical roots, and therefore, should be given special status.

The theological approach expresses the belief that God intervened to bring the New Testament into existence and preserve it for the church, identifying God as the librarian. The historical approach describes the phenomenon as it unfolded over time, avoiding any grander purpose or perspective, counting many (often nameless) Christians as librarians. The historical approach reflects the point of view of Enlightenment scholarship and its historical method. A fundamentalist would emphasize the theological view; the historical view would not be denied but would be made secondary, insisting also that everything was written in the first century. He or she would add that because of God's intervention, the New Testament is God's word in ink, true and without error. Catholic statements from Vatican II do not share the fundamentalist's adjustments but link the two perspectives, recognizing what happened in history, yet affirming the hand of God in guiding. At a general level, this accommodation is possible, but digging into the details makes it increasingly difficult to reconcile the two perspectives. Whichever perspective one prefers profoundly affects how the New Testament is read.

Though both perspectives mention the importance of catholicity and orthodoxy, they value them differently. For the theological description, recognition is key to the process. Some documents contain truth; others do not. The role of the church in constructing Christian scriptures was to recognize the difference and champion texts with correct teaching. Thus, catholicity confirms orthodoxy. For the historical perspective, however, correct teaching is being constructed by individuals and congregations in dialogue with texts over time, so that catholicity creates orthodoxy.

In thinking that the church was embracing divinely appointed texts, the theological definition also sees the church weeding out apostolic writings from the non-apostolic. Whether a text bears the name of an apostle or not is not the final test, for the threat of forgery exists and was, in fact, widespread. A text has to agree with what the dominant churches think is appropriate Christian teaching for the churches to embrace it as authentically apostolic. From the theological perspective, it is important to cut back the weeds and find only the apostolic writings. This, in turn, confines the dating of the New Testament to the first century, though to a historian many appear to come from the second. For the historical process, the church had to select which texts to bring into the Christian scriptures. Selection, not recognition, is key, with the result that something is created. This contrasts with a belief that the church had simply to recognize and bring to light what already existed.

Most importantly, the two perspectives approach the New Testament differently. The theological description is trying to prescribe what had to have happened. The New Testament was inevitable, for God was responsible. The purely historical view seeks only to describe what happened. The New Testament is simply an outcome, one that perhaps could have gone differently.

So, was there a librarian? The answer to this question rests entirely on one's point of view. Some might see God; others, nothing but the outcome of the church's literary habits and politics. Focusing on God and eliminating people from the picture yields a definition that is entirely unhistorical, one that fails to respect

- how the different documents came into being,
- how many other early Christian texts were left out,
- the efforts early Christians made to sort out options,
- the uncertainty surrounding some,
- the differing value placed on New Testament texts,
- how long the church took to resolve these questions, and
- the ambiguity as to whether the questions actually were answered.

Few theologians would overlook the historical factors, but the degree to which different denominations embrace them varies. As for history, it recognizes centuries of curation by many but no master librarian. Generations of librarians contributed opinions and habits of use. Curation, then, was similar to open-source software today and reflects the contributions of many people.

Who were some of these curators? Three examples from the second century are Marcion, who allowed only Luke's Gospel and Paul's letters; Irenaeus, who used Paul's letters extensively but whose chief contribution was to argue strenuously on behalf of four Gospels; and Tatian, who wove Matthew, Mark, Luke, and John together to create his single text, the *Diatessaron*. The fourth century provides additional important examples. The church historian Eusebius affirmed the four Gospels, Acts, Paul's letters, 1 Peter, and 1 John. He noted other texts as disputed or spurious. The great ecumenical Council of Nicea made no statement, but a couple of regional meetings of bishops did create lists—one matches the contents of the New Testament as it is known; the other might have omitted Revelation. The most important statement about the New Testament came from Athanasius, an important bishop in Egypt and one of the most significant theologians in the church's history. In his Easter letter of 367 CE, he explicitly drafted a list of texts that Christians should regard as religious authorities and called this collection the New Testament. As important a leader as he was, Athanasius did not speak for the entire church when he created his list. In fact, all of these examples only tell what was happening in different places at different times. None of these people spoke for all churches or was binding on all. The first time the church issued an official, church-wide statement about the content of Christian scripture came at the Council of Trent in 1546, which convened to respond to Protestant teachings.

By eliminating a single librarian and emphasizing the social dimension, the historical perspective demonstrates that the selection of documents gathered into the New Testament is not a foregone conclusion but a custom, a conventional practice. From the broad swath of early Christian writings, the New Testament is but a small selection. When studying history, there is no reason to wall off the twenty-seven books of the New Testament from the dozens of others written by early Christians. The New Testament is a theological construction invented by the community of faith to define, protect, instruct, and inspire itself. History now breaks down the boundaries of canon, requiring use of all evidence, not just filtered evidence. With the boundaries of canon breached, we return to a library, albeit a comprehensive one, where everything is possible. Here, the analogy of a library has broken down and done so twice: Just as I cannot visualize a library without a librarian, I cannot imagine a library that is complete. Then again, maybe the analogy has not broken down, so much as two different libraries have emerged—one to serve an audience asking historical questions about faith, the other to support historical inquiries not constrained by faith.

To summarize the theological and historical understandings of the New Testament, let me repeat the earlier historical view of it, this time inserting comments to highlight both points of view.

> *Historical.* The New Testament is a collection of some (versus inspired) early Christian writings from the first and second centuries (versus first century alone) that many Christians (i.e., catholicity of time and geography) decided (versus recognized) are beneficial, convey appropriate Christian teaching (i.e., orthodoxy), possess significant historical roots (i.e., apostolicity), and therefore, should be given special status (i.e., canonicity).

While it is fine to say what history does, it does not follow that the church must do likewise. The New Testament has influenced Christian faith and practice for centuries, playing key roles in shaping worship, creeds, morality, and identity. To diminish its special status among early Christian literature would change Christian religion. But without relinquishing its privileged collection of writings, Christians have found enormous latitude in articulating faith. The very diversity latent in the texts, even when seeking to impose unity on them, left room for divergent opinions, whether Catholic or Protestant, slave owner or emancipationist, feminist or patrician, liturgical or charismatic, or hierarchical or egalitarian.

Other Historical Analogies to the New Testament

The writing and collecting of texts by Christians did not happen in a vacuum. Other people edited, compiled, and collected texts for a variety of reasons. People can read the results of their work today and see additional analogies to the New Testament. In surveying ancient writings, readers can examine how the New Testament resembles anthologies, the canon of orators, curricula, oracles, and Jewish scriptures.

Surviving from the ancient world is a collection of quotations excerpted from ancient writings and compiled more than four hundred years after Jesus. In a modern edition that spans five volumes, the author, Stobaeus, expended an enormous amount of effort gathering quotations that provided illustrations of many different topics. What, for example, did ancient Greeks think about politics? Stobaeus provides hundreds of excerpts from drama, philosophy, oratory, history, and anything written on which he could get his hands. Numerous topics are addressed and about five hundred ancient authors quoted. Centuries earlier, at the time of Jesus, the Roman Valerius Maximus, to spare other people the effort of hunting them down, undertook a similar effort in Latin to compile words and deeds worthy to be remembered. He, too, clustered examples according to themes, such as religion, politics, virtue, or vice.

The New Testament is different, for it is a collection of entire works, rather than single sentences or paragraphs lifted from their original sources. To an English reader, Stobaeus' work would resemble Bartlett's *Familiar Quotations*. What Stobaeus' anthology shows us about the New Testament is the habit of bringing together materials, written by a variety of people, so they can be used to address questions raised by readers. Jews and Christians, in fact, engaged in this practice. Among the Dead Sea Scrolls are manuscripts containing strings of scriptural quotations. Among early Christians, the popularity of specific texts, such as Psalms and Isaiah, suggests a similar practice of culling from the Jewish scriptures passages that Christians believed foretold Christ. Scholars refer to these as *testimonia* and consider them to have been particularly useful for defending faith. Just as the Jewish scriptures were plundered, so, too, was Homer. The Epicurean philosopher Philodemus, born a hundred years before Jesus, compiled a collection of excerpts and examples from Homer to illustrate the practices of a good king. In sum, Stobaeus' work was an encyclopedic example of a literary habit that many different people practiced.

A better analogy to the New Testament from the ancient world is the collection and preservation of speeches. The ancient Greeks created a canon of outstanding orators, whose written speeches were preserved to provide examples of compelling oratory. A collection could advertise the skills of the orator, while providing pleasure to the reader. The real driving force for collections over time, however, was to assist education. Examples of oratory provided crucial material for ancient pedagogy. Anyone eager to become a better speaker read Lysias, Isocrates, Demosthenes, Aeschines, and others, whose written speeches contributed to curricula and defined rhetoric's appropriate standards. So, even before Christians began collecting their favorite writings, literate people had grown accustomed to collections of texts to be used as authorities in the present.

Still other collections were made. A massive collection of writings by the just-mentioned Philodemus came to light in the Italian coastal town of Herculaneum. This concentration of scrolls by a single author resulted from a personal relationship between the author and the homeowner, who collected the treatises. Scholars in places like Alexandria, a large metropolis with a magnificent library, consciously gathered together the works of ancient playwrights and poets. Philosophical schools read the writings of their masters and predecessors, and then joined them in literary output. When Christians made an effort to collect writings by their founding figures and heroes, they were behaving just like other literate people.

Compilations of religious materials were also made. Rome had the Sibylline Books, oracles written in Greek poetic form and hidden away in a temple of Jupiter to be consulted at portentous moments by an exclusive body of priests. The utterances of a number of sibyls, or prophetesses, were gathered throughout antiquity, even by Jews and Christians. Michelangelo enshrined sibyls on the ceiling of the Sistine Chapel as participants in the unfolding of revelation. Stories about the healings performed by the god Asklepios were inscribed on the walls of the god's temples to advertise his power and benefaction. Many ancient authors put together collections of stories about the gods.

At last, our attention turns to the most obvious of all analogues for the New Testament, which is the Old Testament. It is obvious, yes, but not that simple. To say, "Old Testament," reflects the ingrained, Christian habit of seeing the Jewish scripture as a nice, single book, rather than a collection of disparate writings brought together over time by a community. Much of what has been said already about the New Testament as a library applies equally to the Old Testament, except with a different timeline and actors.

The second problem is that there is no single Old Testament. When one labels Jewish scriptures as "Old Testament," one uses Christian language and refers to the corpus of Jewish religious writings as they existed among and were used by Christians. Not all Christians agree about which Jewish writings to count as Holy Bible. Protestants use only Hebrew and Aramaic writings in their Old Testament, while Catholics follow the Latin Bible, which has an expanded list of documents in its sacred library, based on the example of the Greek translations of Jewish scriptures. Orthodox traditions likewise adopted the Jewish scriptures in Greek translation.

The difference between Protestant and Catholic canons takes us to the third very important issue. The Christian Old Testament is fundamentally Greek. The early church read Jewish scriptures via their translation into Greek because that was the language most early Christians could understand. The corpus of these Greek translations is called the *Septuagint*, the Latin word for seventy, referring to the team of scholars legend says produced the translation. Additional Greek writings were collected together with the texts translated from Hebrew and Aramaic to create a larger collection, which was the basis of the Latin Old Testament.

Early Christians, then, read Jewish scriptures in Greek. What exactly did they read? Did every church have a scroll of every book of the Old Testament? This seems unlikely. Christians favored some texts, such as the Pentateuch, Psalms, and prophets, particularly Isaiah, yet were clearly rifling through the *Septuagint*, and other Jewish texts, for anything and everything they could find to support their beliefs. Every nook and cranny were examined. From the very beginning, Christians held Jewish scriptures in high regard. Long before there was a New Testament, the early church had the *Septuagint*. This was the church's Bible, setting a clear example to Christians for building their own collection of religious texts, a collection that, over time, supplemented the *Septuagint* and then usurped its primacy.

Libraries Change

Returning to our analogy of the library, one final observation arises: Libraries change. Our sense of the New Testament hinges on the state of technology. A collection of scrolls is easier to add to, take away from, and mix up than are the pages of a book. Once individual texts are sewn together and placed inside a single, protective covering, they suddenly look like a single entity whose contents are not random. The volume begs for a title. After binding together a selection of early Christian writings, they look less like a library and more like a book. The codex, therefore, was a game-changing technology.

The printing press, in its turn, stabilized the text and made it accessible. The transition from hand copying to type eliminated random copyist errors, multiplied the number of copies available, and made them more affordable. This ushered in the great era of translation that saw the Bible move out of Latin and into European languages. More people could now read the Bible. What had been mysterious, often forbidden, was now offered up to the reading public.

Chapter and verse divisions also were introduced, breaking the Bible into small, approximately sentence-sized units. Through the centuries people devised a variety of systems to aid in breaking the Bible into sections so passages could be identified and read. Not until the thirteenth century were the chapter divisions seen in modern English Bibles introduced. Verse numbers were not invented until the sixteenth century. With translations also came punctuation, something contemporary readers take for granted, yet a novelty just a few centuries ago.

All these developments have a profound impact on how people read the New Testament. A single book lures people into reading it as if it were written by one person, in one place, at one time. This tricks them into assuming that it has a cohesive unity. Some people, therefore, say easily, "The Bible says," whereas readers with trained historical consciousness hear the many different voices speaking across the Bible's pages. Even closer analysis reveals how the thinking of individual authors evolved. Scholars who study the apostle Paul now pay careful attention to how differently he expresses his ideas over time. Readers who hear but one voice in the Bible compile excerpts to state the Bible's position on a given topic, using verses from here and there to put together a comprehensive set of doctrines. Those understanding the Bible as a library with many authors who sometimes hold differing views, listen for these views, compare them, and try to see why they differ. Very different questions get asked and vastly different answers become acceptable.

Further changes are coming as technology ushers in a new era of interaction with scripture. Just as libraries have evolved in response to digital information, so also will interaction with the New Testament. If one keeps the New Testament on an electronic reader, one ends up closer to the time when each book of the New Testament was an individual scroll, encountering a Gospel on its own without automatic connection to others. If other early Christian writings are added, they mix like peers on these storage devices. When I save them, I have to decide how to organize them. I can respect traditional classification schemes, like the New Testament, or I can organize them in other ways. And my computer will always default to alphabetical order. In addition, word processing makes it easy to edit the text. Will translations proliferate even more? Will text and commentary blend seamlessly? The printing press made scripture more available and set the stage for the Reformation. Will computer Bibles have equally dramatic consequences? What comes next for the church's sacred library?

Not only do libraries change courtesy of technology, but their collections change. Here lie crucial questions for the New Testament: Will its contents change? Will its collection grow or shrink? On the one hand, it seems silly to ask these questions. The entire point of establishing the canon of the New Testament is to settle, once and for all, to which documents the church should grant ultimate authority. Centuries of tradition serve to mute such questions.

It may sound strange to question whether the contents will change. Would anyone dare? Well, yes. Thomas Jefferson did, editing out what he found disagreeable. The church reveres the Old Testament, but few Christians live by it. As for the New Testament, most Christians favor one part of it—and which part varies among Christians. For example, the Episcopal liturgy gives greater respect to the Gospels; the Reformed tradition leans heavily on Paul; dispensationalists explicitly privilege Paul; Pentecostals trumpet Acts and Paul. Christians do not practice all sixty-six, or more, books of their Bibles. As for adding to the Bible, the Book of Mormon serves the

Church of Jesus Christ of Latter Day Saints, whose members are, therefore, referred to as Mormons. At present, the *Gospel of Thomas* is gathering an audience. In fact, as I write this, a new book has come out that reimagines what the New Testament might look like. Hal Taussig and a diverse team chose a wider selection of early Christian writings to bring together into *A New New Testament: A Bible for the 21st Century Combining Tradition and Newly Discovered Texts.* Change is possible.

The question is worth asking because alternatives are available that were not for centuries. Authority is exercised among churches differently today than in the church's early centuries. Moreover, the New Testament is not a functional category for many scholars. They rely heavily on sayings from source Q and the *Gospel of Thomas* to understand Jesus and look outside the New Testament to put Paul into perspective. Since many historians have eliminated apostolicity as a relevant criterion for inclusion in the New Testament, is the door open for other writings to move into the normative corpus of Christian writings? While many would not likely entertain this question, will Christians with greater historical consciousness about their religious literature do so? There may yet be more room on the shelf.

Questions

1. What were early Christians doing in their library? See 1 Cor 10:6 and 2 Tim 3:16. See also 2 Thess 3:14 and 2 Pet 3:15–16. Compare also 2 Thess 2:2 and Rev 22:18–19.

2. Search the Internet for "books of the Bible," and peruse the different lists of books. How many different lists can you find? Whose library has the most books? The fewest?

3. Select one of the texts that appears in the Roman Catholic Bible that does not appear in the Protestant Bible (for example, Sirach, Tobit, or 1 Maccabees). Skim the text and then search the Internet for reasons why the Roman Catholic Bible includes the text and the Protestant Bible does not. Evaluate the pros and cons.

4. Jude is a very short letter in the New Testament. The *Didache* is a longer but still short text from the early church (which you can read online). Read them both. If it were up to you, which would you include in the New Testament? Why?

5. Think about how research differs when you use one book as your resource versus when you use a library. If you were to investigate what the Bible says about a topic, how would you approach the question if you consider the Bible a book, and how would you approach the question if you consider it a library? What differences might this make in the outcome?

6. Consider this question, "What is the good life?" Using the Bible as your resource, how will your research and answer differ, depending on whether you consider the Bible a book or a library?

7. Allusions to and quotations of the Old Testament are commonplace in the New Testament. Some books in the New Testament refer to others. Imagine two consequences of these conversations among texts, which is called intertextuality, and evaluate their impact.

Further Reading

Alter, Robert. *Canon and Creativity: Modern Writing and the Authority of Scripture.* The Franz Rosenzweig Lecture Series. New Haven, CT: Yale University Press, 2000.

Barr, James. *Holy Scripture: Canon, Authority, Criticism.* Oxford University Press, 1983.

Klingshirn, William E., and Linda Safran, eds. *The Early Christian Book.* CUA Studies in Early Christianity. Washington, DC: Catholic University of America Press, 2008.

Law, Timothy Michael. *When God Spoke Greek: The Septuagint and the Making of the Christian Bible.* Oxford University Press, 2013.

Lim, Timothy H. *The Formation of the Jewish Canon.* The Anchor Yale Bible Reference Library. New Haven, CT: Yale University Press, 2013.

Metzger, Bruce M., and Bart D. Ehrman. *The Text of the New Testament: Its Transmission, Corruption, and Restoration.* 4th ed. Oxford University Press, 2005.

Pelikan, Jaroslav. *Whose Bible Is It? A Short History of the Scriptures.* New York: Penguin Books, 2006.

Taussig, Hal, ed. *A New New Testament: A Bible for the 21st Century Combining Traditional and Newly Discovered Texts.* New York: Houghton Mifflin Harcourt, 2013.

The New Testament Was Written in Greek

T hanks to the dedication and energy of thousands of people around the world and throughout history, the Bible has been translated into nearly five hundred languages—the New Testament, by itself, into more than one thousand. The opportunity for people to encounter the Bible in their native tongue has advanced missionary activity and enriched pastoral ministry, while also helping fragment the church and alter indigenous cultures. Many readers remain completely unaware that the text they read and treasure rests on the enormous labors of scholars, rare manuscripts, and foreign alphabets.

No one could tally all the people who have engaged in the enterprise of biblical translation. With diligence, one might calculate all the published translations but still uncounted would be the translators, their teachers, the people who wrote grammars and dictionaries, and the linguists who developed the semantic theories that guided the work. Also to be counted are the copyists, publishers, typesetters, distributors, salespeople, librarians, and even smugglers. Biblical translation is a broad, intensive collaboration spanning centuries, continents, and cultures. By comparison, all the computer code written by Microsoft Corporation is a hobby.

Like every grand undertaking, biblical translation has its heroes. St. Jerome provided the church with a Latin translation that served for more than one thousand years. Other Latin translations existed when St. Jerome set about his work, but he had learned Hebrew and was able to work from a Hebrew text in the Old Testament as well as Greek in the New Testament. His knowledge of Hebrew was unusual among Christians. The quality of his accomplishment stood the test of time, his legacy touching even English translations.

Martin Luther is another luminary in biblical translation, whose fingerprints remain on the German Bible. When Reformers emphasized the interpretation of Scripture as their source of authority, the need to read the Bible gained importance. If the Bible remained in Hebrew, Greek, and Latin, few could have read it. Luther recognized the consequences of the theological positions he had staked out and set himself the task of translating the Bible into German.

The English-speaking world received its champions in John Wycliffe and William Tyndale. Wycliffe and his colleagues translated from the Latin Vulgate while, two centuries later, Tyndale and his colleagues, though influenced by Wycliffe, translated from the earlier Hebrew and Greek texts. The number of handwritten copies of Wycliffe's Bible that still exist testify to its popularity, while the later invention of the printing press allowed Tyndale's Bible to circulate even more broadly. The King James Version of the Bible, completed in 1611, borrowed copiously from Tyndale's work.

Perhaps one could argue that each language had its champion, a person without whom the work would have failed. Jerome, Luther, and Tyndale have won the most conspicuous places in the history books of the West. I sketch this history briefly to make clear that biblical texts have a history. Whether it is an English Bible one reads, or Spanish, Korean, or Zulu, the text is mediated to the modern reader, courtesy of translators, since the Bible was written in Hebrew, with some Aramaic, and Greek.

The New Testament, strictly speaking, was written in Greek. Readers of this essay most likely read the New Testament in English and, therefore, in translation and subject to the myriad shortcomings a translation poses. In Greek, the text reveals subtleties of communication, clues about the authors who wrote the New Testament, and the relationships among the authors' writings. Reading the text in Greek, one also learns about Christian history and how the New Testament came to be. Mostly, one encounters the written artifacts of another culture on their own terms and recognizes them as products of another time and place.

All Translations Lie

Italians have a proverb, "Translator, traitor." A Russian adage says, about translation, "If it is beautiful, it is not faithful. If it is faithful, it is most certainly not beautiful." People who have attempted translation, working with languages they know deeply, understand immediately the truth of these sayings.

Words are cultural artifacts that do not move simply from one language to perfect equivalent in another. For example, what is a *wilderness*? To me, it is a pine forest filled with animals. In Palestine, it is more likely to be a hot, dry, rocky desert. In the United States, the lack of roads is a technical attribute of a federal wilderness area. In Greek, the emphasis falls on the absence of other humans, or absence of one's own ethnic group. The word *wilderness* is a sign that signifies different things as it moves from one place and its people to others.

The interpretation of something as commonplace as a greeting also varies. What kinds of actions are involved? Does it imply a big, hearty hug? A kiss on each cheek? A formal handshake? How do age and gender affect the interaction? In the ancient world, people went out of town to meet visiting dignitaries, as in the stories of Jesus' approach to Jerusalem and Paul's to Rome. These were not unique events but typical, ritual actions that paid due respect to important visitors. The English writer Anthony Burgess described the difficulty of translation broadly: "Translation is not a matter of words only: It is a matter of making intelligible a whole culture."

Words are only one dimension of the challenge of translation. Many times, in the Greek New Testament, authors imply but do not state words, so translators have to infer and add them. These tend to be obvious and easy. More difficult are places where the writer simply fails to finish his thought, leaving the translator to guess how to round it off or leave the gap hanging. Alliteration, rhyme, assonance, and other tools of melodic speech usually defy translation. Translations often obscure Paul's irony and biting sarcasm or his sometimes rapid, clipped rhetoric. The Revelation of St. John is notorious for its grammatical irregularities; translations make these disappear.

A translator certainly cannot replicate sentence structure. For example, in 2 Cor 2:4, Paul explains that he wrote an earlier letter not to upset the Corinthians, "but to let you know the abundant love that I have for you." Literally, this would be: "but *the love* that you might know which I have abundantly for you." The order of Paul's words place great emphasis on the word love. English translation cannot convey this.

To take an extreme example, Eph 1:3–14 is technically one long sentence in Greek, though repeated relative phrases in vv. 7, 11, and 13 provide some relief. The translators of the King James Version used the relative phrases to break this into four sentences. The more modern New International Version, reflecting a contemporary preference for shorter, simpler sentences, breaks the passage into eight sentences. Both translations improve the style of the Greek, an accomplishment that warns that elegance may be as much a product of the translator's skill as the original author's.

On the other hand, imposing English word order on a Greek sentence may strip it of its style and the pleasure it offers. In English, one reads, "But God *proves* his love for us in that while we still were sinners Christ *died* for us" (Rom 5:8). In Greek, the word order is different, as the main verbs are the first and last words in the sentence: "*Proves*, however, his own love to us God that, still while sinners were we, Christ for us *died*." The ugliness of the translation fails to do justice to the pleasure I feel reading the Greek version, which creates anticipation at the beginning as I wait to understand the point of the verb and then, at the end, creates more tension before resolving the sentence with the final verb. The aesthetic qualities of reading this verse in Greek, or any other well-composed verse, evade translation. Translation is, as the Spanish writer Cervantes described four hundred years ago, the back side of a tapestry: The image can be made out, but the details are fuzzy and the color dull.

The great German poet Goethe dramatized the challenge of translation in his version of the Faust story. Sitting at his desk, the protagonist and scholar, Faust, ponders the opening words of the Gospel according to John, trying to translate them: "In the beginning was the Word" (Greek, *logos*). He struggles with the Greek word *logos*. How should he translate it? Whereas a novice Greek student too readily answers, "Word," Faust pauses, for "word" seems inadequate to be the first cause of creation. Perhaps *mind*? No. Then Faust turns to power and, finally, action. *Action* or *deed*, yes, here Faust thinks is the fundamental, generative cause of the universe, and then Faust inks his translation.

In this scene, Faust illustrates the dilemma that every translator faces, choosing whether simply to exchange words or engage the idea at hand. Neither is accurate, but which is more true? This question has no easy answer, for a translator is necessarily an interpreter. With respect to the Gospel of John's use of *logos*, I hear centuries of speculation within Greek philosophy about the origin and structure of the universe. *Logos* played as common a role in Hellenistic cosmology as the Big Bang in ours. Yet how does one convey this in translation? This exemplifies a huge aspect of the problem, which is in part why, as the saying goes, "All translations lie."

Lost in Translation

When I first began to study Greek, I had no idea what was coming. I simply assumed that if the New Testament was worth studying, it was worth the effort to do so in Greek. From preachers I had heard, I expected to learn what words "really mean" and to find many questions answered by gaining a clearer grasp of grammar. Both expectations were met and both were undermined, as obvious mistakes were avoided but new ways of seeing things appeared. To my unexpected delight, the Greek New Testament also revealed dimensions of the cultural world that gave it birth and brought individual authors into focus. Each reader of Greek has his or her own experience of these things. Here are a number of mine.

Greek Words

One of the first vocabulary words I learned in Greek was *doulos*, which my professor emphasized meant "slave" and not "servant" as it is so often mistranslated in older versions of the English Bible. I dutifully accepted this explanation without understanding why. Over time, and with exposure to ancient history and writings, I learned that the Greek word describes people who were owned and controlled absolutely by others, i.e., chattel slaves; creatures whom one was welcome to beat; those whom one assumed to be foolish; and those over whom one harbored a sense of superiority. A responsible reader of the New Testament cannot soften the brutality that slavery represents. This was the point of my teacher's insistence to translate *doulos* as "slave."

In Lk 6:39, Jesus asks, "Can a blind person guide a blind person? Will not both fall into a pit?" What immediately comes to my mind when I read this is, "Why is there a pit? Did these people like to go around digging holes?" The answer lies in the environment. People dug drainage ditches, defensive trenches and, what is most likely relevant here, cisterns, which collected and stored water. In the dry climate in which Jesus lived, people had to capture and store as much rainfall as possible. Scraping a hole out of rock created a compartment where rainwater could be channeled and kept on hand. The very apparent strangeness of "pit" is a clue to think cross-culturally.

That words come woven into a cultural fabric enlivens them with connotation. When Paul formulates an argument by asking the question, "Is it advantageous?" or "beneficial?" he uses one of the most common questions raised in the Greco-Roman world to determine the best course of action. The apostle, therefore, follows a well-worn path of thinking and decision making. When Paul prays that Christians will be able to discern what is truly important, to differentiate between the better and lesser things in life, he uses the philosopher's lenses to view the world and their vocabulary to describe it. In similar fashion, friendship, flattery, bragging, and bold speech have rich associations in ancient culture. In the Gospels, when a demon names itself "Legion," the reference to the Roman military injects criticism of the Roman Empire into the story. Readers look into another world when reading the New Testament, and that world is populated by Greek-speaking people in the early Roman Empire.

The preceding examples of New Testament vocabulary demonstrate that each has connotations and meanings that simply do not transfer from one language to another. Sometimes knowledge of the Greek word solves problems, other times it raises issues that complicate translation. Either way, the experience of reading the New Testament changes.

Greek Grammar

Reading the New Testament in Greek makes the reader much more conscious of its grammar and the nuances of its communication.

Often, Greek grammar communicates things that escape translation. For example, the New Testament asks leading questions, though few translations express just how clearly the correct answer is implied. Let's revisit Lk 6:39: "Can a blind person guide a blind person? Will not both fall into a pit?" The English reader can infer immediately that the answer to the first is, "No," a blind person should not guide another blind person, and the second answer is, "Yes." However, the grammar makes it easy on the Greek reader by suggesting the correct answer. These questions could be translated more literally as, "A blind person can't guide a blind person, can he? They'll both fall into a pit, won't they?"

As another example, the Greek language has four ways of constructing "if-then" statements, each having different nuances about likelihood. For example, when a Pharisee thinks to himself, "If this man [Jesus] were a prophet, he would have known who and what kind of woman this is . . ." (Lk 7:39), the grammar communicates additional information about the Pharisee's point of view: If Jesus were a prophet, and he is not, he would have known, but does not. The reader can infer this in English, but this extra information is explicit in Greek. Does this matter? Think of it as the difference between generic chocolate and taste-bud-exploding chocolate: both are good, but one provides fuller, more exciting flavor.

In general, paying attention to Greek grammar clarifies the logic of arguments, yet often it multiplies the options. For example, in Rom 5:12, the phrase, "because all have sinned" may be translated in a variety of ways. Alternatives include "in whom all sinned," "with the result that all sinned," or "inasmuch as all sinned." These differences create space for competing theological arguments, making it hard to know what Paul wished to say about the effects of Adam's sin on the human race.

One of the most distinctive characteristics of ancient Greek is that it is a highly inflected language, meaning each word takes on many different forms. Concretely, this means the letters at the end and, sometimes, the beginning of words change to communicate something additional about the word. English does this to a lesser degree, for example: I walk*ed* the dog*s*. Adding -*ed* to the end of a verb tells you the action occurred in the past, while adding -*s* to the end of a noun tells you that more than one dog is involved. An English speaker knows this immediately, without thinking. Imagine a language in which the letters change at the end of every noun, every verb, and every adjective, and in which nouns may have a dozen different forms and verbs, hundreds. This is *walk/walked* and *dog/dogs* on steroids. This is Greek.

Aided by varied endings, nouns can play dozens of roles in a Greek sentence. The translator usually has to insert a preposition into the translation to help make sense of these relationships. When Paul refers to the "love of God," he does so with two nouns, *love* and *God*. In the Greek, there is no third word, "of," which an English translator adds to signify a relationship between the two nouns, rendering the two nouns as "love of God." But this remains ambiguous: Does Paul refer to his own love of God or the love God extends? A reader of English can, of course, recognize this question, but, for me, it became more obvious when reading Greek. This same question arises with "faith of Christ." Does this phrase mean one's faith in Christ or the faith Christ demonstrates? Scholars debate the answer. Throughout the English New Testament, then, when one reads two nouns connected by "of," such as "preaching of Christ" or "baptism of repentance," there is a long list of potential meanings to consider. Are translators doing their jobs if they interpret what "*x* of *y*" means (e.g., "Christ's faith" or "faith in Christ"), or should they render it woodenly "*x* of *y*" ("faith of Christ") and leave it for the reader to guess?

A Greek verb can take more than a hundred different forms, and some are spelled the same way, creating ambiguities. Add to this the general lack of punctuation in Greek manuscripts, and we encounter a problem like Jn 14:1. Do Jesus' words (a) affirm, "You believe in God"; (b) command, "Believe in God"; or (c) ask, "Do you believe in God?" Each of the three options is a legitimate and accurate translation. The translator must interpret and then choose.

Languages take their own forms and combine words into sentences differently. These diverging patterns create gaps that no translation can eliminate. Translators make countless decisions with every sentence, most slight and unnoticed, but even these represent change in how a text communicates. This is what makes translation an art and makes literal translation an illusion.

John 3:1–16

It used to be that every time a football flew through the goalposts, an evangelist lurking in the stands held up a bright yellow sign to remind TV viewers of a Bible verse, usually Jn 3:3 or Jn 3:16, which mention "born again" (KJV) and "eternal life." To provide a sense of what reading the New Testament in Greek would be like, let's examine the opening verses of John 3 to see how knowledge of Greek changes how it is read.

John 3, set in Jerusalem, presents Jesus having a conversation with Nicodemus, a ruler of the Jews. Only John's Gospel makes any mention of Nicodemus. Unlike other Jewish leaders mentioned in the New Testament, Nicodemus has a Greek name, which puzzles me. Moreover, Jesus calls this otherwise unknown person "the" teacher of Israel (3:10). Bible translators typically mute this historical problem by calling Nicodemus "a" teacher of Israel (e.g., NRSV), even though the Greek text is unambiguously "the." In v. 11 of the Greek text, Jesus begins to speak in plurals: "*I* say to *you alone*" is followed by "*We* say what *we* know" and "*You all* do not receive *our* testimony." The conversation between Jesus and Nicodemus has morphed into a debate between the followers of Christ and the synagogue. These four observations make me suspect that Nicodemus is a fictional character introduced to discuss the relationship of faith in Christ to the Jewish community, an important topic in John's Gospel.

Nicodemus visits Jesus "by night" (3:2). As noted earlier, by taking different forms, Greek nouns can perform different functions. For example, a noun can suggest the point of time at which something happened, its duration, or a certain quality or kind of time. The letters at the end of the noun provide the clue as to which function is relevant. Nicodemus' visit, therefore, takes place not simply at night or during the night but "by night." The function emphasizes the quality or kind of time in which this visit took place: It was a "nighttime kind of action," a visit appropriate to darkness, which the Fourth Gospel views as a place of misunderstanding and disbelief. And indeed, as the following verses unfold, Nicodemus proves himself to be a person who fails to catch on to what Jesus says.

Nicodemus opens the conversation by recognizing that Jesus is a teacher who came from God (no small concession), as proven by the "signs" Jesus performed (3:2). By calling Jesus' miracles "signs," Nicodemus adopts and expresses the point of view of John's Gospel, which habitually calls Jesus' mighty acts "signs," as opposed to deeds of power or wonder. John's Gospel also does not leave the reader to wonder why they are signs. For example, after Jesus heals a blind man, he proclaims himself the light of the world. After Jesus raises a dead man, he names himself the resurrection and life.

Jesus responds to Nicodemus' opening confession with one of the most famous lines from the New Testament, telling him that he must be born again (3:3). What Jesus actually says, however, is a double entendre: Jesus tells Nicodemus he must be born "from above" (as in the NRSV), but Nicodemus understands Jesus to say "again" (as in the KJV). Both "from above" and "again" are perfectly correct ways to translate the underlying Greek word *anōthen*. How does one decide how to translate it? By opting for "again," the King James Version attempts to make sense of Nicodemus' response: Revisiting a mother's womb is to be born "again." But Nicodemus is mistaken—stupid in fact—for the very absurdity of one's retraversing the birth canal should make clear that *anōthen* means "from above." By telling English readers what Nicodemus heard, "You must be born again," they are left in the dark as to what Jesus actually says, which is, "You must be born from above." This double entendre on the part of Jesus plays a critical role. Failure to see this in English obscures the conversation and its connections to the Fourth Gospel's religion.

A second double entendre appears in v. 8, in which Jesus draws an analogy from nature. "The *wind* blows where it chooses, and you hear the sound of it, but you do not know where it comes from or where it goes." To clarify, Jesus adds, "So it is with everyone who is born of the *Spirit*." This sounds straightforward, but the Greek word for both *wind* and *Spirit* is one and the same word, *pneuma*. So, to explain what it is to be born from above, Jesus describes it as being born of "water and spirit." He then elaborates on what *Spirit* means and, in so doing, turns to another meaning of the word *pneuma*, namely *wind*, to provide an analogy.

Does failure to recognize the double meaning of *pneuma* matter to the English reader? Not to the extent of *anōthen*. But wait, there's more. Where does the wind come from? Where does it go? These questions introduce two different Greek words for *where* that

John's Gospel repeats often: *pothen* and *pou*, which mean "where from" and "where to." Older English translates these clearly as "whence" and "whither," which has the advantage of replacing the single Greek word with a single, clear, accurate English word. Today, we are stuck translating *pothen* as "where . . . from" and *pou* as "where . . . to." This is unfortunate because it obscures the use of *pothen* and *pou* throughout John's Gospel, where these two little words represent profound questions. In fact, they serve as shorthand in John's Gospel to authenticate Christ and to define salvation. The one who comes from heaven brings revelation; the one who returns to heaven can extend eternal life. "Whence" and "whither" are crucial questions in the spiritual quest of the Fourth Gospel, with eternal life hanging in the balance. The person who is born of the spirit participates in a heavenly origin and destiny unknown to those who are not born of the spirit. The simple analogy of wind is not so simple after all.

These comments on Jn 3:1–11 are my attempt to illustrate how reading it in Greek changes the reader's experience as opposed to reading it in English. Reading it in Greek raises questions about the author's contributions to the narrative and brings greater clarity about what is being said and why.

Individual Writing Styles

The biggest surprise I encountered in the Greek New Testament was the different voices of individual authors. Habits of writing style emerged in the words authors chose, how they put together sentences, and how they imagined their readers. Some played with words; some wove complex sentences. Some were calm, some expressive. Taken together, these habits contributed to a unique profile for each writer.

Here is a quick synopsis. The simplicity of John stands on one end, with Mark not far off, while the artistry of Hebrews stands at the other. Improvement appears over time, as Matthew and Luke edit Mark and add touches of refinement, while the letters written outside the Pauline corpus show more literary care in their writing, so that James and 1 Peter have more elegance and complexity than Paul, and their styles lie closer to Hebrews. This underscores that different people with varying talents and tastes composed early Christian writings.

The Gospel of John has particularly distinctive traits. We have already observed examples of its fondness for word play, whether puns, metaphors, or symbols. It often indulges in irony. The penchant for simple sentences also distinguishes John, starting with the very first words: "In the beginning was the *logos*. And the *logos* was with God. And the *logos* was God." This is elementary sentence structure, especially for Greek. Sometimes, John does not even bother using "and," providing no conjunctions between clauses, which is strange for Greek literature.

The overriding impression of the style of the Gospel of John is one of simple sentence structure and vocabulary. In his contribution to *A Grammar of New Testament Greek*, the scholar Nigel Turner says of John, "The idiom is the very simplest, and the vocabulary the poorest in the New Testament relative to the size of the book." To spin that more positively, the Gospel of John lacks complexity and elegance, but has a knack for saying much with little.

The Gospel of Mark resembles John in its lack of literary pretension. It is written simply and moves forward quickly, sometimes too quickly, as, on occasion, redundancies appear and grammar breaks down. What is most telling about Mark's style is the way Matthew and Luke improve it when they incorporate Mark into their own work, smoothing some of Mark's rough edges and switching out Mark's simple vocabulary for more literary words. This does not mean that Matthew and Luke are elegant writers, but on a scale on which Matthew and Luke are good not great, Mark is inferior.

Another observation about the style of the Gospels is the evidence of Semitic influence. Luke likes to write, "And it happened that," which is a literal translation of a common Hebrew expression. The simple way John strings sentences together probably reflects Hebrew and Aramaic grammar. In fact, when people talk about the style of the New Testament, the conversation typically turns to ways in which the language reveals Hebrew and Aramaic influences.

Turning from the Gospels, one finds a number of other authors remain. At the opposite end of the spectrum from John and Mark is the anonymous Epistle to the Hebrews. Its use of complex sentences is evident from the beginning and continues throughout the letter. The author is talented, and the letter is a pleasure to read.

The apostle Paul blends simple and complex sentences. His complexity does not approach the elegance of Hebrews, nor is his simplicity like that of the Fourth Gospel. Paul writes as if he might talk fast and expressively. Often, he sounds like he is in the middle of a conversation, using rhetorical questions or pretending to have an imaginary conversation partner who asks him questions, a rhetorical device seen in philosophical writings from Paul's time. His style reflects the give and take of debate—and he was embroiled in many. This apostle likes quick, pithy sentences and does not shrink from irony and sarcasm. In addition to short jabs, he uses complex sentences, and these appear most frequently when his thoughts turn more theologically dense, such as in a prayer or confession. Sometimes, his grammar breaks down as his thoughts seem to run ahead of his pen. On occasion, he simply gets caught in a complex sentence and fails to resolve it well. But the overriding impression of Paul's writing is of immediacy, of a person who is thinking his way through issues and engaged in genuine conversation.

Related to style is the matter of aesthetics. Reading the elegance of the author of Hebrews or the opening sentence of Luke's Gospel is delightful. Recognizing where a writer wished to emphasize a word also enlivens the experience. To be sure, translators can introduce elegance, and biblical translators have done this well, but it is a pleasure to look behind the good work of translators to the creativity of the original authors. Doing this brings their individual voices and personalities into view.

Greek Bore Gifts

The New Testament was written in a particular time and place and in a particular language. The historical context does not simply provide background, however, it provides actual content. Previous examples imply this, but let me comment on two specific types of contribution.

Form Criticism

The Christian scriptures come packaged not only in Greek words and grammar but also in the formal structures of Hellenistic culture.

For example, how does one tell a story about a miraculous healing? The ancient world had a formula for this. When one compares stories in the New Testament with those outside of it, they resemble each other, sharing a common outline. Such habits of communication determined the large and small shapes or forms of material in the New Testament.

In our own culture, there are similar generic patterns. An example is the classic story line: Boy meets girl; girl rejects boy; boy wins girl; love prevails. In a coming of age story, a young person must overcome a challenge or obstacle, often a parent. In school, many learn how to structure a business letter, limerick, or sonnet; compose an essay in five paragraphs; or write a research paper. These are standard forms of writing. In sum, how a person puts together ideas or stories often follows preestablished, recognizable patterns. Identifying and describing these common patterns, or forms, is a practice known as "form criticism."

The canonical Gospels contain many examples of Jesus arguing with rivals. Sometimes, they try to trap Jesus in a verbal corner, as when they, not at all innocently, ask whether Jews should pay taxes to Rome. Jesus responds, saying, "Give Caesar what belongs to Caesar, and give God what belongs to God." Trick question deflected; score one for Jesus. But, interpreters have asked what exactly Jesus meant. How does one turn this witticism into policy? Again, comparison of stories in the New Testament with those in the broader world provides guidance. There are many examples of stories told by wise people in antiquity that climax with a prudent saying. Jesus' debates look just like these. Usually, such stories are just a few sentences long, with enough narrative to set up the punch line. Then, wham, the hero delivers a withering retort that proves who is truly smart, clever, or funny. The answer typically is pithy, like Jesus' response about taxes; and the point is to prove who is wiser. The goal is not to formulate policy, but to win. When apparently trapped, Jesus eludes his antagonists with an unanticipated, effective answer, proof positive that he is the wise teacher. Such stories are also called *apophthegmata* (a Greek word) to emphasize the all-important saying at the end or "pronouncement-stories" that give a nod to both the saying and the story that gives it flesh.

Related to this was the delight ancient authors took in wise, pithy sayings. My Latin textbook was populated with many of these. "Life is short; art endures" is repeated often. Examples appear throughout the New Testament. Here are two from the apostle Paul: "Knowledge puffs up, but love builds up" (1 Cor 8:1); and, "Whenever I am weak, then I am strong" (2 Cor 12:10). The ubiquity of such memorable sayings throughout the New Testament lends it punch and reflects the tastes and preferences of people in the ancient world.

John 3 presents another example. Jesus and Nicodemus engage in a dialogue that, at first glance, is not odd. But in many stories in the other Gospels, conversations tend to be quick exchanges that help drive the plot or climax with a single, pithy saying. In Jn 3 and 4 and subsequent chapters, conversations build or give way to long answers. John's conversations sound more like dramatic dialogue or philosophical interviews. This is another example of the Hellenistic culture providing form, in this case, the form of dialogue.

The moral teachings in the New Testament borrow literary forms from their larger Greco-Roman world. The lists of virtues and vices that appear throughout the New Testament may seem natural and unremarkable, yet they reflect a way of talking about behavior that existed in the broader, Greek-speaking world. In Colossians, Ephesians, Titus, and 1 Peter, there are instructions provided to various members of the household, including specific instructions to masters and slaves, husbands and wives, and children. Each group receives directions appropriate to its conventional household role. Philosophers also used this method of organizing advice, today called "household codes."

Christians also borrowed Greco-Roman forms in composing their writings. Letters in the New Testament identify the author and recipient in their opening words, reflecting how letters in the ancient world were generally written. The use of epistles for teaching also reflects a longstanding practice in philosophical schools. In Galatians, Paul recounts his interactions with the church in Jerusalem. For historians of Paul, this information is golden. Why, however, did he offer this recitation? Again, the practice mirrors how people composed arguments in the ancient world. In a dispute, a speaker had to present the facts that were relevant to the case being argued.

For Paul, his trips to Jerusalem were relevant to the debate so he included them. In rhetoric, this portion of an argument is called by the Latin term, *narratio*.

The opening sentences of the Gospel according to Luke and the Acts of the Apostles also reflect a convention of ancient writers. In multi-scroll works, authors devoted the opening words of each scroll to talking about what they were writing. They looked backward at what went before and anticipated what was to come. They also commented on the work of previous authors. Such openings functioned similarly to the title page, table of contents, and introductory preface of a modern book.

One of the important results of biblical scholarship has been to recognize how the cultural world of the New Testament contributed to the very shape and content of early Christian writings. As a result, one can conclude that Hellenistic culture donated not only vocabulary and grammar but also actual form and content to the New Testament.

The Septuagint (LXX)

Though the "Old Testament" was written in Hebrew, with a little bit in Aramaic, most early Christians read the Jewish scriptures in Greek translation. These translations are called the *Septuagint* because of the stories that were told to explain and legitimate their origin. Legend has it that 72 scholars were invited to Egypt to translate into Greek the Jewish scriptures, so that these texts could be added to the king's library. The number of scholars involved led to calling the Greek translations by the Latin number for seventy, *Septuagint*, and referring to it with the Roman numeral for seventy, LXX. The stories tell of God's intervention in the translation process, thus lending the translation legitimacy and authority. The early church, which relied on the Septuagint, embraced and repeated these myths.

There was no known movement among early Greek-speaking Christians to get back to the Hebrew/Aramaic texts of Jewish scriptures. These Christians were perfectly happy using Greek translations, which influenced the language of the New Testament and early church. For example, in Matthew's beatitude, "Blessed are the meek" (5:5), the use of the word *meek* draws on the novel usage of the Septuagint, when it refers to the people of God whose lives are so typified by powerlessness that the plural adjective, "the meek," became a way of describing and identifying God's people. Jesus then offers a surprising vision by holding out the promise that God's rule will belong to such people.

Psalm 22 describes a person experiencing great anguish, and who, among other things, is "despised by the people." The Septuagint uses a blatantly colloquial word to translate *despised*. Early Christians read this psalm as describing Jesus in his sufferings and referred to it frequently in their writings. As a result, the colloquialism used by the translator(s) of Ps 22 became commonplace in the writings of Christians. Early Christians started quoting Ps 22 and the use of the nonliterary word for *despise*, or *contempt*, exploded. The Septuagint set a precedent that was followed repeatedly.

More substantially, the Christian doctrine of the virgin birth depends on the Septuagint. The Hebrew text of the prophet Isaiah says that a "young woman" will conceive (7:14). "Young woman" was translated into Greek with the word *parthenon*, which added to the meaning of "young woman" the more restrictive connotation of virgin. In the Gospel according to Matthew, when Mary becomes pregnant through divine intervention, Isaiah is quoted as support: "the virgin (*parthenon*) will conceive" (1:23). The Christian story of the pregnant virgin only works in the Greek translation of Isaiah. This confirms that Greek-speaking, Greek-writing Christians were reading and learning from the Jewish scriptures in Greek translation.

The Septuagint's most important contribution to the New Testament was the example of scripture itself. Before Christians collected their own writings and compiled their own scriptures, they had the example of Jewish sacred texts. When surveying the books the early church borrowed from Jews, one finds the longer list of texts that reflects the Septuagint, not the shorter list of Hebrew writings. The Septuagint was the early church's Bible and prepared the way for the creation of the New Testament.

In sum, Jewish scriptures influenced the New Testament enormously, and in general, this means the Septuagint, which contributed canon, content, diction, and vocabulary to the New Testament. Its importance compelled Christians to regard the translation of the Septuagint as the product of divine intervention.

These examples, taken from form criticism and the Septuagint, demonstrate ways in which the Greek origin of the New Testament contributed importantly to the content of the New Testament. If the New Testament had been written in Aramaic or Coptic, or some other language, would it say the same thing, just with a different alphabet? No, emphatically no! A different language would have brought different forms, influences, and content.

Mind the Gap

The previous sections argued that translation hides many things. This leads to a question of degree. Granting that translation limits understanding, how consequential are the differences? I have heard and read assurances that these problems have no impact on Christian doctrine and practice. I disagree.

The Bible

Reading the New Testament in Greek should affect one's views about how the Bible came into being. Mythical explanations run aground on concrete details.

A theologically conservative belief about the Bible comes from the Evangelical Theological Society, whose confessional affirmation states, "The Bible alone, and the Bible in its entirety, is the Word of God written and is therefore inerrant in the autographs." By autograph is meant the original document, the very letter that Paul wrote to the church in Philippi or the very Gospel that came into existence when the author of Matthew's Gospel came to the end and put down his quill.

The "autograph" is a commonsense notion but, at times, fictional. As it stands in the Bible, 2 Corinthians is not the letter Paul wrote. It is made up of at least two letters Paul wrote, and more likely others, as well as a paragraph written by someone else. What then is the autograph of 2 Corinthians? Is it the individual letters as they were written or the initial composite version that is known today? John's Gospel offers a similar issue, as it had a variety of editors with, perhaps, three different editions. A common view is that chapter 21 was a secondary addition, early, but an addition. Is the autograph then the version with or without chapter 21? It seems that if the Society qualifies its belief that the Bible is free of errors with an imaginary autograph, then getting behind one's translation does lead to problems of doctrine for this particular theological point of view, which is not shared by all Christian groups.

Not only are "autographs" mythical in theory, but also in reality for they do not exist. Scholars have done remarkable work coordinating more than 5,700 manuscripts to reconstruct a reliable version of the Greek Testament. While great work has been done, the result is a good approximation of what the New Testament looked like in the fourth century, not in the first and second. The gap between the writing of Mark's Gospel and current critical reconstruction is a bit greater than that between Benjamin Franklin and today. This leaves much time for changes, a number of which scholars have identified.

More importantly, reading the Greek New Testament makes an enormously positive contribution to knowledge of the origins of the New Testament, because it makes clearer the relationships that exist among the various texts. The precise similarities in words and grammar among Matthew, Mark, and Luke stand out in Greek and demand explanation. That three different people culled eye-witness testimony and wrote their stories independently does not hold up when their writings are compared line-by-line, word-by-word. Literary dependence is the only reasonable explanation of the evidence. Such comparisons further show the particular interests of the individual authors. I have found no better way to hear the individual voices of the Evangelists than by comparing them word-by-word in Greek.

Hearing individual voices extends to the letters in the New Testament. For example, scholars have questioned whether Paul really wrote 1 and 2 Timothy and Titus, three letters that are referred to as the Pastoral Letters, since they provide advice about how to guide churches. The bulk of words used in these three letters do not appear in Paul's other letters. The word *Savior*, which seems so natural to Christianity, is not one Paul usually used; yet in the Pastorals it appears often. The word *piety* (Greek, *eusebeia*) also appears in the Pastorals but never elsewhere in Paul. Both of these words are commonplace in Greco-Roman writings, and the latter plays an enormous role in Greco-Roman ethics, describing the proper conduct of one's relationships with people and gods. One ancient writer defined *eusebeia* as observing ancestral customs. If someone wished to talk about appropriate behavior during the Roman Empire, they would very likely have used this word as naturally as a person today would mention justice, tolerance, or family values. Yet practicing piety endorses the status quo, whereas Paul tried to introduce people to a new god and held a critical view of ancestral law. In addition, when Paul describes appropriate behavior, he typically argues from a Christian belief, like of the spirit or imminent judgment, not social convention. It is hard to imagine a word that is further from Paul's way of thinking than *eusebeia* in the Greek text. Use of this word is one hint that we are reading someone other than Paul.

Reading the Greek New Testament certainly changed how I think about its origins. The Greek text provides lenses that bring into focus the origins and history of the text, which inform how one thinks about scripture. Many people who read the Bible in all its original languages find this to be true, as evidenced by the thoughtful statements about the Bible produced by the Second Vatican Council.

The Church

Translation into English also affects how people think about the church. The early church used words common in the ancient world to describe itself. Today the words sound like specifically Christian words, lacking secular connotations. This tricks one into thinking too formally about church leadership and organization in the New Testament.

Today, one reads *apostle* and thinks of a special group of church leaders, typically from the past, though some contemporary groups continue to use the designation. However, the English word *apostle* was invented for the specific purpose of translating the Greek word *apostolos*. More precisely, *apostle* is not a translation but an invention, forming a new word by simple borrowing. English letters replaced their Greek equivalents, a process called transliteration, and voilá, a new English word was born. Nevertheless, the Greek word *apostolos* has a history. Used occasionally in ancient Greek for an ambassador, envoy, or delegate, Christians adopted the word to identify an authorized representative, probably because of the frequent use in Jewish writings of the related verb, *apostellein*, which means "to send" and implies a commission. For the early church, then, *apostolos* identified a person sent in an official capacity, a messenger. These normal uses disappear under the made-up word *apostle*.

Seeing *apostolos* as a normal Greek word, it becomes much easier to recognize that the early church called many people apostles, not just the Twelve Disciples. For example, in Rom 16:7, Paul writes, "Greet Andronicus and Junia, my relatives who were in prison with me; they are prominent among the apostles, and they were in Christ before I was" (NRSV). The overabundance of evidence from the ancient world indicates that Junia is the correct translation, as opposed to Junias, which some translations use. Why might this matter? Junia is a woman, and Junias is a man. Paul describes an otherwise unknown woman, Junia, as a prominent apostle. Given the church's exclusion of women from leadership for the better part of two millennia, recognizing Junia as both an apostle and woman certainly surprised me.

Deacon is another example of transliteration. Though it meant a servant, attendant, helper, or messenger, the Greek word *diakonos* was not really translated but simply borrowed. The result is that some readers are tricked into seeing the contemporary diaconate when encountering this word, as people frequently read the present back into the past, a common mistake called anachronism. Many readers make the further error of leveling the entire New Testament so every appearance of *diakonos* means the same thing. These misreadings stumble most clumsily in Paul's letters, in which the apostle uses this word to describe his own preaching.

Paul refers to a woman, Phoebe, as a *diakonos* and helper, by which he does not mean a member of the ladies' auxiliary or the diaconate. With the word *diakonos* Paul is calling Phoebe a preacher. As for *helper*, much cultural information about leadership has been lost in translation: Paul is calling Phoebe a "patroness," which is not a trifling word. This implies social superiority and clout, which means Paul regarded Phoebe as a church leader. Had the idea existed in Paul's mental map, he would have regarded Phoebe as an officer of the church, which, yes, is an anachronistic analogy. Add to this the aforementioned example of Junia, and a very different picture from what has prevailed for the majority of church history emerges, one of women involved in church leadership.

The word *church* is yet another problem. The Greek word for church, *ekklēsia,* pointed to a gathering of citizens for a meeting of the body politic. Early Christians adopted this word to describe their new social group. Today, we are fully comfortable translating the word as "church." In so doing, we anachronistically bring all of our own assumptions about buildings, clergy, membership, ministries, budgets, and programs to bear that simply did not exist when Paul used the word, while the political connotations for Paul's readers have vanished. If a city displeased the emperor, he might abolish its *ekklēsia,* or conversely, express his pleasure by allowing one. The members of the *ekklēsia* enjoyed privileges not extended to nonmembers. As component parts of God's kingdom, Christian groups paralleled the civic assemblies that existed within the Roman Empire. When the early Christians said "church," they heard very different connotations than people of today.

English translation obscures what the church is and who its leaders are. This affects how people think about these questions. Failure to understand the Greek text has certainly helped exclude women from leadership.

Salvation

Common words for *salvation* are also problems for translators. For example, the words *expiation* and *propitiation* translate what is literally "mercy seat," a reference to the ancient Ark of the Covenant (e.g., Rom 3:25). Translators consistently import theories of atonement, all of them later developments, into their translation of the "mercy seat."

Righteousness, in Greek *dikaiosynē,* is a bigger problem. If I were translating non-Christian writings, I would likely use "justice" to translate *dikaiosynē,* a frequently used word and, in fact, one of the most common virtues in the Classical world. If a Greek writer presented a list of admirable qualities, *dikaiosynē* was likely to be on it. Christians had no special claim to this virtue.

A further problem is that speakers of English have no word to express righteousness as a verb. I might pretend this problem does not exist by saying "I do righteousness," but that only works around the problem and is unnatural sounding. "I make it right" would be a better way of talking, but now I could just as easily be setting the thermostat or fixing a wobbling table as balancing the scales of justice. An actual verb would be something like "I righteousize," which, thankfully, does not exist.

The English Bible worked around this problem by translating the related Greek verb *dikaioō* with the word "justify." Translators had to do something, but the relationship between the verb *dikaioō* and its noun *dikaiosynē* vanished beneath their English counterparts "justify" and "righteousness." Now, however, there is a problem because we are using two different sets of English words to cover a single set of Greek words. This creates misunderstanding for readers of the English Bible. The reader of Greek recognizes that "justification" and "righteousness" are one and the same and that the wider pagan world valued them just as highly, though the translation "justice" captures better how they would have thought of it.

Faith is yet another challenging translation. The customary translations of the noun *pistis* and its related, or cognate, verb *pisteuō*, namely "faith" and "believe," entail the same kind of problem seen with "righteousness" and "justify," i.e., two sets of English words translate a single set in Greek. A second problem arises from the historical-social context. While "faith" and "believe" are entirely valid and accurate as translations, they represent only one aspect of meaning. "Trust" and "loyalty" are equally common ways to gloss the Greek noun, *pistis*, to emphasize the social connotations it may express. Loyalty played an enormous role in ancient social relationships, not just in the household but also in the public sphere, even up to geopolitics. Low-ranking people expressed loyalty to their superiors, who returned loyalty in exchange. In the movie *The Godfather*, when Don Corleone fixes a supplicant's problem, the expectation is established that the beneficiary will help Don Corleone when requested. Loyalty calls forth loyalty. The cult of the Roman emperor played a similar function, allowing imperial subjects to express their loyalty to the emperor and, thereby, leverage generous expressions of the emperor's loyalty in return.

What then is faith in Christ? Intellectual assent, ritualized actions, or social solidarity? All are relevant; as a result, a modern person's reading about faith and a historian's thinking of *pistis* as a cultural artifact are two very different things. Long lost is the important nuance of responding to beneficence and power with a display of loyalty. I find this hard to reconcile with a view of *pistis* that regards faith as opposed to and void of any work or deed.

The word for *disciple* more typically translates as "student." Jesus had disciples the way his contemporary philosophers had disciples. Or to say that differently, Jesus had students the way ancient philosophers had students. In antiquity, philosophy contained a moral component such that emulation of teachers was common. Contemporary education functions differently, so finding the right English word to translate *student/disciple* is difficult.

In sum, many factors impede the understanding of words in the New Testament. Present knowledge of the church, lack of knowledge of ancient culture, and the absence of appropriate target words in English inevitably skew how the New Testament is read. To claim otherwise fails to think in Greek or historically.

Greek Is Translation

In this final section, I offer a surprise twist: The Greek New Testament reflects a stage of translation. The texts themselves are not translated, but they represent a linguistic shift among the early Christians, from Aramaic to Greek. This change invites one to think about the historical consequences, not simply of the fact that the New Testament is written in Greek but of the language in which it is was not written.

The New Testament was not written in Aramaic, the language Jesus spoke. This puts distance between the texts we read and Jesus. Before the Greek texts behind our English texts could be written, the religion of Jesus and his first followers had to move out of Aramaic and into Greek. The Greek New Testament implies a historical and cultural gap between the New Testament and Jesus.

Aramaic was the language of the Persian Empire and was a Semitic language, like Hebrew, which it displaced as the spoken language of native people in Palestine. Jesus spoke Aramaic in his home and, presumably, taught in Aramaic. I qualify this because archaeological evidence shows that Greek and Latin were also present in Palestine.

That Jesus spoke Greek does not stretch the imagination, though whether he used it for teaching remains a question. At times in the Gospels, Jesus speaks Aramaic, which suggests this was what he commonly spoke. The examples, however, are not clear cut. Using a foreign language to speak a magical word is typical, and quoting Scripture in Aramaic adds authenticity and drama, so these examples do not say as much as we would like. More helpful is the use of the Aramaic phrase *marana tha* in the early church, which expresses the wish that the Lord would come. The evidence for this liturgical expression appears at the end of 1 Corinthians, where the apostle Paul writes, "Our Lord, come!" (16:22). Paul does not express this wish with Greek words but with the Aramaic phrase *marana tha*, which must have been a popular saying among Christian communities, since Paul assumed his Greek-speaking audience could understand it. This, in turn, points to an earlier circle of Christians who coined the phrase and thus spoke Aramaic. It seems reasonable to situate Jesus and his followers in this community, given some of their names, such as, John, James, Matthew, Bartholomew, and most obviously Kephas, known more commonly by the Greek equivalent, Peter.

Scholars also have uncovered examples in which understanding what Jesus said makes more sense if translated back into Aramaic, further suggesting that Jesus taught in Aramaic. An important example appears in Jesus' self-designation, "son of man." On occasion, this expression alludes clearly to a prophetic vision of the biblical prophet Daniel (7:13, KJV), who saw a figure who looked like a "son of man," that is to say, human, descending from heaven to render judgment. In still other places, the phrase looks like a way to express one's humanity, one's identification with and connection to other people. This meaning is an idiom with its roots in Semitic languages; this usage is precisely why the figure in Daniel is called a "son of man." The scholar Geza Vermes uncovered yet a third meaning in Aramaic sources, where "son of man" serves as a circumlocution for "I," that is a roundabout way for Jesus to refer to himself. Vermes provided a way of interpreting the origin and evolution of Jesus as "Son of Man" that extends from a natural way of self-reference (son of man) to the application of a title (Son of Man) and a way for interpreting the significance of Jesus. It places Jesus squarely in a world where people spoke Aramaic.

If one assumes that Jesus did, in fact, teach in Aramaic, then his teachings are encountered in translation, for scholar and layperson alike. The Greek New Testament remains one step removed from Jesus' actual words. If one assumes everything I have written here about how the shift from Greek to English resembles the change from Aramaic to Greek, one should exercise humility and caution in asserting knowledge about Jesus.

The move from Aramaic to Greek also brings profound consequences. If each Gospel author presents Jesus' words in translation, then the numerous examples of shared wording become a puzzle. Translations are dynamic, variable exercises. There is rarely one and only one accurate and acceptable translation. The flexibility inherent in the order of words in a Greek sentence and the options afforded by Greek grammar to organize a Greek sentence make precise agreements between Gospels all the more remarkable. Only one conclusion is possible: The Evangelists were copying written sources, whether one another or other now-lost writings, or both. As observed earlier, the relationships between the canonical Gospels must be literary, not simply oral.

Jesus' speaking Aramaic also casts suspicion on the authorship of the Letter of James and the Letter of Jude. If Aramaic was the language of Jesus' home, how did his brothers learn to write Greek? Speaking workplace Greek would be just a baby step. Speaking Greek fluently represents a much larger stride. Writing it required education, and writing it well was an advanced skill requiring time and practice. The quality of James and Jude precludes an uneducated author as well as translation from Aramaic. Are we to imagine Jesus toiling long hours to earn the money to put his brothers through school? It is much easier to imagine that the Letters of James and Jude were not really written by Jesus' brothers, but are pseudonymous writings only pretending to have been written by James and Jude.

If Jesus spoke Aramaic, yet the Christian scriptures are written in Greek, a consequential cultural gulf exists between the originator of Christian faith and its documentation. Readers cannot hear Jesus directly.

Conclusion

That the New Testament was written in Greek is a cautionary tale. Translations are but the dull backside of a rich tapestry. No matter how good the translation, much gets muted. Many have studied Greek and can testify to the differences between the English Bible and the Greek New Testament. I have tried to illustrate a number of differences. This reflects a general problem of communication between languages.

More specific problems exist with reference to Christian history. Without Aramaic sources for Jesus, our investigation of Christian origins relies on translation. Not only must readers wonder what they miss in the move from Greek to English but also what was lost in the shift from Aramaic to Greek. People often find that the more they learn, they more they realize how much they do not know. For me, this played out when I realized that Jesus spoke Aramaic.

Readers also must recognize historical blinders. Reading Greek allows one to read the original New Testament but does not allow one to take in the full sweep of the early church. Greek and Latin texts focus our eyes on the church as it grew in the dominant languages of the Roman Empire, yet, within the Mediterranean world and beyond it, churches took root in other languages. Coptic texts from Egypt reveal a vibrant Christianity long absent from textbooks. Along a dramatic eastward arc from Syria to Iraq and on to India, Christianity took root just as profoundly as it did in the Roman Empire. Had these eastern Christians written in Greek or Latin, perhaps they would not have disappeared from the European version of the church's history.

This essay seeks to put into context the experience of reading the New Testament in English by making sure the reader understands that behind the English text is a Greek one. Although translations blur problems of language and history, people continue to produce and read translations, for a translation is far better than the alternative—nothing. I, for one, am glad I did not have to learn Russian to read Tolstoy. Returning to the great poet Goethe, let's give him the final word: "Say what we may of the inadequacy of translation, yet the work is and will always be one of the weightiest and worthiest undertakings in the general concerns of the world."

Questions

1. Some people think the Bible should be translated literally, along the lines of the King James Version. Others think that translators should focus on conveying the meaning, such as the New International Version attempts to do, a method called dynamic equivalence. From your own experience, which view of translation do you think is better?

2. The apostle Paul addresses his readers as *adelphoi*, a plural, masculine noun. Traditionally, *adelphoi* has been translated as "brothers." Many people recognize today that this noun was a friendly term of address that encompassed all of Paul's readers, much as we used to say "mankind" to refer to all people, male and female. Paul did not mean to refer to "all of you men—and not you women," but rather, everyone. So, in the spirit of gender inclusion, many would now translate it as "brothers and sisters" to reflect that everyone is in view. This inclusion creates its own confusion, however, tricking people into thinking Paul explicitly thought to include women as well as men, as if he had actually written "brothers and sisters" in Greek. This inference that Paul explicitly acknowledges each gender is incorrect. How then would you translate *adelphoi*? Why?

3. Translators of versions of the English Bible tend to be more conservative in their work (e.g., Revised Standard Version, as opposed to translations that lack the word *version* in their title, e.g., New English Bible). They tend not to deviate from previous versions without a compelling reason. Do you think it is better to advocate for stability or variety in translations of the Bible? Why?

4. Do the examples in this chapter justify the author's position that reading the New Testament in Greek makes a significant difference in how one understands the Bible? Explain your response.

5. What are some implications of the observation that individual authors wrote parts of the Bible, but their work is credited under the names of others?

6. We have no records of Jesus' teaching preserved in his own language. How would you assess this situation? Do you think this is a problem?

7. The New Testament was written in another language nearly two millennia ago, in another region of the world, and in a different culture. Given that, how directly do you expect it to address your situation in life? How did the examples provided in the essay affect your thinking about the space between the Bible and you?

Further Reading

Issues discussed in this chapter typically appear in literature that assumes a reader's knowledge of Greek, particularly in advanced grammars and dictionaries.

Bakker, Egbert J., ed. *A Companion to the Ancient Greek Language*. Blackwell Companions to the Ancient World. Chichester, West Sussex; Malden, MA: Wiley-Blackwell, 2010.

Horrocks, Geoffrey. *Greek: A History of the Language and Its Speakers*. 2nd ed. Chichester, West Sussex; Malden, MA: Wiley-Blackwell, 2010.

McKnight, Edgar. *What is Form Criticism?* Guides to Biblical Scholarship. New Testament Series. Philadelphia: Fortress Press, 1973.

The New Testament Was Written

To say the New Testament was written in Greek is to make two statements. We just considered the first, namely, that Greek is the language of the New Testament. The second may be too obvious to note, but it, too, merits consideration: The New Testament was written. Period. This simple observation requires people with income, education, and leisure to read and write; the technology to facilitate both activities; and distribution channels linking all. The writing extends throughout centuries and occurs in a cultural context with many dimensions. This essay focuses on the social and technological.

". . . Written" Requires Writing

Every book in the ancient world was written by hand, not only an author's drafts and finished manuscript but also every subsequent copy. In the modern age, the first copy produced on a printing press is expensive, but subsequent ones cost pennies on the original outlay. No economy of scale existed for hand copying. To speed the process, one person could read aloud while a few others wrote what they heard, as happened in a scriptorium, a room where scribes created multiple copies at the same time. Still, each listener produced only one copy and did so by hand. This has important consequences for publication and quality control.

Mistakes Were Inevitable (or, Scriptures Sin)

Copying by hand introduces error. I remember the challenge of copying what I had already written, as a primary school student, to improve penmanship and eliminate errors. The penmanship improved slightly; the errors were fixed; but new errors were created. It was a challenge to copy something by hand and not introduce an error of some sort. Little did I know that I was not alone in my experience.

Even Codex Sinaiticus has mistakes. This beautifully copied manuscript, written in uppercase letters called *uncials*, is the oldest complete copy of the New Testament to have survived. At a glance, even the casual observer can see that great care was taken in its production. Dated to the fourth century and produced by three or four scribes, Sinaiticus is arguably the most important written witness to the text of the New Testament. The manuscript takes its name from Mt. Sinai, where it was discovered at the monastery of St. Catherine. In 1844, Constantin von Tischendorf rescued some of its pages from a bin of materials to be burned. Two visits later, in 1859, he finally laid eyes on the entire manuscript. This was followed by the delicate work of negotiating removal of the manuscript from the monastery to Cairo and then Russia for scholarly examination, culminating in a lavish publication in 1862. In 1933, Sinaiticus moved from St. Petersburg to London, purchased by the British Museum from the former Union of the Soviet Socialist Republics, which preferred the cash to the artifact. Anyone now may see Sinaiticus in the treasures room at the British Library or online in its digitized version.

As became clear when von Tischendorf reviewed the manuscript, editors had fixed the text. The first corrections were made immediately upon completion; a quality control measure taken after the original scribes finished their work. Modern scholars, using ultraviolet light, revealed one of those corrections at the conclusion of John's Gospel. After finishing Jn 21:24, the scribe made a decorative flourish and wrote the subscription "Gospel of John." There was just one problem: He forgot v. 25. He had to erase the flourish and subscription and copy the overlooked verse, then rewrite the end matter. This scribe was neither the first nor the last to make a silly mistake despite taking great care.

Scholars have collated and compared thousands of ancient manuscripts, more than 5,700 for the New Testament, and found consistent patterns of errors made by copyists. For example, some Greek letters looked alike, so it was easy to confuse them. Also, a scribe might move from the end of one line to the beginning of the wrong line or might leave off at a word and return to a second, later occurrence of the same word leaving out what came between. For example, Codex Sinaiticus lacks Lk 10:32, because it ends with the same word as v. 31, *antiparēlthen*. After the scribe finished copying 10:31, his eye returned to *antiparēlthen* but mistakenly skipped ahead to the use of *antiparēlthen* at the end of v. 32, and he continued copying with v. 33. Poof! Luke 10:32 was gone. A later corrector, however, wrote v. 32 into the margin.

The mind can trick a scribe into errors. It is easy to substitute synonyms, switch the order of words, and switch around letters. In Jn 5:39, a scribe meant to write the Greek word *martyrousai* but, unfortunately, wrote *hamartanousai*, changing the text from "Scriptures testify" to the humorous assertion that "Scriptures sin." Another common problem among the Gospels is the intrusion of memory, as the version of a story from one Gospel comes to mind when copying the story in a different Gospel. Suddenly, what is unique to Matthew enters the story as told by Mark. Such examples are normal, innocent mistakes.

The scribes who actually thought about their work might be more troublesome than the ones who copied thoughtlessly. Thinking scribes too often corrected mistakes of grammar and vocabulary. Some scribes wrote notes in the margin that confused later scribes, who then introduced the marginalia into the actual text as they copied. Some scribes altered or enhanced the theological teachings of a text to make them conform to a favorite doctrine.

The difference between accident and intent is not always clear. In 1 Tim 3:16 a Christological confession begins with the relative pronoun "who," which the NRSV translates as "he" to produce a clearer English translation. In Greek, "who" looks like this: *OC*. In later manuscripts, this changed from "who" to "God," which in Greek is usually abbreviated to look like this: *ΘC*, with an additional line drawn over the top that signifies an abbreviation. A tiny bar in the middle changes the uppercase omicron, *O*, to an uppercase theta,

Θ, which is the difference between "who" and "God." Codex Sinaiticus reads OC, but a later hand scribbled in ΘC, reflecting the change throughout time from "who" to "God." The older reading clearly is "who," which is confirmed by other confessional passages in the New Testament that likewise begin with "who." The change in 1 Tim 3:16 could have begun with an accident, but its spread suggests scribes who preferred that the text say something grander about Christ and all too willingly adjusted the text.

Throughout the centuries, hand copying introduced tens of thousands of mistakes into New Testament manuscripts. John Mill was one of the pioneers who compared manuscripts and catalogued discrepancies. In *The Greek Testament* (1707), he presented thirty thousand variants! Critics, of course, pounced; but their zeal did not change a single variant. Important work followed in 1734 from Johann Albrecht Bengel, who expanded the database of textual variants and developed important principles for analyzing them. He created the idea that among variant readings of a text, the more difficult reading likely gave rise to the others. Thus, it is more likely that bad grammar was improved, an unusual word replaced, or problematic theology adjusted than the reverse. Such work led, a century later, to Karl Lachmann's edition of the New Testament (1831), which was based on the most ancient manuscripts. Although the choice may sound obvious, it was an important innovation at the time. Half a century later (1882), F.J.A. Hort and B. F. Westcott published the first critical text of the New Testament based on careful examination of the relationships among manuscripts and the types of family relationships they reflected. Hort and Westcott also incorporated the testimony of Sinaiticus. In the next decade, Bernhard Weiss produced a text that paid close attention to intrinsic probability, at each variant asking which best fit the context and author's style. His results meshed well with those derived by Westcott and Hort's emphasis on the general quality of individual manuscripts and the groups of manuscripts to which they belonged.

The results of the work just surveyed, at times, are dramatic and surprising. For example, Mark's Gospel ends at 16:8; corrected texts omit Mk 16:9–20, considering it a later addition. The story of the woman caught in adultery in Jn 7:53–8:11 does not appear in early versions of the Fourth Gospel. The reference to the divine Trinity in 1 Jn 5:7–8 likewise lacks any credible manuscript evidence.

The advances in understanding the Greek text of the New Testament reached the English-reading public decisively when the Revised Version (RV) of the New Testament came out in 1881, led by the great textual scholars Westcott and Hort. Based on a significantly improved knowledge of Greek manuscripts, the RV introduced thousands of changes in its translation. While many adopted it gratefully, some howled in protest, including John Burgon, an Anglican divine whose published response came immediately. Even today, there exists a Dean Burgon Society, a small group that approves only of the King James Version of 1611 and rejects the progress made by textual scholarship and translational theory. Fortunately, the great majority of Bibles now published do reflect a critical consensus about the text of the New Testament.

The tedious, hard work of scholars in analyzing variants and reconstructing a reliable text has been admirable. For many Christians, it reassures faith. An important argument, one frequently encountered on college campuses, has arisen, asserting that the enormous volume of surviving manuscripts of the New Testament brings them unrivaled certainty and historical veracity. It draws added confidence from comparison to classical texts. For example, two fourteenth-century manuscripts preserve Euripides' play, *Bacchae*, and are supported by about eight partial papyri witnesses from the second century BCE to the fifth century CE, which together still do not preserve the entire play. The text of the play rests on slim evidence next to the thousands of New Testament manuscripts. Thus, the argument concludes, broad-based evidence, carefully sifted, assures readers that the text, as reconstructed today, reproduces the New Testament as originally written.

These arguments are reasonable, but overstated. The critical edition of the New Testament affords an excellent sense of the text as it existed in the fourth century—even a good window into the second century. But there is an over-confident jump from what can be inferred from the second century to the original manuscripts. This is important because scholars have nagging suspicions that, today, the Gospel of John and 2 Corinthians are not read in their original forms. The argumentative flow of John improves greatly if some parts are moved around, and 2 Corinthians makes much more sense if read as an edited compilation of five different letters. Opponents counter that these views lack manuscript evidence, a fair point but not conclusive, for it demands greater access to the manuscript history than exists. It also skips the problems of writing, publication, and distribution that lie at the beginning of each text.

To say the New Testament is written points beyond its birth to its transmission. For more than one thousand years, it was copied by hand. Every copy possessed by anyone had to be made by hand. As already noted, this created an unstable text, since errors crept into every manuscript—some repeated from the copied manuscript, some newly minted by the scribe. Manuscripts had a habit of looking like those with which they shared geographical and temporal proximity. Centuries passed before scholars began to compare texts and figure out what were the earliest readings.

Publication and Distribution Were Haphazard

Decades from now, some readers will recall, fondly, the late-night parties they attended to celebrate the release of the latest installment in the *Harry Potter* series. Stacks of freshly printed books awaited young readers as the clock struck midnight. Such memories have nothing to do with publication in the ancient world, which lacked publishers, printers, distribution networks, marketers, chain stores, and J. K. Rowling.

If a person looked hard in a large city of the Roman Empire, one might find a bookseller. We know, courtesy of mention by ancient authors, there were a handful of retailers. These scarce references raise the issue of whether they actually suggest a much larger set of booksellers or, indeed, reflect their scarcity in the Roman Empire. The surprise expressed in a couple of texts at encountering a bookseller hints that the retailers concentrated in the very largest urban centers, the same places one would expect to encounter a concentration of philosophers, declaimers, teachers, and libraries. This concentration increased the likelihood of a market and access to manuscripts, which was crucial, because inventory required finding texts to copy. There were no wholesalers. Keeping up with the latest writings required a network of connections so one could secure a copy to make a copy. Today, copying an entire book is considered a violation of copyright; the fair thing is to purchase the book. In the Roman Empire, making an individual copy was the only way to get one, whether people made copies themselves, hired a scribe, had a slave take pen in hand, or purchased a copy made by the bookseller—who in turn paid no royalties to the author. What did the author receive? Only fame.

Though publication in the Roman Empire did not have Potter-like scale, it was an event. "Publication" involved a public reading of a new work to one's friends. Perhaps after dinner or during the day, friends would assemble to listen as a new work was read, possibly by the author, maybe a slave. Depending on the venue, others might be present. With this reading, a work debuted. An author might then have given copies to his friends as gifts or, less often, to a trusted bookseller to ensure correct and accurate copying. A friend could also borrow the original to copy. One hand copy at a time, the work slowly built its circulation. A first run of more than one million, like the later Potter volumes, would have been unimaginable.

This was even more the case for early Christian writings, knowledge of which would have spread by word of mouth from Christian to Christian. As one considers the distribution of Christian writings, one enters the realm of speculation. To me, it seems plausible that many writings spread as gifts, with one Christian offering a copy of a text to another as a gesture of friendship, perhaps to initiate a personal relationship or to link one Christian community to another. Perhaps some even donated books in their role as a patron to a church. Others might have given a book to advertise themselves as Christian teachers, in exchange for hospitality, or another reason. As individuals and churches sought to build their collections of apostolic writings, providing copies to one another would have strengthened relationships. In general, the Christians involved in copying and distribution were those with the greatest means.

In some cases, luck may have been the determining factor in distribution. While traveling or entertaining visitors, a Christian might have encountered a text and taken the opportunity to copy it or, again, assigned the task to a slave. Christians might have heard a text read in public and later written down what they remembered of it.

However a Christian discovered a new writing, he or she had to take initiative to produce a copy. Running to a bookstore was not an option. Throughout the first century or two, relationships were key to the distribution of texts.

". . . Written" Results in Reading

In a civilization such as ours that provides free education and assumes general literacy, it seems perfectly natural that the early church created a book, or library, such as the New Testament. But the church took root in a very different environment from ours, such that the simple fact of writing at that time should give pause.

Few Could Read

A clever aphorism about Christian origins asserts that Jesus proclaimed an approaching kingdom, but the church arrived instead. In similar fashion, I would suggest that Jesus promised a kingdom to the poor, but people of means reported. Though I say this with some exaggeration, the majority of evidence for the early church comes in written texts, so we necessarily encounter the early church through its writings and, therefore, hear the voices of Christians who wrote, a skill that placed them in a distinct minority.

By one estimate, the literacy rate in antiquity rarely topped 10 percent. Variations existed. The western half of the Roman Empire might have had rates of literacy as low as 5 percent. Higher rates prevailed where the Greek civic institutions provided public education, but the rate still falls below one-third of the population because only part of the population received education, namely, the freeborn, male citizens.

The people who wrote the New Testament were among the literate minority. Unfortunately, Paul is the only author who can be named. A glance ahead at the second and third centuries reveals the kinds of Christians who wrote: Justin, Valentinus, Marcion, Irenaeus, Tertullian, Clement of Alexandria, Hippolytus, Origen, and Cyprian, among the best-known Christians of their time, were all educated, a pattern that continued into and beyond the fourth century. Of course, these men remain known precisely because they wrote, so literacy actually filters our knowledge of early Christians. Still, their visibility underscores what may pass as unremarkable when one reads the New Testament, namely, educated people wrote it.

Who Learned to Read?

Education was a privilege. This does not mean that only the rich could read, but it does imply life's circumstances obstructed many potential students.

In Sirach, the author provides a clue to scholarly success. He writes, "The wisdom of the scribe depends on the opportunity of leisure; only the one who has little business can become wise" (38:24). He acknowledges the important contributions of farmers, artisans, smiths, and potters, noting that "without them no city can be inhabited" (38:32), yet asserts the superiority of the scholar, who enjoys audiences with rulers and whose memory endures. Though Sirach wrote in Hebrew, his recognition of leisure directs attention to the Greek word *scholē*, which means leisure and from which the word *school* is derived. An important qualification for education was having the time to pursue it. This reflects one limiting factor on literacy.

A common attitude held that the father provide his children's education. Some included their daughters in this. At its literal level, the ideal was that the father served as instructor. If this were the case, it would result in a limited circle of literate people, for only the children of literate people would, in turn, become literate. In reality, mothers and grandparents might also have served as instructors. More frequently, fathers engaged tutors, so the ability to afford a tutor was the more pressing constraint. A lesser alternative was to pay tuition to send a child to a school, which still required means. The lucky few lived in a city that funded education. Money, then, was another obstacle to literacy.

Despite the need for money and leisure, literacy could still be found among slaves. Some of these entered slavery by way of conquest and were literate before enslavement, making them valuable as teachers or secretaries. Some received education from their owners who sought to enhance their slaves' value. Others became literate because, as boys, they were companions to their owners' sons and thereby participated in the sons' education.

The nature of ancient literacy encourages one to consider who wrote early Christian writings. The majority of literate people were men, though the ratio became more balanced at elite levels of society. Many enjoyed the leisure and means as youths to pursue education and saw education as a path to greater wealth as adults. The apostle Paul was literate, yet worked with his hands, which suggests his family had the means to educate him but lacked social prominence. Another large group of literate people were slaves whose literacy provided valuable services for their owners or freed slaves who probably relied on their literacy to make a living. Their services likely supported some Christian correspondence and the distribution of Christian writings. Perhaps a slave took dictation when one of the Gospels was composed.

Professionally, literacy allowed men to work as architects, doctors, lawyers, scribes, and teachers. The author of Luke-Acts appears to have written for a patron, so the author represents a literate Christian whose skills served a wealthier believer—whether for remuneration, room and board, or goodwill. Literacy also opened doors for service in the imperial administration. This reflects the important role of church leaders in connecting individual churches to one another, a task for which literacy was critical. Together with wealth and rhetorical skill, literacy propelled people into leadership positions in the church.

How Did People Read?

A longstanding generalization about reading in the ancient world claims that reading was oral. This means that when people read, they did so aloud. In the modern world, parents read aloud to their children, news anchors read teleprompters, and lectors read scriptures to worshipping communities. People on buses, however, read silently—one hopes—as do people in libraries and probably readers of this book. If true, a significant disjuncture exists between modern and ancient readers. However, in an important scholarly article, A. K. Gavrilov has called this bald generalization into question and done so with sufficient evidence. Ancient readers could and did read silently, if they chose.

That said, there was more public reading in the ancient world than today. Slaves read to their owners. Dinner parties featured reading or recitation as entertainment. Readers might have preferred to do so orally to interact with and enjoy more fully the poetry they read. They might also have needed practice for an oral performance. Not surprisingly, reading aloud was an important part of the educational curriculum. Students had to learn not simply to pronounce words correctly but when to take a breath, when to pause, where the sense began or ended, when to raise or lower the voice, when to speed up or slow down. Poetry complicated this, for it shaded into song, and poets considered themselves singers. An ancient Roman author, Quintilian, writing about education, warned students not to "degenerate into sing-song" while reading. He expanded on his opinion by recalling a *bon mot*, or "good word," from Caesar's youth: "If you are singing, you sing badly; if you are reading, you sing" (*Institutio Oratoria* 1.8.2; trans. H. E. Butler; Loeb Classical Library).

Reading aloud would have played an important role in how most early Christians encountered the New Testament. If only 5 to 30 percent of a congregation could read, the majority could only hear it. Neither, during oral reading, would the rest of the congregation read along silently, because no printed programs, bulletins, missalettes, or Bibles existed to pass out to attendees. The congregation would share the experience of hearing their sacred texts, as reflected explicitly in Rev 1:3, "Blessed is the one who reads aloud the words of the prophecy, and blessed are those who hear and who keep what is written in it. . . ." Few had the opportunity for private reading—and doing so silently if they wished.

". . . Written" Requires Education

Two thousand years ago, just like today, literacy required education. A fortunate combination of archaeological artifacts and extant textbooks reveal what education looked like during the early church, providing a good sense of the education received by early Christians. It turns out that their educations influenced how and what they wrote. We will look closely at maxims and sayings in what follows, because they played a central role in ancient curricula and appear frequently in the New Testament.

The Educational Curriculum

Many handbooks from the time of the New Testament survive and provide a sense of the education received by early Christian writers. Around age seven, a child began primary education and around twelve years old, advanced to grammar for about three years. Next, teenagers took on a more specialized course of study for two or more years in rhetoric, law, medicine, or philosophy. The primary curriculum began with reading and writing, along with music and mathematics. In the second stage, literature and poetry were emphasized, along with reading and grammar. Finally, teenagers could advance to the study of rhetoric, or to be more precise, oratory, since spoken presentation was the ultimate goal, not simply composition. This course of education shaped how children learned and how they expressed themselves as adults. This included Christians, for the things they learned in their studies revealed themselves in their writings, as we shall see after reviewing ancient curricula.

Primary education introduced students to the alphabet, just as today. From letters, children moved to syllables and words. When they turned to sentences, teachers taught them model sentences to practice. These were commonly drawn from poets, so their poetic structure made them memorable while their content was compact, pithy, and incisive. Typically, model sentences expressed a moral sentiment, making them life lessons that adults often recalled. Such succinct, insightful sentences are called maxims or aphorisms. (In biblical tradition, these appear in wisdom literature, for example Proverbs.) More literally, they can be called "gnomic" or "sententious" sayings, based on the ancient words used to describe them, the Greek word *gnomai* and Latin word *sententiae*. These maxims, or gnomic sayings, were widespread and worked their way into Christian writings, so we will examine them more closely.

Examples of maxims abound in classical culture. Two well-known are: "Know thyself," and, "In all things, moderation." In his handbook on rhetoric, Aristotle emphasizes that maxims are general statements. They do not say something about Socrates or Alexander the Great but about people-at-large. Nor do they focus on generalities, only on people and their actions, which makes them express some kind of moral statement. For example, "No one is really free," or, "Only the wise are rich."

A good saying pleases the mind. Educated people in the ancient world loved hearing them, so collections of historical and legendary sayings were compiled. The writings of Plutarch (c. 45 to 120 CE) contain many, e.g., *Sayings of Kings and Commanders*, *Sayings of Romans*, *Sayings of Spartans*, and *Sayings of Spartan Women*. The Greek word for these "sayings" is *apophthegmata*, or in the singular, *apophthegm*, which loans itself to English as the obscure word *apothegm*. These provided terse, pointed sayings, which often gave insight about life, much like maxims. In the collections of *apophthegmata*, however, the sayings are attributed to specific people as examples of their wit or wisdom, which may or may not apply to people in general or have moral purpose. Added narrative details make *apophthegmata* little stories. In some cases, "anecdotes" would be a helpful translation.

Two examples lend a sense of how *apophthegmata* expand beyond maxims. Plutarch records twenty-nine clever sayings by Cato the Elder. One is almost a maxim: "He used to say that those who separate honor from virtue separate virtue from youth" (*Sayings of Romans* 198f). Eliminate the opening words that tie the saying to Cato, and the thought could stand on its own as a general expression about human conduct, i.e., a maxim. Another example sets the stage by noting that statues were set up to honor many men. Cato observed this and criticized it, saying, "I want people to ask why no statue of Cato is set up, rather than why one is" (198f). In this case, the insightful saying is tied specifically to Cato and a particular circumstance that gives meaning to the saying and guides its interpretation.

The frequency of *apophthegmata* can be explained not only by the pleasure they afford, but also by their presence in the school curriculum in which they were part of the standard exercises known as *chreiai*. These were concise reports of sayings or actions attributed to a person and suited to the person's reputation, as seen in the examples from Plutarch. A number of ancient textbooks survived and reveal that young people studied *chreiai*, to recognize their form and nature, so as to construct them and use them appropriately.

In his first-century handbook, Theon differentiated maxims from *chreiai* in four ways:

1. The *chreia* is always attributed to a character, while the maxim never is.

2. The *chreia* sometimes makes a general statement and at times a specific one, while the maxim makes only a general one.

3. The *chreia* is witty, sometimes containing nothing useful for living, while the maxim is always concerned with matters useful in life.

4. The *chreia* is an action or saying, while the maxim is only a saying.

Theon offers many examples of *chreiai*. Here are four (as translated by Hock and O'Neil, pp. 85, 87, 91, and 89):

1. "Diogenes the philosopher, on being asked by someone how he could become famous, responded: 'By worrying as little as possible about fame.'"

2. "Socrates, on being asked whether the Persian king seemed happy to him, said: 'I can't say, for I don't know where he stands on education.'"

3. "Damon the gymnastic teacher whose feet were deformed, when his shoes had been stolen, said: 'May they fit the thief.'"

4. "A Laconian, when someone asked him where the Lacedaemonians consider the boundaries of their land to be, showed his spear."

The fourth example shows how action can replace a pithy saying. The third provides a specific point that is funny but provides no insight into life. The first two offer general wisdom but are attributed to specific people, Socrates and Diogenes. As these two suggest, philosophers liked to use *chreiai*, which permeated education, for they demonstrated wit and often delivered valuable insight.

At first, the *chreia* received simple elaboration—a saying received a speaker and brief context to provide an introduction and interpretive frame, as in the first three examples in the preceding paragraph. Throughout time, the elaboration grew more complex, becoming a short essay through the use of standard strategies. Hermogenes' treatise, *On the Chreia*, lists eight: praise the speaker, paraphrase the saying, provide a rationale, express the opposite sentiment, present an analogy and then an example, state an authority, and conclude with an exhortation. Hermogenes illustrated these steps using Isocrates, who said of education, "The root is bitter, but the fruit sweet." Hermogenes then expanded this saying by noting Isocrates' wisdom (praise) and reasoning that important matters usually require toil (rationale), whereas ordinary matters do not (opposite), just as farmers must work the land (analogy), just as Demosthenes labored long and hard (example), and just as Hesiod testified (authority). Teachers trained students with this exercise in elaboration as a preliminary step to composing full speeches.

Not only did the *chreia* change throughout time but also so did maxims. The earlier definition lost its grip and almost any well-turned phrase, whose use displayed verbal cleverness, came to count as a gnomic or sententious saying. Traditionalists insisted that *sententiae* remain relevant to the topic at hand, while some orators sprinkled them wherever they could to elicit approval from their audience. They marked a person as urbane and suggested sophistication.

The *chreia* was one exercise among many that formed the *progymnasmata*, a curriculum of exercises that prepared students for rhetoric. The entire series of exercises trained students in a dozen different mental aspects of creating speeches, like prerequisite study modules that, when mastered, prepared students to advance to the difficult art of composing full-blown speeches. The *progymnasmata*, i.e., these preliminary exercises, included fable, narrative, speeches in the voice of other characters (i.e., impersonation), arguments for and against a thesis, praise, and the aforementioned maxims and *chreiai*. Originally, teachers of rhetoric handled instruction in the *progymnasmata*, but by the time of the Roman Empire, many grammarians had brought *progymnasmata* into their curriculum, leaving the rhetoricians to focus on teaching students actual oratory.

The two goals of education as outlined so far were literacy and oratory. A minority of people attained the former and fewer still progressed to the latter. This educational path centered on rhetoric. Unlike contemporary higher education, which emphasizes written composition with a nod to public speaking, ancient curriculum employed written exercises to educate orators. Writing served the larger outcome of speaking persuasively, which could bring a person social clout and wealth. The most extensive ancient treatise on rhetoric, written by Quintilian, whose youth overlapped with the apostle Paul's life, introduced history to students during their oratorical education. Philosophy and law had to wait for later, following oratory for those young adults with leisure.

Education Influenced Christian Writers

Recognizing what young people studied demonstrates the ways adults wrote. Children studied maxims, and adults wrote them. Young people practiced *chreiai* and later used them to construct speeches. Similarly, the adults who wrote the New Testament used the lessons they learned in school in their writings.

Many maxims appear throughout the New Testament. A particularly noteworthy one appears in 1 Cor 15:33, "Bad company ruins good behavior" (REB). This maxim is variously attributed to the Greek playwrights Euripides and Menander, which means the apostle Paul did not invent it but quoted it. He likely learned it as a schoolboy.

Elsewhere in his letters, Paul shows himself a fan of such sententious statements, as demonstrated in the interesting research of P. A. Holloway, who identifies many dozens. At times, Paul went on long, gnomic riffs, as in Rom 12:9–21, Gal 5:12–6:10, and 1 Thess 5:14–22. The way Paul uses maxims reflects their broader use by others, as illustrated in the following examples.

* A slightly modified King James Version of 1 Cor 10:12 provides crisp, though old, form: "Let him who thinks he stands take heed lest he fall." Paul uses this saying to summarize and interpret historical examples, as did others.

* "Do not let your good be spoken of as evil" (Rom 14:16 NRSV) is a paradoxical *sententia*, as it combines opposite ideas; moreover, it improves on Paul's earlier attempt to formulate the idea in 1 Cor 10:30. Both paradox and revision are typical of maxims.

* Paul's use of *sententiae* to round off paragraphs or provide transitions between topics reflects an important and changed use of *sententiae* in his day, as in Rom 4:25: "who was handed over because of our transgressions and raised because of our

justification." This phrase provides a hinge between two major sections of Romans, namely, 3:31–4:25 and 5:1–8:39.

It also appears that Paul's rivals used maxims, which Paul rebutted with his own. For example, Paul appears to quote someone else's claim, "All things are lawful," to which he retorts, "But not all things are beneficial" (1 Cor 6:12). Later, he quotes a slogan, "All of us possess knowledge," only to undermine it with his own *sententia*, "Knowledge puffs up, but love builds up" (8:1). Constructing short, elegant, insightful statements was taught in school and encountered throughout life. Paul reflects this cultural habit in his use of them.

The important and ubiquitous role of *chreiai* in philosophy and education influenced Christian teaching and the development of Christian traditions about Jesus' sayings. Burton Mack, among others, has demonstrated the surprising correlations between texts about Jesus and the guidelines presented in the textbooks about *chreiai*. Mack draws attention to Lk 12:22–31, a group of verses that, at first glance, looks like a series of topically related ideas, otherwise randomly strung together.

> [22]He said to his disciples, "Therefore I tell you, do not worry about your life, what you will eat, or about your body, what you will wear. [23]For life is more than food, and the body more than clothing. [24]Consider the ravens: they neither sow nor reap, they have neither storehouse nor barn, and yet God feeds them. Of how much more value are you than the birds! [25]And can any of you by worrying add a single hour to your span of life? [26]If then you are not able to do so small a thing as that, why do you worry about the rest? [27]Consider the lilies, how they grow: they neither toil nor spin; yet I tell you, even Solomon in all his glory was not clothed like one of these. [28]But if God so clothes the grass of the field, which is alive today and tomorrow is thrown into the oven, how much more will he clothe you—you of little faith! [29]And do not keep striving for what you are to eat and what you are to drink, and do not keep worrying. [30]For it is the nations of the world that strive after all these things, and your Father knows that you need them. [31]Instead, strive for his kingdom, and these things will be given to you as well.

A reader might infer that statements attributed to Jesus were floating freely in churches, and someone clustered together a handful that shared a theme. Using the ideas found in the *progymnasmata*, however, Mack demonstrates the presence of an argumentative flow in these verses:

Thesis	Do not worry about your life, what you will eat, or about your body, what you will wear. (v. 22)
Reason	For life is more than food, and the body more than clothing. (v. 23)
Analogy	Consider the ravens: They neither sow nor reap, they have neither storehouse nor barn, and yet God feeds them. Of how much more value are you than the birds! (v. 24)
Example	And can any of you by worrying add a single hour to your span of life? If then you are not able to do so small a thing as that, why do you worry about the rest? (vv. 25–26)
Analogy	Consider the lilies, how they grow: They neither toil nor spin. (v. 27a)
Paradigm	Even Solomon in all his glory was not clothed like one of these. (v. 27b)
Analogy	But if God so clothes the grass of the field, which is alive today and tomorrow is thrown into the oven, how much more will he clothe you? (v. 28)
Conclusion	And do not keep striving for what you are to eat and what you are to drink, and do not keep worrying. (v. 29)
Example	The nations of the world strive after all these things. (v. 30)
Exhortation	Instead, strive for his kingdom, and these things will be given to you as well. (v. 31)

Mack demonstrates that these sentences correspond to the different ways students were instructed to develop a *chreia*. A rhetorical logic, taught to young teenagers in school, guides the flow of thought in these verses, a logic that is not abstract and timeless but a cultural artifact of the Greco-Roman world.

Other aforementioned exercises also affected the authors of the New Testament. For example, many have recognized the rhetorical device of narrative in Gal 1:11–2:14. The exercise of making a speech in the voice of an ancient or mythical person of historical significance also spilled over into Christianity, as a number of people wrote texts in the name of respected Christian worthies.

Textbooks for advanced rhetoric also influenced Christian writers. Methods used to open and close speeches and gain an audience's goodwill were taught, and examples can be found in the New Testament. The textbooks covered figures of speech with care, providing definitions and examples. Among these was the parable. For me, parables are something Jesus told. Only later did I encounter them elsewhere, whereas educated members of the early church would have recognized parables as one of many literary figures and one that featured prominently in the sayings of Jesus but was not peculiar to Jesus. In short, educational curriculum influenced writers in the early church.

The Culture of Educated People Influenced the New Testament

Some students grew into particularly well-educated adults, who were called *hoi pepaideumenoi*, which literally means, "The people who have been educated." Today, one might call them the educated elite (minus the pejorative connotations common in the United States). Such people fostered a distinct culture among themselves, purposefully displaying what they had learned in their social and public lives. Similar habits appear in Christian writers.

Participants in educated cultures competed in erudition and performance. Oratory was a spectator sport with substantial rewards and honor, as speakers vied to deliver the best speech in public displays of their prowess. Festivals often featured contests for the best speech in praise of the emperor or a member of his family. In live performance, before a potentially unruly crowd and without the aid of microphone, teleprompter, or visual aids, an orator had to capture and hold the attention of the audience, offering new and familiar content in pleasing ways. Those who succeeded enjoyed good lives.

The better one's skills, the more status one attained. The second-century author, Lucian of Samosata, seemed destined to apprentice as a sculptor but turned to education. Through hard work, he erased all evidence of his eastern accent and learned to delight people with his wit and brilliant reworking of traditional stories. He testified that education brought him honor, praise, and esteem from people preeminent in birth and wealth. He held a position in the imperial administration of Egypt and aspired to supervise a Roman province. Similar things could be said of Dio Chrysostom, whose education elevated his status. He rose to local prominence and eventually became a friend of emperors. His nickname, Chrysostom, means "golden-tongued" and reflects the esteem he won through his powers of speech.

With so much on the line, the competition to succeed could get the better of people. One ancient critic remarked that oratory required deceit, lies, and a persona that was brash, boisterous, and contentious. Talk radio would provide a modern counterpart, only add the need for grammatical perfection for, in the Roman Empire, the slightest verbal mistake provided an opening for enemies. The aforementioned Lucian of Samosata wrote an essay to defend himself after expressing a greeting incorrectly, wishing someone health instead of joy. People of good taste just did not wish others "health" in the morning! Few today would note such a slip, let alone make a big deal out of it. Not so in Lucian's circles, for precision and propriety of speech were important markers of an educated person. On another occasion, Lucian was criticized for using an obscure word. He defended himself, arguing that he had, in fact, used the correct word and then exploded in accusations that his critic was immoral and ignorant. The taunt hurled at Lucian seems trivial, and his response extreme, yet the stakes were high, which explains Lucian's outburst and underscores the coin in which he and his rivals traded. In a world where orators had to compete for students and honor, a grammatical *faux pas* could undermine one's career.

These matters affected the ministry of the apostle Paul, as appears in his Corinthian correspondence. Particularly in 1 Cor 1–4,

Paul competed for the hearts of his readers, many of whom found other Christians more compelling speakers. Similar problems bubble to the surface in 2 Corinthians. The charge that Paul's rhetoric was deficient is explicit, leaving people to wonder about his qualifications and prefer other Christian teachers whose verbal prowess commanded their admiration. Such matters may strike contemporary readers as superficial, but they cut to the core of ancient values. If a person prized powerful speech, then Paul's inferiority in this department justifiably hurt his reputation.

Among educated people more generally, a number of intellectual habits appear. They liked to sprinkle echoes of antiquity in their speech and writing. They would imitate the great historical orators, poets, and playwrights, copying their diction, vocabulary, themes, and genres while quoting their writings. The epic poems of Homer were standard works throughout ancient educational curricula. To say that every educated person read them requires no qualification. Homer's *Iliad* and *Odyssey* were better known in the ancient world than the Second Amendment at a gun show today. Also popular were the plays of Euripides and the speeches of the orator Demosthenes. One could facetiously describe education as learning to quote ancient works.

Ancient sources could dominate and overwhelm the writings of educated people. Even when thinking about contemporary issues, the writer's use of ancient sources to illustrate and discuss these issues could crowd out references to the world around. An example that illustrates this appears in Lucian's essay *Charon*, named for the underworld ferryman who, in this story, comes up to see what makes human life so wonderful that people are always sad to leave it. The god Hermes guides Charon. Many examples are introduced to illustrate human folly, but none from Lucian's lifetime. All come from ancient Greece, including many quotations from Homer. Could Lucian cite no examples of human folly from his own day? Certainly, had he so wished, which is precisely the point: Given the choice, he preferred to use material from ancient tradition, not the world around him. Such was the method of educated people in Lucian's day; and it lent gravity, rhetorical delight, and persuasive power.

This same habit of mind appears throughout the New Testament, though with a Christian twist. Instead of quoting Homer and other Greek worthies, early Christians drew on the ancient resources of Jewish scriptures. An extreme example appears in the letter of Jude, in which readers encounter a rapid redeploying of Jewish writings. Allusions to Cain, the Watchers, Sodom and Gomorrah, the Exodus, the wilderness wanderings, Korah, the death of Moses, and Balaam come quickly and with scant explanation. The apostles, as a generic group, are quoted, as is the prophecy of Enoch. These stories are not probed, neither are their applications given precise elaboration. For example, when Jude compares the Christian interlopers to Cain, he does so with little evidence, which does not matter, for Jude's innuendo hovers slanderously over the accused, smearing them. More to the point, in writing about the present with the resources of the past, Jude is talking like his secular counterparts, filling his perception of reality with examples of antiquity.

Besides the quotation and imitation of ancient worthies, the rhetoric of praise and blame provided another distinct component of educated speech during the early church, more so than in previous centuries. There was nothing even-handed about ancient speeches of praise or blame. They took a specific position and emphasized it, overstating the positive in praise, the negative in blame.

The vituperation directed against rivals in Jude fits into this historical trend. The rivals are insiders, people who slipped in undetected and participated in the church's worship and fellowship (v. 4). Apparently, the threat is obvious to no one but the author of Jude. These people are impious, which is close to the stereotypical accusation of godless and, perhaps, sexually promiscuous, another commonplace accusation leveled against people one does not like (vv. 4, 8). They are greedy (v. 11), a motive typically attributed to rivals, as is accusing them of serving their own interests (v. 12). Accusations of boasting and flattery are two more clichés (v. 16). All of these could be said about any rival throughout the history of Greek literature. Calling them grumblers, malcontents (v. 16), and divisive (v. 19) is not quite a cliché, but typical. To score additional points, the author throws in that they are subject to passions (v. 16) and devoid of spirit (v. 19). The only item in this litany that is particularly Christian is the accusation that they are devoid of spirit. The presence of these people at love feasts is also specifically Christian, yet elsewhere the context of meals as the place of fraudulence is a delicious theme for satire. Thus, for all the author of Jude has to say about these people, he says little. The bulk of the letter trades in the rhetoric of blame and, thereby, reflects a broader cultural trend.

Educated people also paid attention to oratorical style. On the one side were purists who prized standard vocabulary, elegance, and restraint—traditionalists if you will. Showmen held the opposite opinion, playing to the applause of the crowd and filling their oration with figures of speech. These two positions were labeled Atticism and Asianism; the former arose from the home of Athens and the classicism it represented, the latter from Turkey and points east. Atticists took fifth and fourth century BCE Athenian sources (playwrights like Aeschylus and orators like Lysias and Demosthenes) to guide their sense of appropriate and tasteful Greek style, while the Asian style reflected the changes in grammar, diction, and vocabulary brought to the Greek language by centuries of use throughout the Mediterranean world. Asianism had an expressive, some might say bombastic, quality that made it entertaining and captivating. To purists, however, the Asian style was simply vulgar and excessively ornamental, too much of a good thing.

While no author in the New Testament was imitating Attic Greek, the choices represented by Atticism and Asianism appear. The Letter of Jude provides an example of Asianic exuberance, when the author piles on analogies for those he condemns. In v. 11, he draws three from Jewish scripture to attack his imaginary opponents, writing, "Woe to them! For they go the way of Cain, and abandon themselves to Balaam's error for the sake of gain, and perish in Korah's rebellion." Then, in v. 12, he demonstrates how their behavior expresses itself: "These are the blemishes on your love-feasts, while they feast with you without fear, feeding themselves." But wait, there is still more to be said:

> They are waterless clouds carried along by the winds; autumn trees without fruit, twice dead, uprooted; wild waves of the sea, casting up the foam of their own shame; wandering stars, for whom the deepest darkness has been reserved forever." (vv. 12–13)

These four analogies illustrate an over-the-top quality of rhetoric. Why use one analogy when you can think of four? Clever interpreters of Jude justify the use of all four, but they fall victim to the author's vivid, excessive rhetoric. This overkill may not strike the English reader as unusual, but there is a rhetorical history embedded in Jude v. 13.

The apostle Paul fell into a trap of Attic versus Asianic Greek. In describing the kind of people to whom God mercifully shows favor, Paul wrote that God has chosen weak and contemptible things of the world to shame the things that are not (1 Cor 1:28). The thought is beautiful, unless you happen to be among those who compete for honor and have achieved some. Such a person struck back at Paul. Like Lucian wishing someone health in the morning hours, Paul was in trouble over trivia; the word he used for *contemptible* was nonliterary, and from an Attic perspective, nonstandard. In extant ancient writings, the word appears most frequently in writings from the Eastern Mediterranean and never in any respected Attic authority. When Paul used it in his letter to the Corinthian church, it rang out loudly to an educated person, as loudly as if I were to use the word *ain't*. We all know what *ain't* means. There's a good chance we have all used it in conversation, but anyone with just a little formal education knows better than to use it in writing. This is precisely what happened when Paul used the Greek word *exouthenein* instead of *kataphronein* for "contemptible." This came back to haunt him when a person of superior literary and rhetorical taste took up Paul's word and threw it back in his face, accusing him of "contemptible" (*exouthenein*) speech (2 Cor 10:12). Bazinga! Paul did not actually know what hit him. He had not simply been criticized but also mocked. He had been ridiculed and (contraction alert) didn't see it coming. These kinds of cultural wars will not emerge in a translation.

Thus, in rhetorical battle and exuberance, praise and blame, and reliance on the writings of ancient worthies, the New Testament participates in the cultural habits of the educated people of its era.

". . . Written" Results in Interaction

The digital economy has introduced the idea of interaction as an activity in which people engage with technology and, thereby, find opportunities for innovation. Obviously, interaction happens between humans as well as within technology. By virtue of writing, important aspects of interaction also have played a role in the church's history.

The Codex

"Technology is anything invented after you were born." So suggested the visionary computer scientist Alan Kay. His statement expresses the truth that people fail to see the commonplaces of life as technology. People buy technology at the Apple store, not Macy's; yet clothing represents a technology, as do forks, and pencils. The next time a Luddite rails against technology, think about life without toothbrushes and deodorant.

Another ubiquitous technology is the book. By book, I mean those paper-filled objects that line the shelves in homes and libraries. Look carefully at one, and you will see that the pages divide into a number of sections, each comprised of pieces of paper folded over and nestled inside others. In a hardbound book, each section has stitching in the fold to hold the pages in place; the different sections, in turn, are sewn together to create the text block of a book. Place these pages inside hard covers for protection, and a book results. Alternatively, the many sections of paper may have glue run down their spines to hold them together and attach them to a cover. Sometimes, the individual pages are backed with glue to hold them together, creating a cheap paperback, which leads most quickly to books with loose pages. These methods for putting pieces of paper together represent technologies that did not exist for the majority of human history. The book is something that had to be invented.

We cannot say who invented the form of the book or when, but judging by the oldest books that exist, the book came into being about two thousand years ago. It emerged and became popular during the Roman Empire, which means that the book and the church grew up together. The book format appears to be a particularly Roman invention; so today, the Latin word *codex* is used to describe it. When a book migrates to a Kindle, conceptually it remains a book but physically is no longer a codex.

The book, or codex, was first created to serve as a notebook, more useful for ephemeral jottings than for formal literature. Scholars have drawn attention to the curious fact that Christians were among the earliest adopters of this new technology. In *Books and Readers in the Early Church*, Harry Gamble suggests that Christians were motivated to do so by the early collection of the letters of Paul. They may have been circulated in notebook format early on, making a larger book form a natural progression. Bundled together, Paul's letters would have created a larger-than-normal scroll. A scroll also would not have allowed them to be referenced easily. Individual pages in a book permitted both obstacles to be overcome. In Gamble's view, then, Christians took advantage of a fairly new technology, the codex, to serve a new purpose.

Formatting

Much thought and effort lies behind the pages of the Bible. How they appear is but one of many possibilities pursued in its history. The New Testament read today, whether Greek or English, is not what Christians read for centuries.

Readers, in the time of the early church, picked up some texts and encountered a format called *scriptio continua*, "a river of letters," in which one letter followed immediately the one before, without any intervening punctuation or spaces and no regard for line breaks. Imagine reading Mt 5:1–6 in this way:

WHENJESUSSAWTHECROWDSHEWENTUPTOTHEMOUNT
AINANDAFTERHESATDOWNHISDISCIPLESCAMETOHIMT
HENHEBEGANTOSPEAKANDTAUGHTTHEMSAYINGBLES
SEDARETHEPOORINSPIRITFORTHEIRSISTHEKINGDOMOF
HEAVENBLESSEDARETHOSEWHOMOURNFORTHEYWILL
BECOMFORTEDBLESSEDARETHEMEEKFORTHEYWILLIN
HERITTHEEARTHBLESSEDARETHOSEWHOHUNGERANDT
HIRSTFORRIGHTEOUSNESSFORTHEYWILLBEFILLED

Romans considered it an accomplishment when their children could read such texts at first sight.

The absence of chapters and verse divisions makes the ancient text even more unlike today's versions. For example, I referred to the quoted text as Mt 5:1–7a. Chapter and verse, as in "Mt 5:1," is one way of referencing scripture. Another is to refer to the first word(s) of a story, as in the Paternoster or Magnificat. The former is Latin for "our father," the opening words of the Lord's Prayer, which many, therefore, refer to as the "Our Father." Magnificat is the opening word, in Latin, of the beautiful expression of praise uttered by Mary, who, upon learning that she would give birth to Jesus, said, "My heart magnifies the Lord." The first word is a handy way of referencing famous texts, but would not work well with the thousands of paragraphs in the Bible.

Chapters and verses have proven useful. The former most often came first. The oldest example appears in Codex Vaticanus, which resides in the Vatican Library and is one of the most important of all biblical manuscripts. Copied in the fourth century, Vaticanus inserts section breaks more frequently than those found in modern Bibles. It also provides evidence of competing systems of chapters, offering two different systems in Acts and indicating that Hebrews was once positioned after Galatians, as in Codex Sinaiticus and unlike modern Bibles. In addition, this manuscript provides no chapters for 2 Peter, indicating that whoever created the system of chapters did not include 2 Peter in the New Testament. A century after Vaticanus, another manuscript, which scholars designate Alexandrinus, was copied. Here is found an entirely new set of chapter divisions, which resembles those found in most Greek manuscripts. Each section in Alexandrinus also has a title written in the margin that describes the chapter content. Christians were inserting aids into their Bibles to facilitate reading, and around 400 CE, these were still evolving.

To reach the origin of contemporary chapter divisions, one has to jump ahead eight centuries to Stephen Langton, Archbishop of Canterbury from 1207–28, during which time he devised his scheme of chapter divisions. These caught on and remain the chapter divisions in the modern English Bible. More than three centuries passed before these were broken into verses, a task performed by Robert Estienne, a famous printer, when he produced his fourth edition of the Greek New Testament in 1551. He used them again in 1553 when he published a Bible in French. William Whittingham, an English reformer living in exile in Geneva, followed suit in his 1557 translation of the New Testament into English. He continued working in Geneva on the translation of the entire Bible, which came out in 1560. Known as the Geneva Bible, it, too, used Estienne's verse divisions. As one of the most consequential English Bibles ever produced, it established the chapters and verses common to all English Bibles. As for Mt 5:1, credit Langton for labeling chapter 5 and Estienne for v. 1.

The Printed New Testament

The Gutenberg Museum in Mainz, Germany, celebrates the technological breakthrough of its distinguished citizen, Johannes Gutenberg, who, a bit before 1450, devised metal moveable type and changed the course of history. At the time, it meant that a day's work no longer produced mere pages but perhaps, hundreds. This new technology changed Christianity. Throughout the next couple of centuries, the Bible was translated into many languages and printed for distribution across Europe, a crucial ingredient in the Reformation.

The first Greek New Testament printed was part of a multilingual Bible, a beautifully crafted book called the Complutensian Polyglot, after the Spanish city in which it was produced. It presented the New Testament in Greek and Latin. Great editorial care went into the preparation of this work, which began in 1502 and was printed in 1514. Papal sanction, however, did not arrive until 1520, so the multivolume Bible did not circulate until 1522.

Into that delay stepped competitors. Publisher Johann Froben conferred with the famous scholar Erasmus to bring a Greek New Testament to market. Together, they undertook and completed the project in less than a year, producing the first printing in 1516. Though the second Greek New Testament to be printed, it was first to market.

Erasmus's text anticipated Silicon Valley by more than four and a half centuries, proving that first to market is a winning strategy. Though he offered an inferior version of the Greek New Testament, Erasmus captured the market. To call his text beta would give it too much credit. He drew on manuscripts conveniently at hand, relying on two twelfth-century texts, which he compared to a few others. For Revelation, he had but one manuscript to use, and it lacked the last six verses. Not to worry, though, for great scholar that he was,

Erasmus just translated the Latin Bible into Greek to supply what was missing!

Given how fast Erasmus and Froben worked, the printed piece had many mistakes. A technology that promised to cut down on typos came out of the gate with hundreds. The second, third, and fourth editions came out in 1519, 1522, and 1527. Even the fourth edition remained inferior to the Complutensian Polyglot, but Erasmus's earlier, more conveniently sized edition held fast to market share, forming the base for what came to be called the Textus Receptus, the commonly used Greek New Testament. In a sign of the inertia when sacred texts are concerned, it took four hundred years for scholars to dislodge Erasmus's work, which provided the Greek text for the great German and English translations of Luther and King James.

This history does reflect a new stage of interaction with the New Testament. The very human process of textual transmission was acknowledged and investigated. The conservative reaction came from people who assumed that divine providence had protected the text during the centuries of copying. Once scholars went from library to library comparing texts, that view crumbled. The detailed work of comparison and analysis would have to be done.

This also marks a new stage of interaction for the public, for the Greek text became the basis for vernacular translations of the New Testament. As Hebrew and Greek were displacing the Latin Bible for scholarly study, they became the texts on which translators of the Bible drew. A millennium of tradition was being overturned, as modern-language Bibles were produced, and done so on the basis of Hebrew and Greek, not the Latin Vulgate. This changed profoundly how people would interact with scripture.

Conclusion

Little could be more obvious about the New Testament than that it is written. This essay has demonstrated how this simple observation actually says much.

Writing draws attention to the technology of the New Testament. Hand copying slowed and limited distribution, while introducing scribal errors into the text, causing the text to evolve. The codex changed the nature of how Christians stored and experienced their scriptures. Throughout the centuries, formatting also varied, affecting how people read the New Testament. The printing press accelerated access and stimulated the process of correcting the accumulated errors of scribes. Writing made technology a significant part of the history of the New Testament.

Writing also underscores the social context of literacy and literary production. The people who wrote the New Testament were not average people. By virtue of their literacy, they were part of a fortunate minority in the Roman Empire, privileged to pursue education, equally privileged to be educated. The curriculum they studied affected how and what they wrote, while aspects of their literary activity reflect a culture of educated people. In recognizing that the New Testament is written, a social context that affected its form and content is discovered.

Questions

1. Biblical scholar Dennis MacDonald made a daring attempt to link the New Testament to educated culture by arguing that Mark's Gospel drew on and imitated the epic poetry of Homer. For example, both Odysseus and Jesus were called carpenters, both suffered many trials, and both endured fickle, cowardly companions. The disciples James and John play the role of the mythical twins Castor and Pollux, seated on either side of Zeus, while blind Bartimaeus in Mark parallels the blind poet Tiresias, both serving as blind seers. Judas Iscariot parallels Odysseus' disloyal servant, Melanthius. Jesus' courage in the face of certain death reflects that of Achilles, while Jesus' violent death resembles that of Hector. These suffice to suggest the sweeping vision MacDonald offers for reading the Gospel of Mark as a recasting of Homer in prose with a new vision of the heroic. As you read the parallels just proposed, what do you think counts as a valid parallel? How do you determine the relevance of proposed parallels?

2. Think about the occasions in which you read out loud, or others read aloud to you. Why, at these times, is the reading oral and not silent? What are the purposes for reading out loud? How do you interact differently with what is read out loud? How does social context affect the activity?

3. Is it surprising that education shaped how and what is written in the New Testament? Compare your own experience. How does your education affect your oral and written communication? What influences do your social groups have on how you communicate? What forms or genres do you use in your own writing that you learned from others?

4. What are the different ways you interact with the Bible? Do different formats or technologies change the nature of your interaction?

5. "No two manuscripts of the New Testament are exactly alike" is a standard claim. Assuming it is true, assess and react to the statement.

Further Reading

Anderson, Graham. *The Second Sophistic*. Routledge, 1993.

Casson, Lionel. *Libraries in the Ancient World*. New Haven, CT: Yale University Press, 2001.

Gamble, Harry Y. *Books and Readers in the Early Church: A History of Early Christian Texts*. Yale University Press, 1997.

Gavrilov, A. K. "Techniques of Reading in Classical Antiquity." *The Classical Quarterly*, new series, 47 (1997) 1: 56–73.

Harris, William V. *Ancient Literacy*. Harvard University Press, 1989.

Hock, Ronald F., and Edward N. O'Neil. *The Chreia in Ancient Rhetoric*. Volume 1: *The Progymnasmata*. Texts and Translations 27. Graeco-Roman Religion 9. Atlanta, GA: Scholars Press / Society of Biblical Literature, 1986.

Holloway, Paul A. "Paul's Pointed Prose: The *Sententiae* in Roman Rhetoric and Paul." *Novum Testamentum* 40 (1998) 1: 32–53.

Johnson, William A. "Toward a Sociology of Reading in Antiquity." *American Journal of Philology* 121 (2000) 4: 593–627.

———. *Readers and Reading Culture in the High Roman Empire: A Study of Elite Communities.* Classical Culture and Society. Oxford University Press, 2010.

Kennedy, George A. *New Testament Interpretation through Rhetorical Criticism.* Studies in Religion. Chapel Hill, NC: University of North Carolina Press, 1984.

MacDonald, Dennis R. *The Homeric Epics and the Gospel of Mark.* New Haven, CT: Yale University Press, 2000.

Mack, Burton L. *Rhetoric and the New Testament.* Guides to Biblical Scholarship. New Testament Series. Minneapolis: Fortress Press, 1990.

Winsbury, Rex. *The Roman Book.* Classical Literature and Society Series. London: Duckworth Publishing, 2009.

Whitmarsh, Timothy. *The Second Sophistic.* New Surveys in the Classics. Oxford University Press, 2006.

Winter, Bruce W. *Philo and Paul among the Sophists: Alexandrian and Corinthian responses to a Julio-Claudian movement.* Grand Rapids, MI: W.B. Eerdmans, 2002.

To See Images of Greek Manuscripts

Codex Sinaiticus—*www.codexsinaiticus.com*

The Pauline Epistles—*www.lib.umich.edu/reading/Paul/*

There Are Four Gospels

There are four Gospels in the New Testament. This seemed unremarkable until I heard a preacher attempt to explain it. At first, I thought it strange that the preacher was even explaining it, all the more that he felt the need to defend it. He wanted to dispel any worries that four Gospels somehow indicated disagreements among the apostles. In fact, he argued, four witnesses were superior to one because they provide a surer base for faith and more knowledge about Jesus than only one Gospel would afford. Four Gospels, he concluded, represent a fourfold benefit for the church.

As it turns out, the preacher raised a real problem, one even older than the New Testament and which has elicited a number of reactions. Some readers, like the preacher, uneasy about the existence of four Gospels, feel compelled to defend why four versions of Jesus' ministry are necessary. Others, as early as the second century until the present, take the four Gospels and weave them into a single, super-sized life of Jesus. They assume that this fuller story presents a clearer picture. In fact, what they gain with their amalgamated Jesus is misleading; what they lose by harmonizing the differences and muting the individual testimony of each Gospel cuts deeply.

Other people have achieved the same result as the harmonizers without the effort, unconsciously blending the four into a single account when they repeat stories about Jesus. This happened often when scribes hand copied the New Testament and occurs today when Sunday school teachers give their lessons. Intermingling the Gospels goes hand-in-hand with a common-sense attitude that assumes each Gospel tells the same story because—it is assumed—each simply states what happened. This results in a new version of the story and contributes to the ongoing, constructive creation of mythology about Jesus.

This essay will insist on four Gospels and refuse to take four as a simple fact. Four is a correct count but not a necessary total. It is an outcome, not a plan. To understand and appreciate that the New Testament has four Gospels, each needs to be understood individually. In refusing to blend the four Gospels together, we will see their authors' individual ideas and perspectives. Hearing four clear voices will change how we think about early Christian history and the significance of Jesus.

The Emergence of Four Gospels

Whether contemporary readers think twice about having more than one Gospel, the earliest Christians did. Their comments reveal the difficulties the early church faced by possessing multiple accounts.

The Gospel according to John recognizes that it competes with other traditions and allows room for competitors, while implying its own superiority. It asserts that there simply is too much to say but encourages the reader to be satisfied with what the text of John provides, for it reveals what one needs to gain eternal life. John's Gospel also sets itself up as conveying insider information that privileges those who possess and understand it. This position rests on the experience of John's community of believers, who believed God provided ongoing revelation. The story of Jesus continues beyond his Resurrection as his teachings unfold among those who believe in him, requiring a very different story than the other evangelists provide.

The author of the Gospel according to Luke says up front that he knows of many written texts that compete with one another for an audience, and that he wishes to supplant them with his own superior narrative. Careful reading of Luke's account reveals that one of these inadequate texts the author wishes to replace is the Gospel according to Mark.

Luke thought Mark left out too much material, an opinion shared by Matthew. In the eyes of his critics, Mark's too-brief account lacked many of the best stories about Jesus and his most profound teachings, failed to express crucial themes and ideas, lacked a sufficiently broad historical horizon, and did not anchor Jesus adequately within Jewish tradition. Mark's failure to include stories about Jesus' birth and Resurrection must have bewildered the other Gospel writers. Matthew, in particular, made changes to Mark that corrected Jesus' teachings. Yet, both Matthew and Luke generally followed the outline of Jesus' life that Mark provided, a tacit endorsement that kept Mark in good stead and provided credibility to all three texts.

Others in the early church agreed with the authors of Matthew and Luke that Mark's Gospel did not tell enough of the story. In particular, Mark did not relate any of Jesus' appearances after he rose from the dead; this begged for correction. Unknown editors provided remedies, adding a few more sentences at the end of Mark's text. These alternate endings featured teachings by the risen Jesus so the story would end "appropriately." The longest of the additions was written with an eye on the other Gospels and helped update Mark's Gospel so it spoke more directly to later Christians. Among other things, it reasserted, correctly, the politics of Mark's Gospel after they had been muted by Matthew and Luke: Authority rests not on respected apostles but in the power of the divine spirit acting in the midst of Jesus' followers, in exorcisms, healings, speaking in tongues, and immunity to poison. This improved version of Mark passed down through the manuscript traditions and entered the English Bible.

The additions to the end of Mark's Gospel reveal a strange twist in the evolution of the written gospel. Even though Mark invented the genre, Matthew, Luke, and John redefined it such that Mark had to be revised to fit the new model. This reflects an assumption that there is but one correct way to tell the story of Jesus. But if this were so, there would not be four Gospels, each telling a unique story. The reality of four Gospels contradicts the assumption that the story of Jesus must be told in a single fashion.

In the late second century, Irenaeus of Lyons, a bishop in France, directly addressed the issue of multiple Gospels, arguing on behalf of four. On the one hand, Irenaeus argued, using only one Gospel was a clear sign of heresy. The Ebionites, a group that tried to stay inside

Judaism, restricted their reading to the Gospel of Matthew. Marcion, who tried to purge Christianity of anything resembling Judaism, read only the Gospel of Luke. Those who tried to disentangle Jesus' humanity from Christ's deity preferred Mark's Gospel, whereas Gnostics, for whom cosmology was important, had a strong preference for John's Gospel. For Irenaeus, four Gospels were enormously positive, because those who read only one missed correct doctrine. Reading only one Gospel was a path to idiosyncrasy and error.

Against heretics, then, Irenaeus attempted to argue for the necessity of four Gospels. He found ammunition for his arguments by analogy with the natural world. The world, he argued, divides into four zones, and there are four principal winds. Therefore, the church requires four Gospels to serve as four pillars. Irenaeus next argued for a fourfold text with analogies from scripture. As there were four general covenants with humankind given through Noah, Abraham, Moses, and Jesus, so there also should be four Gospels. Then, at much greater length, Irenaeus argued that the fourfold Gospel is like the four heavenly creatures, unusual beings that protect heaven's majesty, described by the prophet Ezekiel and repeated in Revelation. These four multi-winged creatures are described as resembling a lion, calf, man, and eagle. Irenaeus took up each of the four, in turn describing their qualities and how each resembles the work accomplished by Christ. Because they resemble Christ, the creatures express the character of the Gospel. For Irenaeus, the four were not simply a helpful analogy but a cosmic thread linking heaven and Jesus. He saw an underlying necessity in the comparisons so that he concluded, "For the living creatures are quadriform, and the Gospel is quadriform, as is also the course followed by the Lord." To Ireaneus, then, a fourfold Gospel was not a mathematical accident. As surely as there is more than one Gospel, there cannot be three or five. Four are not simply a historical accident. In Irenaeus' view, there *must* be four.

In summarizing Irenaeus' arguments, much has been left out. To his credit, Irenaeus tried seeing something unique in each Gospel to warrant the need for four. He made general observations that have influenced preachers, as well as Christian iconography, ever since. The lion, calf, man, and eagle commonly adorn church interiors as symbols of the canonical Gospels. But these images, like Irenaeus' comments, are superficial and too closely tied to the heavenly creatures to provide insight into the unique characteristics of each Gospel. Ireanaeus had the right impulse but was too quick to tie scriptures, old and new, together with nature into a single, neat package to work out the particular characteristics of each Gospel.

Each Gospel has its own story, and it is to these individual stories we turn to see what Irenaeus and many others missed. We begin with Mark, the first of the canonical Gospels to be written, then look at Matthew and Luke, which are revisions and expansions of Mark. We will examine John last, because it takes a different and more independent approach to its story.

The Gospel According to Mark

The author of the second canonical Gospel is the first to put together a lengthy story about Jesus. Much was said and written about Jesus in snippets prior to Mark's Gospel. Perhaps some Christians threaded a few of these snippets and short narratives together into slightly longer units. Mark probably had a collection of parables with which to work, perhaps also collections of miracles and apocalyptic sayings. Someone may have drafted material about Jesus' death, but the author of Mark appears to have been the innovator who compiled these individual pieces, stories, and anecdotes into a lengthy narrative about Jesus.

The story Mark's author wishes to tell is a familiar one, yet not the story one expects to hear. For one thing, Mark has esoteric elements. Though today the parables are considered a superb method of communication, the author of Mark does not consider them such. For him, parables obscure Jesus' teaching in order to shield it from outsiders. Whereas evangelical impulses motivate simple and clear preaching, Mark suppresses Jesus' identity during the course of his story.

In another oddity, Mark's Gospel presents Jesus as a teacher for Gentiles. For example, Jewish dietary regulations are set aside in Mark, and Sabbath observance is moderated. The Gospel even explains Jewish practices, suggesting that its audience is not Jewish. To think about this in general terms, then, by the time anyone got around to writing a life of Jesus, the Jewish roots of the Jesus movement were being eclipsed, leaving it to a Greek writer to present a Jesus for a Gentile readership. This is already a good way downstream from the source of Christianity.

Another surprise in Mark's story is how closely he intends for Christians to identify with Jesus. To be precise, Mark never uses the word *Christian* but disciples or, more literally, "students," and followers. This is partly why Mark introduces Jesus at his baptism, for this is the entrance point into discipleship. Jesus sets the example of baptism for his followers, his reception of the divine spirit illustrating what will take place in the baptism of the many disciples to come. In Mark's story, then, *Jesus sets an example for Christian discipleship*.

Although humility is one aspect of following Jesus, Mark has much more in mind. Since Jesus' followers were a threatened minority making their way through a hostile world that did not welcome Christian preaching, Jesus provided an example of how to persevere in this life and reach a transformed, heavenly existence in resurrection—in a word, a way to apotheosis. Struggling ahead, despite suffering, disciples of Jesus won godlike immortality.

As the story of Jesus unfolds in Mark's Gospel, words and, specifically, Christological titles are turned upside down. Mark likes to designate Jesus as the Son of Man and does so to emphasize the connection between Jesus and the Christian audience. That Jesus, as Son of Man, forgives sins does not mean that he occupies a superior position from which he dispenses forgiveness but that God has graciously allowed forgiveness to be dispensed among the community of his people by people. When Jesus asserts the lordship of the Son of Man over the Sabbath, he does not claim a unique position for himself. He claims for all of his disciples, who are equally sons of men, freedom from Sabbath regulations. When Jesus predicts his fate—three times no less—he presents himself as a model for his followers: He is the Son of Man who serves others and suffers but, ultimately, rises from the dead. In Mark's Gospel, Jesus is not a uniquely transcendent entity, but an exemplar. Jesus represents existence within the community of faith and embodies the blessings it enjoys, the difficulties it faces, and the destiny that awaits it.

The story of the Son of Man, however, culminates on a surprisingly upbeat trajectory when Jesus reveals the Son of Man is not only the innocent sufferer but also the eschatological judge. The latent potential of God's people becomes clear. God entrusts them with the work that is normally thought of as God's own work. At a pivotal moment in Jesus' trial, the author of Mark, having neglected throughout his Gospel any connection between his Son of Man and that of the prophet Daniel, invokes Daniel's image of the Son of Man who descends from heaven with the people of God to judge the world. The intimate connection between Jesus and his followers, expressed in Jesus' identity as Son of Man, receives a crucial, final dimension that recognizes human potential. Human destiny may lie in the heavens.

Jesus, as Son of God, likewise takes an unexpected turn. We meet Jesus as God's son right at the beginning of Mark, when a heavenly voice identifies him as such at his baptism. Demonic voices similarly recognize and, with fear, confess Jesus' familiarity with the divine. God identifies Jesus as a special son on a mountain, where Jesus' heavenly potential shines through in a physical transformation, and God again identifies him as son and asserts that this makes him superior to the immortals, Moses and Elijah. This episode may well serve as a resurrection story for Mark, an example of what happens when God raises a person from the dead to immortality. As such, both examples of God's testimony on behalf of Jesus, at baptism and transfiguration, prefigure crucial moments in the path of Jesus' followers. These moments not only reveal Jesus, but also they present mileposts in the experience of his followers, who become God's children in the baptism of the spirit and realize their full destiny as God's children in resurrection.

Mark's presentation of Jesus as Son of God reaches its climax when Jesus hangs battered and humiliated on the cross, and a Roman soldier acknowledges what, at that moment, seems so preposterous: Jesus truly is God's son. In a surprise move, a close relationship with God results less in fearsome power than in guiltless endurance in the face of difficulty. Yet over this hang the words "Son of God," again inviting disciples to bring themselves into the picture. "Son of God" is not a status that distinguishes Jesus from his followers but an aspiration. Where the power of the divine spirit (baptism) and immortality (transfiguration) are concerned, pursuit seems reasonable—frightening perhaps, but worthwhile. On the cross, this point of connection with the teacher turns around completely and becomes repulsively frightening. Here, where it seems most likely that weak humans could identify with their master, they flee. Here, insists Mark's Gospel, is where one truly finds the Son of God.

Mark presents a picture of life that is very Greek. The human condition is difficult, tragically infused with suffering. In the face of this difficulty, what should one do? Mark answers this question religiously. The more difficult life becomes, the more it is to be embraced and endured. Such is the path of God's children, but the suffering endured leads to the life of heaven. In the language of Greek mythology, through the heroic enduring of extreme challenges, of life-threatening ordeals, successful endurance leads to immortality.

Mark's answer presents more than the typical struggles of human life. Death looms as a threat, perhaps remote but still frightening. More significantly, a crucial moment approaches, heralded by Jesus' ministry: God will soon judge the world through Jesus. The power seen in Jesus' life and among his followers is the evidence of how close this decisive judgment is and should motivate people to endure life's trials and follow Jesus.

The author of Mark's Gospel argues for an interpretation about the significance of Jesus. At the time he wrote, alternative traditions about Jesus existed. From what can be inferred, one could see in Jesus a Jew who taught people the correct way to live under the law of Moses or the revealer of divine wisdom who brought life-transforming truth. To accord with these traditions about Jesus, end-time judgment need not have figured prominently. Mark argues differently.

Just as Mark uses Jesus to model the way for his followers, so he uses *Jesus' disciples as bad examples to be avoided*. Jesus' inner circle is portrayed as cowardly and obtuse. Repeatedly, they fail to understand Jesus, a recurring theme. They need help understanding his parables. After Jesus feeds thousands of people—twice, no less—the disciples fail to comprehend the significance. When he tells them he will die, they do not understand. When he emphasizes the necessity for suffering and death, they show how utterly incapable they are of hearing this hard truth, three times. Asked to keep watch, they fall asleep, three times. In the end, one disciple betrays him; all flee; and Peter denies knowing Jesus, three times.

Nor does the Gospel of Mark rehabilitate the disciples. Either readers assume to know something that lies outside the text that makes everything better, or they take the text at face value and assume the reliability of Jesus' immediate followers is suspect. Jesus asks one thing of them, one difficult thing to be sure—namely, that they follow. Instead, they run away. They do not understand, and they do not follow, making them unreliable teachers of the gospel.

Readers can, therefore, observe that Mark champions no particular follower of Jesus, which provides another key feature of his book. Most gospels place one or a few founders in its spotlight. Peter, James, John, and Thomas figure in the New Testament; others take the stage later. These central figures anchor Christian teaching to Jesus to guarantee its authenticity or provide a channel for revelation. Not so in Mark.

The Gospel of Mark situates authority not in historical proximity to Jesus but in contemporary experience of the divine spirit. The exorcisms and healings featured in Mark reflect the religious experiences of Jesus' followers. These provide assurance of the presence of God's spirit and affirm the conferral of the spirit in baptism. God's rule is at hand. Difficult though the path may be, immortality approaches.

Since authority does not lie in what the inner circle has to say, the gospel needs another foundation. The Gospel of Mark finds this in the example of Jesus. This is precisely where the creative genius of Mark rests. The author took traditions about Jesus, which had been primarily things he said, and crafted a narrative to provide an example for disciples to imitate. Jesus provides a model of faithfulness to God, which the gospel calls for his followers to live out in their own circumstances. Given what Jesus taught about humility and impending judgment, one expects those circumstances would involve hardship and indignity. Whatever the obstacles, however, faithfulness leads to immortality.

The Gospel of Mark, then, represents something new on the stage of Christianity, for in it, the life of Jesus is presented for the first time in written, narrative form. The author did not do this frivolously but with purpose, not lured by an amazing story worth telling but driven by the nature of the message. To produce obedience, teaching could suffice; apotheosis, however, requires courage and accomplishment. Jesus models the way. Constructing a story to present Jesus' example forever welded Christian theology to the lived life of Jesus.

Q—Which Matthew and Luke Both Mined for Material

The canonical Gospels were not the first four documents written about Jesus. Each author had written materials to use. For example, scholars suspect that Mark started with a collection of parables; John had a collection of stories about miracles performed by Jesus (the so-called "Signs Source"); and Matthew and Luke used a variety of documents, one notably in common, a written collection of Jesus' teachings, that is referred to conventionally as Q, short for Quelle, the German word for "source."

The idea of Q developed through the nineteenth century and became a commonplace working assumption. The content can be described, generally, as the material that appears in both Matthew and Luke but is absent from Mark. The majority of today's scholars think that both Matthew and Luke used Q, and many have attempted to reconstruct and interpret its text.

Even skimming Q quickly would correctly reveal that it records things Jesus said and little else. For this reason, it is called a "sayings source." It contains things such as the Lord's Prayer and the Beatitudes but makes no effort to create a storyline to bind the various sayings, instead stringing them together with the meager logic of a grocery list. On occasion, repeated words or similar ideas cause sayings to be linked, but often, the sequence lacks transparent rationale.

In the twentieth century, scholars expended a great deal of effort analyzing their reconstructions of Q. They identified repeated motifs, such as poverty and judgment. Analysis of such themes led scholars to reconstruct the evolution of Q in three historical stages, beginning with a collection that focused on sayings about discipleship, to which was added apocalyptic expectations, and later, things such as the brief story of Jesus' temptation.

Investigation of Q has been ingenious and industrious, and the results are important, as reconstructed Q provides the earliest window into the teachings of Jesus and dominates contemporary reconstructions of the historical Jesus. Q alerts readers to the fact that the four Gospels did not emerge from a vacuum but were built on collections of material composed by earlier writers.

The Gospel According to Matthew

The Gospel of Mark, the first attempt at an extended narrative about Jesus, won an audience within the early church in competition with other texts and traditions. It made sufficient impression on the author of Matthew's Gospel that he made it the backbone of his own book about Jesus; yet the significance of other texts and the shortcomings of Mark compelled Matthew to write his own replacement text. In Matthew's view, Mark's Gospel fundamentally failed to communicate Jesus' teachings sufficiently. As a result, Mark inadequately characterized Jesus and failed to embed him within Jewish community and tradition. In looking at these last two deficiencies, the difference made by the teachings Matthew added to his story can be seen.

To enhance his *characterization of Jesus*, Matthew adds biographical information. The most immediate and obvious addition is his opening birth narrative. Matthew's stories about Jesus' birth enriched Christian tradition with memorable imagery; more to the point, they satisfied curiosity about Jesus' origin. As in biblical stories about Jewish heroes, God intervened to bring about the surprising birth of Jesus. Hellenistic traditions contributed their influence, making explicit divine paternity. At the opposite end of the Gospel, Matthew's resurrection narratives provide a fuller, more satisfying conclusion, including a defense against accusations of fraud and a farewell commissioning from Jesus that sets the church's agenda.

Throughout Matthew's Gospel, quotations and allusions to Jewish scriptures add to the portrait of Jesus, demonstrating the divine purpose being realized in Jesus' life. A recurring motif is a comparison of Jesus to Moses as ruler and lawgiver. This resembles the ancient Jewish writer Philo, whose *Life of Moses* portrays Moses as king, lawgiver, priest, and prophet. Matthew's birth narrative quickly links Jesus to kingship by tracing Jesus' lineage through King David and providing the explicit testimony of the Magi (the three wise men) that Jesus is born king of the Jews. Jesus' birth in Bethlehem, the city of David, adds to this, and the star that announces Jesus' birth associates him with other divine rulers. The qualities of a good ruler appear in Jesus' refusal of Satan's offer of power and, again, in the characterization of Jesus as gentle. The triumphal entry into Jerusalem adds to the picture, which becomes explicit in the image of final judgment when Jesus sits as judge over the nations of the earth. It reaches its climax in the final paragraph when Jesus asserts that all authority in heaven and earth has been given to him.

Many details paint Jesus not only as a ruler but also, specifically, as a second Moses. Just as the baby Moses escaped Pharaoh's attempt to kill all baby boys, the baby Jesus eludes King Herod. As a result, Jesus spends time in Egypt, as had Moses. As Moses spent forty days and nights fasting on Mt. Sinai awaiting the law, so Jesus goes hungry for forty days and nights in the wilderness awaiting trial by Satan. When the three temptations come, Jesus responds to each with words from the fifth book of Moses, Deuteronomy. Both Moses and Jesus control wind and sea. Moses judged his people; Jesus will judge the world. According to Jewish traditions, nature mourned Moses' death, as it does for Jesus.

Matthew also organizes Jesus' teachings into five discourses, a number that answers to the five books of Moses. In the first, the Sermon on the Mount, Jesus explicitly interacts with the Law of Moses, endorsing its continued validity, stipulating that not a single stroke of the pen will pass away. Jesus demonstrates an alternative way to interpret the Law of Moses to achieve righteousness, one that is personally rigorous. Jesus also offers guidance on essential religious practices, such as prayer and almsgiving, and formulates priorities and values for his followers. In my opinion, the Sermon on the Mount is the most profound and challenging of any of Jesus' speeches. The scholar Hans Dieter Betz argued that differences in ideas between the Sermon on the Mount and the rest of Matthew's Gospel indicate that the Sermon existed as a literary summary of Jesus' teachings prior to Matthew, who copied it into his narrative, thereby anchoring his Gospel to the church's Jewish past and present.

By situating the Sermon on the Mount on a mountain, hence the name, Matthew creates an allusion to Moses, who received his law from God on a mountain. Mountains reappear in Matthew's Gospel in other critical events: once when Jesus is transfigured into a glorious body of light, like heavenly beings in general and Moses in particular, and again at the end of the story, after his Resurrection, when he commissions his successors and promises his abiding presence. Matthew tightens the correlation between Jesus and Moses in the transfiguration story by adding the detail that Jesus' face shone, as had Moses' after he was on Mt. Sinai. In all three mountain settings, Jesus is like the great Moses, only better.

Linking Jesus to Moses is key to Matthew's story, as he wants to position Jesus as the great teacher, the reliable guide to righteousness. Whereas Mark's Gospel assumes a Gentile readership, Matthew's reflects followers of Christ who remain within the broader *Jewish community*, arguing with their kinsmen about the correct way to live.

A decade or two before Matthew wrote, Roman armies conquered Jerusalem and destroyed the temple, eliminating a key aspect of Jewish life. We know from Josephus and the Dead Sea Scrolls that many had criticized the Temple and warned of God's displeasure with it. Its destruction in 70 CE called for insight into how Jews should live going forward. During this crisis, various groups, the Pharisees and followers of Jesus among them, stepped forward to provide answers and lead. The Pharisees appear to have set the stage for rabbinic Judaism, but the followers of Jesus gave us the Gospel of Matthew, an expression of faith in Jesus as developed among Jews.

This Jewish context influences what Matthew wrote. From the opening sentence, readers are introduced to Jesus as the son of Abraham and David, followed by a genealogy that illustrates this statement. Just as fourteen generations passed from Abraham to David, another fourteen passed from David to Jesus, placing Jesus at an auspicious moment in Jewish history. This Jesus then goes on to appear as a second Moses. From the point of view of Matthew's social situation, there could be no better person to teach and lead people to righteousness. Incorporating the Sermon on the Mount into his text emphasized traditions about Jesus as formulated among Jewish Christians. Matthew also rewrote Mark to eliminate Mark's dismissal of kosher food laws. Matthew's focus on Jews continues in the second sermon, in which Jesus sends his followers to evangelize only Jews. In the fifth sermon, Matthew adds to his story lengthy denunciations of the Pharisees, teachers with whom followers of Jesus were in competition.

The Jewish character of Matthew's Gospel is reflected in its emphasis on righteousness, unlike in Mark's. This appears in the description of righteous Joseph, is elaborated in the Sermon on the

Mount and culminates in the concluding paragraph in which Jesus commissions his disciples to preach obedience to the entire world. The Jewish character of Matthew's Gospel is further apparent in the intertwining of mercy and righteousness. Mercy is, for Matthew, the true face of righteousness and the quality by which one escapes final judgment.

This ethic extends to Matthew's discussion of the church. Matthew's explicit references to the church are unique among the four Gospels. While the church is certainly relevant to each Gospel, the appearance of the actual word is striking. It appears in Matthew's fourth sermon, which focuses on life in the Christian community. This sermon does not focus on church polity or liturgy but on practice, emphasizing humility, mercy, and forgiveness to create a community living together successfully. God grants this community the power to forgive and petition.

Matthew's other mention of the church is a key passage in which Jesus identifies Peter as the rock on which he will build the church. Jesus then grants the power to confer forgiveness. Matthew alone records these words. They provide evidence of the church's growing self-awareness and an example of how individual apostles are beginning to be singled out as a community's link to Jesus. A very different attitude toward Jesus' first followers, a positive one, appears in Matthew as compared to Mark.

Given the prominent position of Jewish law in Matthew's Gospel, it seems fitting that he also plays down Jesus' miracles. He relates fewer, and the ones he tells are shorter. He also clusters them together to get them out of the way and colors them with words from Isaiah to make them tools of compassion not displays of power. In fact, those who rely on deeds of power (like an exorcism) to authenticate their faith in Jesus will be sorely disappointed at the final judgment. This resembles the story from Jewish tradition in which a rabbi tried to persuade other rabbis of his interpretation of Torah by successfully invoking many signs, including a voice from heaven, in proof of his position. The other rabbis, however, refused to side with him, preferring what they read in Torah to miraculous evidence. Similarly, Matthew departs from Mark to present a different kind of faith in Jesus, one in which righteousness and mercy trump miracles.

For all of its focus on Jewish community and tradition, Matthew's Gospel does not ignore the expansion of the church into the Gentile world. As early as the opening genealogy Matthew provides clues to this by inserting a few Gentile women into the list of Jesus' ancestors, hinting at the broader consequences to come. These clues become clearer when the Magi appear, indicating the extension of God's kingdom to the broader world. The kingdom of heaven benefits not only Jews but also all who come to Jesus. Matthew sees in Jesus one who would lead Israel to the heights of its imagined greatness, such that the entire world would look to it, offering honor and tribute. Jesus is king of heaven and earth and welcomes into his kingdom people from all corners of the earth. In Jesus' kingdom, ancient Jewish aspirations come to fruition. The Magi are but the first to acknowledge this.

From Mark to Matthew, then, surprising social and literary paths have been followed. The Gospel of Mark stimulated another Christian who continued to live according to Jewish traditions (though he wrote in Greek) to write a "better" Gospel that would present a more Jewish Jesus. Matthew makes explicit Jesus' relationship to Jewish traditions and more effectively communicates what Jesus taught. In Mark, Jesus, the model human, is a teacher for Gentiles and communicates by action and example; while in Matthew, as a second Moses, Jesus instructs Jewish Christians in lengthy speeches.

Matthew uses Mark as the narrative backbone for his Gospel, but he is not a slave to Mark. Matthew reaches back to traditions earlier than Mark does for sayings of Jesus to incorporate into his new, improved Gospel. Matthew clusters teachings to create longer sermons and miracles to redefine their relevance. Whereas Mark makes a bold statement that what Jesus had done was vitally important, Matthew endorses the view of earlier traditions that what Jesus said was fundamental. Linking word and deed is frankly unremarkable. Most thinkers in the ancient world would have insisted they correspond. Yet one should pause and congratulate Matthew for making this a literary reality in Christian literature. Drawing liberally on traditions about Jesus' teachings, Matthew unites sayings and narrative, giving the church a Jesus—a Jewish Jesus—who speaks and acts.

The Gospel According to Luke

Mark's Gospel asks the question, "How does a Gentile follow Jesus?" Matthew's asks, "How does a person live righteously according to Jesus' teaching?" Turning to the Gospel of Luke, readers find a text that asks, "What is the correct version of Christian faith?" Written some decades (in my opinion) after Matthew, the Gospel of Luke arises in a situation of significant diversity among versions of Christianity. Is the faith Jewish or is Jewish tradition irrelevant? Is it an alien faith or at home in the Roman Empire? How does one know which version of Christian teaching is reliable? Luke embarked on a project of historical investigation to settle these questions.

To understand what Luke accomplished, we will consider three aspects of his writings. By examining the material Luke added to Mark expanding Jesus' biography, one can see the thematic core of the gospel as Luke understood it. By paying attention to other themes Luke emphasized, one will recognize how he made his story seem so natural and persuasive. Finally, considering the scope of his entire project, one can differentiate it from those of his predecessors.

Luke sets out to portray *Jesus as the prophet who brings God's salvation to people in need.* Clues appear in the birth narrative. Like Matthew, Luke deepens the connection between Jesus and God with a story of the virgin birth, yet their stories diverge. Gone are the Magi, who are replaced by shepherds, shifting the focus of Christ's kingdom away from a Jewish monarch to its concern for outsiders and especially the poor. It is not simply bad luck or inadequate planning that keeps Mary and Joseph from getting a room in the inn; rather, the stable is the birthing room appropriate for Jesus, and the shepherds are the perfect court and subjects. Despite the irony that "a Savior, who is the Messiah, the Lord" (Lk 2:11) was born in humble surroundings, the lowliness actually signifies the message he will bring.

The mercy Jesus extends to the poor and needy comes to the forefront in Luke's Gospel. "Blessed are the poor in spirit," Jesus tells readers in Matthew's Gospel, whereas in Luke Jesus says, "Blessed are you who are poor"—end of sentence. The poor. Luke later adds, "Woe to you who are rich." In Luke's view, riches are ill-gotten and a pernicious distraction from God's priorities. Jesus instructs the wealthy Zacchaeus, whom readers meet only in Luke, to make restitution to those he defrauded. The beggar, Lazarus, another person met only in Luke, rests in the bosom of Abraham after death, while the nameless rich man who ignored Lazarus when he was alive dies and suffers torment. God's mercy targets the poor, which establishes an ethic for religious believers to practice. Pious people must be merciful and generous.

This reflects the broader platform of Jesus' kingdom in which fortunes are reversed. The high are brought low, the humble exalted. The ancient world was sensitive to the whims of fortune, keenly aware that states rise and fall, as do the lives of individuals. Fate could turn on a dime. The Magnificat, the beautiful praise Mary speaks when she learns of God's plan for her (Lk 1:46–55), anticipates this cardinal tenet in Luke's theology: God brings down the mighty and lifts up the humble.

This reversal of fate is not something delayed into the distant future or afterlife. Jesus demonstrates the salvation God offers in the course of his ministry. Not surprisingly, repentance and forgiveness are common motifs in Luke's writings. But Luke's conception of salvation is broader than forgiveness. For example, the lame walk, the sick are healed, and lepers are cured. A widow, mourning the death of her only son, is rescued from likely ruin by Jesus when he brings her son back to life. People on the margins are not left to themselves; Jesus reaches out to them. The other Gospels, of course, recount such deeds in the course of Jesus' ministry, but it is the Gospel of Luke that clearly labels these as acts of salvation.

Such deeds of salvation form part of the prophetic ministry of Jesus, as Luke presents it. In an early story riddled with thematic significance (4:16–30), Jesus stands in the synagogue to read from the prophet Isaiah about an anointed prophet who heals the blind and preaches to the poor. When he finishes, Jesus identifies himself with the figure in the text and adds more commentary to compare himself to the great prophets Elijah and Elisha. Later in Luke, Jesus again summarizes his work by alluding to the words of Isaiah: "The blind receive their sight, the lame walk, the lepers are cleansed, the deaf hear, the dead are raised, the poor have good news brought to them" (7:22). The prophet Jesus brings God's salvation to people in need.

Luke's portrait of Jesus as the prophet of salvation sits in *a larger, more complex story designed to assure the reader of its reliability.* The roles of scripture, divine spirit, and apostles in Luke's account work together to give the reader confidence that the author has indeed established the correct view of the gospel.

Luke opens his Gospel promising to present a reliable story about "the things that have been fulfilled among us." This reveals a lot about his historical method. He will understand current events through their relation to ancient texts. We have already seen how Luke uses the words of the prophet Isaiah to interpret Jesus' deeds. He also advocates this method for interpreting Jesus' death and Resurrection. At the end of his Gospel, two disciples walk away from Jerusalem to the little town of Emmaus (24:13–35). The resurrected Jesus joins them along the way. Unrecognized, he strikes up a conversation with them and learns of their sadness over his crucifixion. Jesus then scoffs at their ignorance and, drawing from Moses and all the prophets, begins to explain the correct way to understand these recent events. Among competing views of Jesus at the time Luke wrote, he therefore argues that the correct view of Jesus must align with the words of the ancient Jewish prophets. If this seems obvious, credit Luke for helping it seem so, for it was not so when he wrote.

The words of scripture are one example of God's mind and plan. Many times in his writing, Luke refers to things Jesus had to do: He had to heal a woman, stay with Zacchaeus, and go to Jerusalem. He had to preach and to die. To Luke, divine initiative lies behind events, directing them. The story of the Gospel could not be only "a" story; it had to be "the" story.

Many times in Luke's story, necessity becomes more directly identified with the agency of God's spirit. Luke's Gospel tells readers that John the Baptist is full of the spirit, as is Jesus, and that God will give the spirit to anyone who asks. The gift of the spirit empowers Jesus to do mighty deeds and, in turn, enables his disciples to do likewise. The spirit also helps people speak in praise, prophecy, and defense. Luke stands in complete opposition to anyone who would discount the evidential value of the spirit's work.

The apostles stand as the final guardians of Luke's views. As he presents them, they all stood in agreement on the nature of the gospel. Peter, John, James, and Paul could find common ground and cooperate. Individually and collectively, the apostles' accounts serve as witness, providing a link back to Jesus. This link works geographically as well, as it is important that the gospel went out of Jerusalem and remained connected to Jerusalem as it spread. Luke believes this happened and bases his story on it. Therefore, he presents a story based on reliable witnesses empowered by the divine spirit, guided by the hand of God, and sent to preach about a series of events that unfolded according to scripture and are understood through the interpretation of scripture. Modern history would balk at these criteria, but Luke told a story that has stood for centuries.

Turning to the scope of Luke's project, there is much more to Luke than has yet been mentioned—twice as much, actually. After writing a Gospel, *the author filled a second scroll with an investigation of the early church*, the Acts of the Apostles. Whereas Matthew anachronistically placed the church in Jesus' lifetime, Luke correctly pushed it forward, subsequent to Jesus' life, and continued writing to do so. This second volume is what, above all else, sets the Gospel of Luke apart from the other Gospels. The combination of Luke-Acts makes the author the most prolific contributor to the New Testament and arguably the most articulate theologian of the early church. Though Jesus, Paul, and John usually receive the most credit for the New Testament, the anonymous author of Luke-Acts is just as important, and arguably more influential, as he created the picture of early Christian history that has dominated thinking for centuries.

Luke's theological ideas also helped set the stage for centuries of Christian thought. On the question of the church's relation to Jewish history and tradition, Luke answered by embracing them; yet he mapped a clear historical narrative that accounted for Christianity's evolution out of Jewish religious practices, thanks in great measure to a heavenly vision given to Peter and a reasoned summit of church leaders in Jerusalem. To his credit, Luke recognized that Jesus and the first Christians were Jews who lived like Jews, attending synagogue and worshipping in the temple, and did not force a Gentile church into the life of Jesus. At the same time, interweaving the stories of the births of Jesus and John the Baptist helped root Christianity in Jewish history, while narrative parallels between Jesus and both Peter and Paul provided continuity between Jesus and the early church. Luke gave Christian faith a pre-history, one rooted in ancient writings and traditions.

Luke also created space for Christian faith within the Roman Empire. On occasion, Luke's comments about dates and rulers clue readers into events on the larger world stage. In Acts, when Roman officials sit in judgment on Christians, they rule favorably. Moreover, the climax to Luke's story takes place when Paul arrives in Rome. Luke did such a good job making Christianity look at home in the Roman Empire that some (not including me) think this was a main reason he wrote.

I do admire the accomplishment of the author of Luke-Acts. In combining God's powerful spirit with the actions of the earliest Christians and footnoting with scripture, Luke hits upon a way of tracing the trajectory of authentic Christianity. Actions empowered by God's spirit provide clear evidence of God's will and the legitimacy of the people acting on God's behalf. The specific ability of Christians to defeat evil spirits further validates Christianity. Luke ties the workings of God's spirit to an orderly succession of witnesses, beginning with the apostles in Jerusalem and continuing with Paul, whom Acts connects to Jerusalem. Linking contemporary events to works of ancient scripture establishes the legitimacy of the events and their interpretation. In fact, the sequence of fulfilled events provides the overarching theme that guides Luke's history and holds it together. For the author of Luke and Acts, the nexus of spirit, apostle, and scripture provides Christianity with a profound story and sound historical footing. From such a position, the author confidently asserts that he offers a reliable view of the gospel.

The Gospel According to John

The first three Gospels surveyed here reveal the diversity that existed among early Christians and the variable texts used to express their differences. Though the authors of Matthew and Luke had good reason to replace Mark's Gospel with newer, expanded, more satisfying stories of their own, they still respected their predecessor by using his text as their base. The author of the Gospel according to John takes an entirely different approach.

The Gospel of John *rejects the Synoptic Gospels' story*. John does not rescue Mark's text with additions and emendations but replaces it. John does not take the outline of his story from Mark, nor does he take any core material. John includes no exorcisms or parables. In John, Jesus makes multiple trips to Jerusalem, as opposed to Mark's one. Jesus cleanses the temple at the beginning of John's story, not just before the crucifixion where Mark places it. John creates his own storyline and, with it, offers many stories that are unique to his Gospel—such as Jesus' turning water to wine, Jesus' washing the disciples' feet, and Thomas's doubting Jesus is risen. John has his own story to tell and does so in his own way.

John's Gospel also appears to criticize the synoptic tradition. For example, in the story of Jesus' agonized prayers in the Garden of Gethsemane just before his arrest, a key to Mark's ideas about discipleship, Jesus prays, "Remove this cup from me" (Mk 14:36). This story does not appear in John; worse, it is criticized: Jesus says, "Now my soul is troubled. And what should I say—'Father, save me from this hour'? No . . ." (Jn 12:27). Where Mark's story focuses on the necessity for Jesus to suffer, John's Gospel does not but, rather, changes Jesus from a victim to the one who orchestrates the final, climactic days of his own life. As such, Jesus refuses to pray to avoid his impending death, and the crucifixion becomes the path to glorification, a repeated and important insight in John, for it brings a return to the divine realm.

Where miracles are concerned, John advances the conversation far beyond the Synoptics. John calls miracles "signs," by which he tells readers that deeds of power are not simply eye-popping spectacles but events with much to communicate. Therefore, in John's story, shortly after Jesus feeds the five thousand, he says, "I am the bread of life. Whoever comes to me will never be hungry" (6:35). As his sermon continues, Jesus adds, "I am the living bread that came down from heaven. Whoever eats of this bread will live forever" (6:51). The skeptics in the crowd naturally ask how one is supposed to eat Jesus' flesh, to which he responds, "Those who eat my flesh and drink my blood have eternal life" (6:54), pointing the reader to the Eucharist. A similar interaction between sign and revelation takes place when Jesus heals a blind man and raises his friend Lazarus from the dead. Miracles yield insight into Jesus, his work, and his ongoing significance.

The beginning of the Gospel of John provides the most telling difference between it and the synoptics. Each Evangelist, like every author, had to decide where to start his or her story. The Fourth Gospel takes a much more expansive approach than the other three and thereby critiques their lack of vision. Mark begins, "In the beginning of the gospel . . ." (1:1 KJV) and moves quickly through prophetic traditions to Jesus' baptism. Matthew and Luke thought the story should begin earlier, going back to Jesus' birth and, even further, by connecting Jesus to ancient Jewish history. John looks back to an even more remote time, to the day of creation, echoing the opening words of Genesis: "In the beginning . . ." (1:1). This is not just literary artifice or pretentious allusion. Pointing to creation announces a cosmological point of view that informs John's entire Gospel and signals a fundamental shift of perspective from the other three.

What does it mean to say that *John's Gospel has a cosmological point of view*? John does not tell a story about Palestine or the Roman Empire, but about the totality of the universe. The text has a point of view from outside the world that allows the reader to see what is going on in heaven and on earth, not just a small corner of the Mediterranean basin.

One simple observation is that John's Gospel frequently uses the Greek word *kosmos,* significantly more often than the other three Gospels combined. *Kosmos* translates into English as "world," denoting a variety of things—sometimes all of creation; other times all living things in creation, perhaps only gods and humans or just people; and other times to the physical creation, either earth or both heaven and earth. These meanings are slippery and shift easily, as in John 1:9–10: "The true light [Jesus] was . . . coming into the *kosmos*. He was in the *kosmos*, and the *kosmos* came into being through him, and the *kosmos* did not know him." John sees Jesus as a figure who moves into and out of the *kosmos* and who, in fact, is creator. This point of view fundamentally changes the story John's Gospel tells.

This cosmological perspective correlates with John's view of Jesus. John drew on a Greek tradition that identified Reason as the divine presence within the created order and identified Jesus with this. The Greek word for *reason* is *logos*, which the English Bible has stubbornly rendered as "Word." Although this translation keeps readers' ears attuned to Gen 1, in which God speaks and creation happens, and allows interpreters to make connections with the prophetic word, it obscures the connection of *logos* with Greek philosophy and cosmology in which *logos* is a ubiquitous technical term. It is inconceivable that *logos* could be used in the opening verse of John's Gospel, an explicitly cosmogonic cluster of clauses, and not be read in dialogue with Greek cosmology. Even if one listens only to Gen 1, the opening line, "In the beginning was the Word," alerts readers to John's cosmological horizon and places Jesus on the cosmic stage, not simply the soil of Palestine.

John says things about Jesus as a cosmological figure that identify him as a divine being. For example, "The *logos* was with God. . . . The *logos* was God. . . . All things came into being through him"(1:1–3). Elsewhere in John's Gospel, Jesus claims participation in God's fundamental works of creation and judgment, including the power of life. In a climactic utterance at his arrest, Jesus identifies himself to those who come to arrest him, saying, "I am" (18:4–6), which is usually translated as "I am he" to accommodate English style. This seems innocent enough, but again there is an allusion to Jewish tradition and specifically to the divine name in the Hebrew scriptures. The four-letter name of God, traditionally translated with small capitals as "the Lord," as opposed to "the Lord," and variously referred to in English as Jehovah or Yahweh, appears related to the verb "to be." Thus in a play on this name, God told Moses in Ex 3:14, "I am who I am." When Jesus says, "I am," it is an allusion to this divine name. So powerful was the revelatory effect of those two little words that those who had come to arrest Jesus fell to the ground. This also explains Jesus' earlier statement, "Before Abraham was, I am" (8:58), and why people picked up stones to throw at him after he said it. Jesus straddles and transcends time. It comes as no surprise, then, that this Gospel reaches a crescendo with the disciple Thomas's unique confession, "My Lord and my God" (20:28).

When Jesus refers to himself as "I am," it is an example of his role as revealer. Jesus has specific credentials that qualify him for this role. As he says, "My testimony is valid, because I know where I have come from and where I am going"(8:14). Jesus' origin, where he is from, is another criticism of the Synoptic tradition; for however correct it might be to say Bethlehem or Nazareth, these geographic locations are irrelevant. Jesus is from above; he comes from the Father. This self-knowledge equips him to reveal the Father and the way to the Father.

Jesus' role as revealer accounts for two ways Johns' Gospel differs from the Synoptics: Jesus speaks about himself and engages in discussions with his disciples. It is in John and only John that one hears Jesus talk about his relationship to the Father and say things about himself like, "I am the good shepherd," "I am the light," and "I am the resurrection and the life" (10:11; 8:12; 11:25). John's story also presents question-and-answer dialogues between Jesus and his disciples. To be sure, in the Synoptics, one encounters conversations. But in Jesus' interaction with his disciples before his arrest, the dialogue is less conversational and more a device for teaching, as disciples ask questions and Jesus provides answers. Thomas complains the disciples do not know where Jesus is going. Philip asks Jesus to show them the Father. Judas asks why Jesus reveals himself to them but not to the world. These read more like an interview than a conversation. This form would become popular in later Christian writings.

Another result of the cosmological horizon is that the nature of "eternal life" must be rethought. In Matthew, Mark, and Luke, eternal life is mentioned occasionally and is something that lies in the future, whereas in John, eternal life is now. It is not something to await but something encountered in the present. Judgment likewise looms in John's present, not in the Synoptics' future. The same can be said of the kingdom: In the Synoptics, it is approaching, while in John's Gospel it is already "in you." By way of analogy, the Synoptic Gospels have a horizontal storyline, moving from present to future, and the Fourth Gospel, a vertical one, stretching between heaven and earth.

The Gospel of John, like the others, also has an interest in *the church*. This becomes explicit in Jesus' prayer on behalf of his followers, when he includes a petition for those yet to come. The focus of Jesus' petition is their unity. Turning to the letters of John, we learn why unity is a problem. The community has fractured. Perhaps this is reflected in the Gospel through allegiance to the figure called "the beloved disciple" versus Peter or Thomas. Perhaps it is related to the growing split between Jewish Christians and the synagogue. Given John's teaching that the world will hate those who practice loyalty to Christ, the community of John clearly sees itself as put upon and excluded.

The church's relationship to Jews in John's Gospel is complicated. Placing the episode in which Jesus chases the money changers out of the temple at the beginning of the story puts Jesus in immediate opposition to the temple and its authorities. The first miracle in John, in which Jesus turns water into wine, heralds the surprising superiority of the new wine, a metaphor for faith in Jesus. Scripture scholar Raymond Brown did much work showing how, in John's Gospel, Jesus reinterprets or replaces Jewish institutions and festivals. The most obvious is Jesus' claim that the true worship of God takes place in spirit, not in a specific temple or place. Many have observed how odd it is, historically, to name Jesus' opponents as "the Jews," as if all his kinsmen stood in united opposition against him. They argue that this clues readers in to the debates taking place near the time the Gospel of John was written. An identity crisis had arisen, as those who believed in Jesus found themselves at heated odds with the Jewish community, some even expelled from the synagogue. Despite these antagonisms, believers clung tenaciously to the Jewish scriptures and God. The church in John claims to be heir to Jewish traditions, while members of the Jewish community disagree and begin to ban Christians from community gatherings.

In Mark's Gospel, Jesus is identified as the "Son of God." This title clearly establishes Jesus' special relationship with God, but it finds clearest expression in suffering and is held out to others as a goal for which to strive. In Matthew and Luke, Jesus is more uniquely God's son by virtue of Mary's miraculous, divine impregnation. John's Gospel tops them all by asserting that, at the time of creation, Jesus existed and was the agent of creation. Jesus, the *logos*, is how God is present in the universe. Jesus is divine and shares the divine name; therefore, he cannot be a model but becomes a guide. The cosmological dimension of John's Gospel eclipses the others, turning Jesus into a creator, revealer, and cosmic Savior. This takes Jesus beyond what members of the Jewish community were willing to tolerate, bearing witness to an important stage in the evolution of the church from a Jewish to Gentile phenomenon.

Conclusion

We return now to a basic observation: There are four Gospels. Four were written, because four different authors had different audiences, different views of Jesus, and different senses of the human condition and its need. Mark wrote for Gentiles; Matthew brought Mark back onto a Jewish stage; Luke changed the stage to the Roman Empire and gave it a historical framework; and, while John presented a Jewish-Christian context, he made the entire cosmos the stage.

The Christianity evidenced in Mark left behind its Jewish social origins, including the leadership of Jesus' family and earliest disciples. Matthew claimed a Jewish past, respecting the Twelve and privileging Jewish practices and aspirations. The roots of Christianity within Judaism fascinated Luke, but these origins serve to anchor a Gentile religion historically, not impose a Jewish identity in the present. The earliest disciples provided fundamental witness to Jesus, but the story Luke told requires moving beyond them to another figure, the apostle Paul. Only by adding Paul and his preaching to non-Jews can Luke's story reach its climax.

For Luke, the movement from Jew to Gentile lay in the past. This transition is still fresh in John's Gospel and remained a wound in the psyche of John's community. But the view of Christ "the creator" demands a Christianity that stands above any ethnic designations. The Gospel of John is self-conscious about the development of its ideas but takes confidence in its connection with the disciple whom Jesus loved, a figure it alone introduces into the story of Jesus, whose superior witness justifies the views of the Gospel and its community.

In Mark, Jesus is one of us, while Matthew and Luke gave him the advantage of divine paternity. John took a giant leap forward and identified Jesus as the divine creator, God's very presence within the universe.

Mark agrees that the human condition is difficult. Following Jesus adds further hardship, yet endurance leads to God's approval and immortality. Matthew saw a world that needed to choose righteousness and practice mercy, as grounded in Jewish tradition and taught by Jesus. The kingdom of heaven became a reward for the humble and merciful, which is to say, the righteous. Luke saw people divided by inequities in which the rich and powerful abused those beneath them. This would not last. Ancient oracles pointed to Jesus as God's agent for reversing inequity. The spirit of God brought this about in the present, while judgment awaited the rich and powerful. John presented a world of people blinded by darkness, people who need the illumination Jesus brings. As the divine creator, who was better than Jesus to alert the world to God's judgment and open the door to heaven? Few people recognized who Jesus really was. Most were blind. Those whose eyes were opened enjoyed heavenly life right away and had no fear of death.

There are four Gospels because different early Christians had their own stories to tell about Jesus. The early church grew comfortable with these four stories and gave them a place of privilege in worship and ministry. Changing technology bound individual stories together into books and centuries of continued use enshrined the four texts as the four canonical Gospels.

What the collection of four canonical Gospels says is that for the message of Jesus to be relevant to different social groups or to people experiencing life in different terms, a new Jesus is necessary. One Gospel will not suffice. Additional ones are needed. At the same time, if every group were to have its own unique Gospel, the church would fragment, as was happening. Four Gospels, therefore, is a statement about church diversity and unity. By holding the number of accepted Gospels at four, the early church decided that some coherence was necessary among Gospels to hold intact the larger organization of the church. How churches move from the enshrined, canonical four Gospels to contemporary relevance has been and is a challenge each faces in its teaching and practice.

Questions

1. How should one read the attitude of Mark's Gospel toward the disciples? Should attention be focused on how the Gospel portrays their relationship to Jesus when he was alive and among them, or should one also consider the relationship one assumes they had with Jesus after the Resurrection?

2. There is another way of reading Matthew's Gospel. One can take the strong affirmations of Jewish traditions and community in Matthew as representing the views of the sources used by the author, not the actual views of the Evangelist himself. Thus, a Gentile composed the Gospel of Matthew but drew on sources from Jewish Christianity and took care not to change them when he incorporated them into his new work. Jesus was a Jew who ministered to Jews. Not until after the Resurrection did he turn his attention to Gentiles and send his disciples to evangelize them. Do you think this is more likely or that Matthew emerged inside the Jewish Christian community?

3. Read Mt 28:16–20. If Matthew's Gospel reflects a group of Jews who followed the teachings of Jesus, how would you interpret these verses? If these verses explain how the church left behind its Jewish roots to follow Jesus, how would you interpret them?

4. Which Gospel resonates most with the world as you experience it? Explain.

5. What problems confront people today that require salvation? If you wrote a gospel that provided deliverance from these problems, would it look like a canonical Gospel? How similar or different would it be?

6. In Lk 4:16–30, Jesus preached in the synagogue in Nazareth. Mark 6:1–6 was Luke's source. The number of verses alone tells us Luke expanded the story significantly. Read and compare these two texts and see if you recognize the broader themes Luke added to the story.

7. Both Matthew and Luke provide the same summary of the preaching of John the Baptist (Mt 3:7–10; Lk 3:7–9). Consider that John preached in Aramaic, yet Matthew and Luke wrote in Greek. How would you account for the similarity between Matthew and Luke in this case?

8. What is the attitude of John's Gospel to Peter and Thomas, especially in 20:24–29 and 21:15–22? Add Mt 16:13–19 and Jn 20:19–23 to your consideration.

Further Reading

Ashton, John. *Understanding the Fourth Gospel*. 2nd ed. Oxford University Press, 2009.

Betz, Hans Dieter. *Essays on the Sermon on the Mount*. Trans. L. L. Welborn. Minneapolis, MN: Fortress Press, 1985.

Brown, Raymond, and Francis Moloney. *An Introduction to the Gospel of John*. The Anchor Yale Bible Reference Library. Yale University Press / Doubleday, 2003.

Kingsbury, Jack D. *Matthew as Story*. 2nd ed. Minneapolis, MN: Fortress Press, 1988.

Luz, Ulrich. *The Theology of the Gospel of Matthew*. New Testament Theology. Cambridge University Press, 1995.

Rhoads, David, Joanna Dewey, and Donald Michie. *Mark as Story*. 3rd ed. Minneapolis, MN: Fortress Press, 2012.

Tannehill, Robert. *The Narrative Unity of Luke-Acts*. 2 vols. Facets and Foundations. Minneapolis, MN: Fortress Press, 1991.

Telford, W. R. *The Theology of the Gospel of Mark*. New Testament Theology. Cambridge University Press, 1999.

Tyson, Joseph B. *Marcion and Luke-Acts: A Defining Struggle*. Columbia, SC: University of South Carolina Press, 2006.

White, L. Michael. *Scripting Jesus: The Gospels in Rewrite*. New York: HarperOne, 2010.

The Gospels Are Anonymous

Centuries of tradition have ingrained the habit of referring to the four canonical Gospels as Matthew, Mark, Luke, and John or, to use their full names, the Gospel according to Saint Matthew, the Gospel according to Saint Mark, etc. This tempts readers to believe the titles indicate who wrote the Gospels, which is why the heading of this chapter is not obvious, as it seems on the surface that the Gospels do state the names of their authors. They do not. The titles they bear link them with the early church's heroes and certify that the Gospels' teaching and the church's preaching are one.

Titles Are Misleading

The titles of the Gospels present an innovation. Unlike other ancient literature, they are neither called "The Sayings of Jesus according to St. Matthew" nor "The Life of Jesus" nor "An Account of Jesus." They bear the title "Gospel," which is something relatively new.

To be precise, two things are new. First, no literary category of "gospel" had existed for Christian gospels to join. Second, Christians went for more than a century before using the word "gospel" to refer to writings. One looks in vain through early Christian writings before 150 CE for the word *gospel* to denote a written text. Two generations of Christians referred to Mark as something other than "Gospel." In a scholarly journal François Bovon has suggested that, at first, Mark was called "Memoirs," and perhaps the earliest readers called Matthew "Beginnings" or "Life" and Luke "Narrative" (HTR 81 [1988]: 23). For nearly a century, the word *gospel* referred narrowly to a preached message focused on Christ's death and Resurrection or, more broadly, to Jesus' message. Only in the second century did Christians look backward and designate some of their writings as "gospels." If, therefore, Christians did not even start to call written works "gospels" until decades after the first few were written, then the titles known so well today could not have been original.

The form of the titles supports this. If there were only one Gospel, it could be called simply, "The Gospel." To add the prepositional phrase, "according to *X*," implies the knowledge of more than one and the need to differentiate them. That all four take the same form of title, namely, "The Gospel according to *X*," betrays that the titles have been standardized and, therefore, are secondary.

Accepting their titles as a secondary addition means that one does not know, from the titles of the Gospels, who wrote them. This does not mean the Gospels are silent where authorship is concerned. Two point to their authors; nevertheless, none provides a name. If one discounts the traditional titles as historical evidence, as this essay will argue, then one can say that the four canonical Gospels are anonymous.

Two Completely Unknown Authors: Mark and Matthew

Nothing in the Gospels of Matthew and Mark indicates who wrote them. No names are put forward and no self-references appear.

The Gospel According to Mark

As indicated previously, Mark was the first of the four Gospels to be written. Internal evidence provides some guidance about its origin. For example, it was written in Greek, in a simple style, presumably addressing a Greek-speaking audience for whom literary art was not a priority. In it, Mark explains Jewish customs, indicating an audience for whom such things needed explanation, namely, Gentiles living in a place where they comprised the primary local culture. That

Mark overturns food regulations and Sabbath observance underscores a primarily Gentile audience.

The recurrent theme of suffering throughout Mark has led people to see the audience as Christians facing persecution. This is an
important consideration but difficult to define. First, life might have
been harsh enough that people could suffer without persecution.
Human frailty, the vicissitudes of fate, and the inevitable difficulties of life were and have been common assumptions about human
existence. Second, persecution comes in degrees, ranging from the
slights incurred by not participating in the activities of others to a
bloodlust sanctioned and enforced by the government. A common
claim is that Mark's Gospel addresses Christians in Rome as they
faced persecution by the emperor Nero. This view picks up on the
repeated encouragement to endure suffering, but the degree of speci-
ficity goes far beyond any internal evidence linking it to Nero. As we
shall see, this view is not likely to be true.

The view of Neronian persecution owes much to the ancient
identification of Mark's Gospel with the city of Rome and the apostle Peter. The second-century testimony of the Christian Papias provides the earliest existing, explicit commentary on the origin of the
Gospel according to Mark. Papias wrote his work on early Christianity sometime between 100 CE and 140 CE. What is known
about Papias comes from other Christian writers who refer to him.
In his history of the church (about 320 CE), Eusebius quotes Papias'
remarks about the origin of Mark's Gospel, which derive from what
an elderly Christian, the Presbyter, had said to Papias:

> "And the Presbyter used to say this, 'Mark became Peter's
> interpreter and wrote accurately all that he remembered, not,
> indeed, in order, of the things said or done by the Lord. For
> he had not heard the Lord, nor had he followed him, but
> later on, as I said, followed Peter, who used to give teach-
> ing as necessity demanded but not making, as it were, an
> arrangement of the Lord's oracles, so that Mark did nothing
> wrong in thus writing down single points as he remembered
> them. For to one thing he gave attention, to leave out noth-
> ing of what he had heard and to make no false statements

in them.'" (Eusebius, *Ecclesiastical History* 3.39.15; Kirsopp
Lake, trans., Loeb Classical Library)

This important testimony has influenced the reading of Mark's Gospel for centuries but requires critical reflection.

Papias' comments about Mark's Gospel reveal that, by the end
of the first century, controversy surrounded it. The first problem with
Mark's Gospel was that an eyewitness did not write it. Papias concedes
the point but defends Mark by arguing that the account rests on the
eyewitness testimony of Peter as recorded by one of the apostle's companions, and not just any companion but Peter's interpreter or translator. The assumption appears to be that Peter preached in Aramaic; then
Mark translated it into Greek. Regardless, this invites the rebuttal that
Mark filtered Peter's teachings and, in the process, edited and amended
them, introducing error. Papias counters this by asserting Mark's inno-
cence and simplicity as the recorder of Peter's preaching, Mark's only
goal being to pass on what he had heard and to do so truthfully.

Papias' account fits into a larger pattern of controversy surrounding early Christian gospels. Who wrote them mattered in the
arguments about what texts Christians should read and trust. To
be written by an original eyewitness was a key argument in eval-
uating the reliability of gospels. The authors of other early Christian writings claimed association with people who knew Jesus, for
a text needed a good pedigree to win an audience. What is encountered in Papias is a concession that Mark was not actually written by
someone from Jesus' inner circle, which was a problem for the text's
authority and reliability. Papias provides a solution by conceding the
author was not an eyewitness himself, but the scribe for someone
who was—namely, Peter! By making a connection between Peter
and the Gospel according to Mark, the early church rescued Mark
and gave it solid footing in the face of its competitors.

Reading the Gospel according to Mark, however, makes it hard
to believe the tradition about its connection to Peter. In Mark's story,
Peter is no hero, no sage, and no figure of special merit. He is, in fact,
a fool and coward who elicits censure from Jesus and, in the end,
denies his teacher. In this, he looks like the other disciples who also
misunderstand Jesus and fail to stand with him at the moment of
crisis. The Gospel of Mark lacks connection to any particular early

apostle. More to the point, Mark's Gospel pushes early followers to the margin to present its own message about Jesus. Mark does not want to be connected to Peter, the Twelve, or even Jesus' family and argues against any such necessity.

Papias' attempt to connect Mark with Peter further stumbles over the claim that Mark's Gospel contains everything the author heard Peter teach. Allowing for the possibility that Mark did not hear all of Peter's sermons, it still seems unlikely that Peter did not have more to say than is found in Mark. Furthermore, the Gospel's assumption of a Gentile audience that follows Jesus free of Jewish legal observances sounds like it came from the apostle Paul, not Peter. According to the testimony of Paul, in his letter to the Galatian churches, during a particularly testy incident in Antioch, Paul criticized Peter for not participating in table fellowship with Gentiles. This precipitated an agreement in which Paul preached to Gentiles and Peter evangelized Jews. While the Gospel of Matthew reads like a text that might rest on the man who preached to Jews, the Gospel of Mark certainly does not.

The most important criticism of Mark's Gospel in Papias' report is how Mark ordered events. Faced with the accusation that Mark did not place the elements of the story about Jesus in correct order, Papias concedes this point, arguing that it is unimportant and misses what Mark was doing. The author of Mark was simply and naïvely transcribing, as the memories came to mind, what he remembered Peter to have preached. If Papias were correct, one would expect a story whose elements are haphazardly ordered. This is not what is encountered.

A great deal of order appears in Mark's arrangement of materials. Chapters 8–10, in particular, have a careful organization that underscores the points the author seeks to make in his story of Jesus. Through the first eight chapters, Mark notes the disciples' inability to understand Jesus. They fail to understand the parables, the feeding of the five thousand, Jesus' teaching about unclean foods, and the feeding of the four thousand. After the second feeding, Jesus launches into a withering critique, demanding, "Do you still not perceive or understand? Are your hearts hardened? Do you have eyes, and fail to see? Do you have ears, and fail to hear? And do you not remember?" (8:17b–18). Exasperated, Jesus reiterates, "Do you not yet understand?" (8:21). Then Mark's story pivots.

In 8:22–26, Jesus heals a blind man. This is the first story Mark tells of Jesus healing a blind man. The next is in 10:46–52. Situated between these two stories are Peter's startling confession and three parallel units of text. In the case of the first blind man, Jesus needs a couple of attempts to perform the healing miracle. The first attempt helps, but the result is still poor, blurry vision. After the second application of healing, the man's vision clears. This is a metaphor for the disciples who were blind and needed Jesus' help to see, which apparently was provided, for in 8:27–29 Jesus asks them who people say he is, then who they think he is, to which Peter answers, "You are the Messiah." This sounds like an excellent answer, but I'm not entirely sure whether Peter got this right or whether he was like the blind man with improved but still foggy vision.

Following Peter's confession, Jesus begins teaching the disciples that he is about to undergo great suffering and death. Jesus repeats this prediction two more times for a total of three (8:31; 9:31; 10:33–34). After the second prediction, Mark notes that the disciples did not understand—again—what Jesus was saying (9:32–34). This editorial statement is not needed because the stories illustrate it. After each of these predictions, the disciples do something stupid, something that demonstrates a complete inability to grasp what Jesus is saying. In the first case, Peter rebukes Jesus for his crazy talk about death (8:32–33). After the second prediction, the Twelve fail to understand and then spend the afternoon arguing about who will be the greatest in the coming kingdom (9:32–34). Following the third prediction, the brothers James and John ask for the seats of privilege and honor in Jesus' kingdom (10:35–41). These three predictions of Jesus' death are followed by three examples of the disciples' obtuseness.

Death Predicted	Disciples Misunderstand	Teaching on Discipleship
8:31	8:32–33	8:34–9:1
9:31	9:32–34	9:35–49
10:33–34	10:35–41	10:42–45

The pattern continues. After Jesus sets Peter straight, he calls everyone around and says, "If any want to become my followers, let them deny themselves and take up their cross and follow me." Jesus goes on to teach what good discipleship looks like (8:34–9:1). Similarly in chapter 9, after the argument about who would be greatest, Jesus sits down and offers more lessons about good discipleship, beginning with, "Whoever wants to be first must be last of all and servant of all" (9:35–49). The pattern holds for the third time, as the disciples' foolish ambition calls for yet another lesson on discipleship, concluding with the words, "For the Son of Man came not to be served but to serve, and to give his life a ransom for many" (10:42–45). Next comes the second and final story in Mark of a blind man being healed.

What is seen in Mark is a pattern of prediction, misunderstanding, and teaching about discipleship that repeats three times. This is not an example of random memory on the part of the author but clear evidence of literary composition.

Other structures appear in Mark's Gospel. One is a habit of clustering similar materials. Mark strings together two or more miracle stories in three places. He includes two clusters of controversy stories, five in 2:1–3:6 and six more in 11:27–12:40. Chapter 4 presents a series of parables.

The author of Mark's Gospel is also fond of ring structures, in which he opens with a topic, moves on to others, but then returns to the opening motif. A number of these can be identified. Rejection is the topic of 3:30–35, and Mark returns to it in 6:1–6. Herod is the topic in 6:6b–32, and Mark returns to Herod in 8:21.

We will linger over a final device Mark likes to use because it so clearly demonstrates careful planning and symbolic communication. Mark's Gospel uses a "sandwich," or an ABA structure, in which one story is embedded inside another. The first story (A) begins, the second (B) is inserted, and then the first story (A) concludes, hence ABA. This structure invites the reader to compare or contrast the interconnected stories.

Mark made half a dozen such sandwiches; we'll sample four. In 5:21–43, a man asks Jesus to come to his house to heal his twelve-year-old daughter. En route, Jesus encounters a woman who has suffered twelve years of bleeding. She touches Jesus' clothes in the belief that his power will flow to her and cure her. It does. Jesus and the woman talk briefly, and he continues on his way to the man's house where he raises the now deceased girl from the dead. The span of twelve years, the shared gender, and the struggle for life unite the two stories and invite readers to interpret them in dialogue with one another.

Toward the end of Mark's Gospel, there are two more sandwiches. In one story, 11:12–21, Jesus curses a fig tree for not bearing fruit. In the next, Jesus drives the money changers out of the temple. In the conclusion to the first story, Jesus and his disciples walk past the now-withered fig tree. The ABA structure invites us to read the fig tree as a symbol of the failed temple and its impending demise. The analogy may seem odd at first, but the prophet Isaiah used the fig tree as a metaphor for unfaithful Israel centuries earlier. In another sandwich, 14:53–72, Peter enters the courtyard of the high priest, where Jesus stands trial. The action shifts from Peter to Jesus, who is asked, "Are you the Messiah?" Jesus answers, "Yes." The story shifts back to Peter who three times denies his affiliation with Jesus. The sandwich underscores the two very different examples of faithful endurance.

The earliest sandwich occurs in 3:20–35 and involves Jesus' family. They hear reports about what Jesus has been doing and go to bring him home, thinking some madness had taken hold of him and that he needs rest. The story then shifts to teachers of the law who accuse Jesus of being inspired by the prince of demons. Jesus notes the absurdity that Satan opposes Satan, and makes the famous statement that a house divided against itself cannot stand. Then Jesus states that attributing his deeds to Satan is unforgivable slander against the divine spirit. The story picks up with Jesus' family arriving to take charge of him. Jesus rejects their attempt to do so and says that his true family are those who do God's will. This sandwich has the effect of condemning Jesus' family. First, they are portrayed as neither understanding Jesus nor following him during his lifetime. Second, their position is lumped in with the religious leaders who oppose Jesus and are branded unforgiveable. After Jesus' death, his brother James would become a leader in the church, a particularly important figure in the Jewish wing of the movement. This sandwich states that familial bonds give no one an advantage in Jesus' kingdom. Worse, the family members' attitudes during Jesus' ministry absolutely disqualify them.

Perhaps the most significant aspect of Mark's literary artistry lies in the seams he created to stitch together the individual traditions he brought into his Gospel. About a century ago, Karl Ludwig Schmidt published a monograph titled, *The Framework of the Story of Jesus*. He demonstrated that the oldest Jesus traditions consisted of individual, self-contained stories requiring the author of Mark to add connections to hold them together. That they are Mark's contribution is betrayed by the fact that the links between stories are not required by the stories. To say that more concretely, stories are introduced with a time or location, but that information plays no role in what follows.

Early on, an example of the author's handiwork appears. In 1:21–34, the author of Mark constructs a sample day in the life of Jesus by taking two unconnected stories and providing narrative introductions that tie them together as events that happened on the same day. The author then composes and appends his own summary of all the things Jesus did later that same day, in what turned out to be one very busy day in Jesus' life. Throughout his Gospel, the author invents such connections.

Papias utterly misses the fact that Mark is an author with a point of view and a specific version of the gospel to express. As seen, Mark positions stories strategically and links them creatively. He clearly uses characterization to convey his message and dramatic tension. He develops and articulates, in narrative form, distinct theological ideas. His fingerprints are all over his Gospel.

I have taken time to note, in detail, some examples of Mark's literary art to make clear that Mark is a thoughtful composition, not a haphazard jotting of one's memories. To this evidence, one can join the arguments of scholars that the author of Mark used written sources. A collection of miracles seems likely, as well as sayings of judgment. Recent conversations have focused on Mark's use of a written story about Jesus' death. The use of sources and the organization of material undermine the traditional view put forward by Papias. Internal evidence from the Gospel of Mark therefore demonstrates that the theory about Mark's origins put forward by Papias is factually incorrect. Papias is demonstrably wrong, and one cannot trust what he has to say about the origin of Mark.

In fact, reliance on Papias is a detriment to reading Mark for it imposes a misleading frame of reference on the text. By severing Papias' link between the Gospel according to Mark and the apostle Peter, one eliminates the main connection between the Gospel of Mark and Rome. This leaves the Gospel according to Mark untethered to any identifiable circumstances or author, underscoring that it is actually an anonymous text, making all references to "Mark" merely a habit, a convention to help readers talk about someone they do not really know.

The Gospel According to Matthew

Matthew's Gospel, likewise, gives no indication of who wrote it. One can infer the author stood closer to the Jewish roots of Christianity, seeing Christ as King of the Jews, champion of righteousness, and upholder of Moses' law. The author of Matthew stakes out these positions in conscious debate with the author of Mark, for the author of Matthew used Mark as the base of his new Gospel but purged Mark's Gentile elements and asserted Jewish religious practices and beliefs. In addition, Peter receives greater honor in Matthew. To him, Jesus gives the keys to the kingdom, reflecting a different sense of authority behind the text, one more concerned about anchoring itself to Jesus.

For more specific information, there is an ancient tradition that accounts for the origin of the Gospel of Matthew. Again, it comes from Papias, and can be found in Eusebius, together with his comments about Mark.

> These are the views of Papias concerning Mark. As for Matthew these things were said: "Matthew collected the sayings in the Hebrew language, and each translated them as able." (*Ecclesiastical History* 3.39.16)

This claim is perplexing. The Gospel according to Matthew, as we know it and possess it, was written in Greek, not translated from Hebrew into Greek. How do we know this? Translation Greek usually has quirks of style that betray Semitic roots. These are not seen in Matthew. By and large, Matthew is written with a natural Greek style.

Clearer evidence comes from what most scholars agree to be the origin of Matthew, namely, that the author used Mark's Gospel, copying significant portions of it into his own composition. The close similarities between Matthew and Mark can be explained only by a hypothesis of literary dependence of one on the other. For numerous reasons, most scholars today hold the view that Mark wrote his version first and that Matthew subsequently used Mark. In addition, one can see how Matthew improved Mark's Greek style, adding a little polish here and there, using a more elegant word or fixing awkward grammar.

The only way any credence can be given to Papias' words about Matthew is if Papias is referring to a different text than the one known today as the Gospel of Matthew; otherwise, this early tradition is wrong. Counter arguments about the care Papias claims to have taken do not change the fact that he makes a mistake where Matthew is concerned—just as he is wrong about Mark.

Without Papias to fall back on, the identity of the author of Matthew's Gospel, just like Mark's, remains anonymous.

Two "I"s with No Names: John and Luke

Mark and Matthew were the first canonical Gospels written. John and Luke followed and present a different state of affairs. Although Luke and John remain anonymous, their authors speak: In both Gospels, readers discover the pronoun *I*. Though these authors remain nameless, they are not invisible. Because I think the Gospel of John was written before Luke, an admittedly minority view, we will discuss it next.

The Gospel According to John

The Gospel of John reveals a complicated origin that explicitly involves at least two authors and one key source of information. Evidence of additional editing opens the door to more writers. This makes it hard not only to put a name on the author but also to decide who gets final credit for this Gospel.

The Identity of the Beloved Disciple

As John's Gospel draws to its close, the writer pauses to directly address his readers. In cryptic words, one reads:

> [20]Peter turned and saw *the disciple whom Jesus loved* following them; he was the one who had reclined next to Jesus at the supper . . . [21]When Peter saw him, he said to Jesus, "Lord, what about him?" [22]Jesus said to him, "If it is my will that he remain until I come, what is that to you? Follow me!" [23]So the rumor spread in the community that this disciple would not die. . . . [24]*This is the disciple who is testifying to these things and has written them*, and *we know* that *his* testimony is true. [25]But there are also many other things that Jesus did; if every one of them were written down, *I suppose* that the world itself could not contain the books that would be written. (Jn 21:20–25, NRSV, italics added)

In v. 24, the writer points directly at the person responsible for the Gospel of John, the so-called "beloved disciple." This companion of Jesus provided witness to the things recorded in the Gospel; moreover, he wrote them down. After the stone-cold silence about authorship in Mark and Matthew, vv. 24 and 25 are a big step forward. Who, then, is this beloved disciple? John's Gospel refuses to name him. People have typically identified him as John, because he is one of Jesus' closest disciples in the other Gospels, a conclusion that the title of the Gospel reinforces. But the Gospel itself never makes this correlation.

A few people, however, suspect that a clue appears when Jesus raises Lazarus from the dead. Fearing for Lazarus' life, his sisters, Mary and Martha, send word to Jesus, saying, "Lord, he whom you love is ill" (11:3). Two verses later, the Evangelist adds, "Jesus loved Martha, and her sister and Lazarus" (v.5). From the point of view of the Gospel narrative, Lazarus is identified as a friend Jesus loved. This raises the possibility that subsequent references to the beloved disciple are of Lazarus. As the story in chapter 11 progresses, Lazarus dies, but four days later, Jesus raises him from the dead. In chapter 21, readers learn that a rumor circulates that the beloved disciple would not die. If this is indeed Lazarus who rose from the dead, the rumor has additional rationale. Perhaps Lazarus is the beloved disciple, and I emphasize *perhaps*. I introduce this minority view to make clear that there is an alternative way to identify the beloved disciple that does not require introducing the figure of John or looking outside the text.

John's Gospel implies more about the unnamed disciple, but how much more is unclear. He might have connections in Jerusalem. Since he sits next to Jesus at the last supper, which takes place in Jerusalem, he may be the host. It seems likely that he is "the other disciple" who was known to the high priest and, therefore, can enter the high priest's courtyard after Jesus' arrest, which would reinforce his connection to Jerusalem. The beloved disciple appears again at Jesus' cross with Jesus' mother, and Jesus commits her to the care of the beloved disciple. Perhaps this suggests he has a home in Jerusalem or nearby. These are conjectures.

What matters more than the beloved disciple's name is how he is characterized. The beloved disciple displays greater loyalty and courage than Peter. At the final meal, the beloved disciple sits next to Jesus, not Peter. When Jesus is taken to the high priest for trial, Peter and the other disciple follow. The household knows the latter, so he enters. He puts in a good word for Peter, who then is admitted but subsequently denies even knowing Jesus. During the crucifixion, the beloved disciple's courage continues on display, as he remains at the cross whereas all the other men, including Peter, have fled. After the Resurrection, Mary Magdalene announces to Peter and the beloved disciple that the tomb is empty. The two run to the tomb to see for themselves. Upon arriving, Peter, we are told, sees, but the beloved disciple sees and believes. Lastly, in the appended chapter 21, Peter and the beloved disciple are fishing in a boat when Jesus appears at the shore and offers the unsuccessful fishermen advice. Acting on the suggestion, they make an epic catch that they are hard pressed to haul into the boat. The beloved disciple is the one who recognizes the obvious: "It is the Lord" (21:7). In these stories, the beloved disciple displays courage, loyalty, and insight superior to the other disciples in general and Peter in particular. Given these comparisons, the beloved disciple is better qualified to convey the story of Jesus.

John's Gospel compares its hero, the beloved disciple, not only with Peter but also Thomas. The story of doubting Thomas, which appears only in John's Gospel, is well known. As the story goes,

Thomas asserts that he will not believe Jesus has risen from the dead until he puts his finger in Jesus' wounds. Jesus appears and gives Thomas the opportunity, to which he responds with a climactic, "My Lord and my God!" The entire Gospel has been building to such a confession, so Thomas plays a positive role in John's Gospel. But his faith is not as strong as the beloved disciple's, as Jesus makes clear in his response, pronouncing a blessing on those who, unlike Thomas, believe without having to see.

Given the overall scope of the four Gospels, this story about Thomas seems unremarkable. Outside the New Testament, however, there is significant early Christian literature that bears the name of Thomas, whom tradition says travelled to India to preach the gospel. He left a much greater legacy in the early church than the New Testament reflects. In the story of doubting Thomas, however, the Gospel of John presents its champion, the beloved disciple, as superior—not only to Peter but also to Thomas as well.

Neither Thomas nor Peter is left without merit, however. Even in his doubt, Thomas confesses his faith in Christ. Peter is rehabilitated as well, when, in chapter 21, Jesus commissions him to lead the church. Though positioning the beloved disciple ahead of Thomas and Peter, John's Gospel does not deny Peter and Thomas a place of leadership in the church.

We can add one more observation about the beloved disciple. He is not among the inner circle of disciples who travels with Jesus. Jesus predicts that this group will scatter and leave him alone, which happens when Jesus is arrested. The beloved disciple does not abandon Jesus; he is at the cross. Surprisingly, the disciple with greater insight is not someone from Jesus' inner circle.

The Testimony of the Beloved Disciple

Having considered the identity of the beloved disciple, we now have to think more carefully about his role. Is he really the author of this Gospel? It is tempting to think, in 21:24, that the author of John refers to himself in the third person, in which case he validates the text of John even as he writes it: "*This is the disciple who is testifying to these things and has written them*, and *we know* that *his* testimony is true." But aside from how unseemly such self-recommendation would be, v. 25 immediately corrects such a view, as it provides commentary on v. 24, noting that, in addition to the beloved disciple's testimony, Jesus did many other things that would fill countless volumes. Here we encounter the important words, "I suppose," as the writer of the current text speaks directly: "But there are also many other things that Jesus did; if every one of them were written down, *I suppose* that the world itself could not contain the books that would be written." Verse 25, therefore, introduces a speaker who says, "I," who reflects—with a degree of uncertainty—on the beloved disciple and his testimony. We thus have two people involved in the origin of John's Gospel, (1) the beloved disciple through testimony and (2) the person who actually wrote the Gospel as we have it. Unfortunately, both of these suppositions are misleading.

To say "the person who actually wrote the Gospel as we have it" would hide important nuance. There may be more than one author and, possibly, multiple editors. Serious issues with the structure and flow of John's Gospel make scholars suspect it was revised. For example, the location of Jesus in chapters 5 and 6 is disorienting, as he appears to move between Jerusalem and Galilee as if they were next to each other. In 14:31 Jesus says, "Rise, let us be on our way," yet not until 18:1 do he and his disciples depart. The text counts Jesus' miracles, the first in 2:11 and the second in 4:54; however 2:23 says that many people in Jerusalem believed in Jesus because of the miracles (plural!) that he performed. In 11:2, Mary is described as the woman who poured perfume on Jesus' feet but it is not until the next chapter that the Gospel tells the story of where this happens. In 16:5, Jesus criticizes his disciples because they did not ask him where he was going; however, this is exactly the question posed by Simon Peter in 13:36. These oddities in the flow of thought in John's Gospel make scholars wonder what has happened to the text.

Chapter 21 presents one of these problems, such that many scholars believe Jn 21 is a secondary addition to the Gospel, an appendix. The end of chapter 20 provides persuasive evidence for this, because its two final sentences read like a conclusion.

[30]Now *Jesus did many other signs* in the presence of his disciples, which are not written in this book. [31]But these are written so that you may come to believe that Jesus is the Messiah,

the Son of God, and that through believing you may have life in his name." (Jn 20:30–31, NRSV, italics added)

If the Gospel of John ended at 20:31, no one would suspect anything was missing. The words form such a nice, rounded conclusion. Yet more material, which today is labeled chapter 21, follows.

As the additional chapter draws to a conclusion, a familiar phrase is encountered, "But there are also *many other things that Jesus did*" (21:25), which echoes the original conclusion, "Now *Jesus did many other signs* in the presence of his disciples" (20:30). This redundancy suggests that chapter 21 was, indeed, a secondary addition to the Gospel of John. So readers face different possibilities. Perhaps the beloved disciple wrote the first twenty chapters, and another person appended chapter 21. Or, perhaps the same person wrote chapters 1–20 but added 21 at a later time, in which case the information in chapter 21 tells readers that his first twenty chapters were based on the writings of the beloved disciple. Or the beloved disciple wrote traditions that someone else turned into Jn 1–20, followed by a third person who wrote chapter 21. So there are two, perhaps three, people involved in writing the Gospel of John as it is known.

Other problems suggest revisions have taken place. In Jn 5:19–27, for example, Jesus talks about his ability to grant life. He preaches that whoever hears his voice and believes "*has* eternal life"; such a person "*has passed* from death into life" (5:24). After speaking through eight verses about this present reality of life, 5:28–29 recalibrates the conversation to the future tense: The hour comes when people in graves "*will* hear his voice and *will* come out" for resurrection. A similar contrast between present and future reoccurs in John 6, in which Jesus again talks about eternal life in the present, yet three times a version of the phrase "I will raise him on the last day" (6:39, 40, 44) intrudes on the flow of thought. Many take these three repetitions as the work of a later editor, seeking to reconcile the idea of present life in John's Gospel with the idea of future life as taught in other Christian communities.

Bringing the teaching of the Gospel of John into line with churches elsewhere does appear to be a vital purpose for chapter 21. In John's Gospel, Peter and the beloved disciple are compared, to the advantage of the latter and detriment of the former. Peter's disgrace reaches its nadir with his three denials of Jesus. In the appended chapter, Peter is rehabilitated, as three times Jesus asks if Peter loves him and follows each of Peter's affirmations with the instruction for Peter to be a leader for Jesus' followers. In this story, Peter's position within the early church is affirmed, bringing two different groups of early Christians into harmony. A text that formerly celebrated the beloved disciple and his unique testimony and insight, with the addition of chapter 21, makes peace with Peter. Chapter 21 presents a different point of view than the previous twenty chapters and is probably written by a different person.

Regardless of the number of hands involved in John's Gospel, the end of chapter 21 credits the disciple whom Jesus loved. But how much credit should be given to the beloved disciple? One can form a number of hypotheses.

1. If one wants to maintain a single author for John's Gospel, then the author of chapter 21 previously wrote chapter 1–20, and in 21:24, credits the beloved disciple as his source of material like a footnote. The differing views of Peter suggest this is not the case.

2. The next, most simple interpretation is to say that the beloved disciple wrote the first twenty chapters, and someone else wrote and appended chapter 21. However, the way the beloved disciple is described in the third person in 19:35 makes this unlikely.

3. One could modify point 2 and say someone wrote chapters 1–20 using source material from the beloved disciple. Then chapter 21 represents the work of yet a third person.

4. Point 3 is too simple, however, because chapters 1–20 have a complex literary history. First, they draw on a written collection of miracle stories that scholars call the Signs Source or Gospel of Signs. Second, one also must acknowledge the additional emendations made to the Gospel, such as those already noted in 5:19–27 and 6:39–44. There are more stages to the composition of John than point 3 acknowledges.

There are cracks and seams in the preceding options that add still more nuances. At minimum, even if the beloved disciple wrote nothing, his name was attached to traditions that went into the composition of this Gospel. Perhaps his name was attached to one of the written sources. The beloved disciple lingers in the community's view of its history, as is evident from his unique presence in the Gospel of John and the perception of the person who wrote chapter 21. Whether community hero or writer of source material, the beloved disciple serves as the focal personality for John's Gospel. But at least two other nameless people get credit for authorship. We cannot say who they are, other than (1) the person who presented a unique vision of Jesus around the figure of the beloved disciple, and (2) the unknown person who appended chapter 21 and wrote, "I suppose."

Without a name, the Gospel of John remains anonymous. In this case, it is multiply anonymous, though we have a vague outline of the figures responsible for it. Enigmatic as this is, however, it gives readers more to consider regarding possible authorship than do Mark and Matthew.

The Gospel According to Luke

Like the Gospel of John, the Gospel of Luke does not name its author but does reveal something about the author. This happens in the opening lines, again with a pronoun.

In the first sentence of the third canonical Gospel, the author speaks in the first person, *I*, and addresses a specific reader, whom he calls "Theophilus." This elegant sentence, which provides an introduction unlike any of the other canonical Gospels, states the following:

> "Since many have undertaken to set down an orderly account of the events that have been fulfilled among us, ²just as they were handed on to us by those who from the beginning were eyewitnesses and servants of the word, ³*I* too decided, after investigating everything carefully from the very first, to write an orderly account for you, *most excellent Theophilus*, ⁴so that you may know the truth concerning the things about which you have been instructed." (Lk 1:1–4, NRSV, italics added)

These words provide important insight into the author and his literary activity. We will examine them carefully.

Who was Theophilus? The name literally means "friend of God." As a result, many people have taken Theophilus to be a generic designation, an honorary title that applies to and addresses any pious reader. We know from ancient evidence, however, that Theophilus can be a real name, so many regard Theophilus as a specific individual. In favor of this is the entire sentence, which serves as a formal literary prologue. In such a context, an author might very well address his patron, the person for whom he is writing. That he is addressed as "most excellent" implies a social standing that corresponds to what could be expected of a patron. In some cases, a literary patron financially supported a writer. More generally, patrons were social sponsors who advanced a client's cause in the public arena or offered protection. (Compare this with actions in the movie, *The Godfather*, in which Marlon Brando's character extends his assistance to those in need with the expectation of gratitude and loyalty.) Financial support was certainly a possible component. In this Gospel, then, there is an individual writing a text for another individual, his patron and social superior.

If Theophilus is a real person, the temptation to identify him grows. A few imaginative souls have argued that they know who Theophilus was: A Jewish priest, a Roman official, and Paul's lawyer are three proposals. I liken such attempts at identification to assuming that, if you meet a stranger from New York, that person will know the friend you have who also lives there. Asking such a thing of someone you meet may seem reasonable right up until the millisecond the words leave your mouth. Paying attention to how Theophilus is characterized remains significantly more important than pursuing a phantom identification.

Who, then, is the author, the "I," who speaks in the opening verses? These introductory lines reveal a surprising amount of information. First, the author is a man, given the grammatical gender of the words used to describe him, something only evident in Greek, not English. Second, something to which the reader is already alert, the author could read and write, so he is better educated than at least 90 percent of the Roman world. Third, his use of an introductory prologue indicates familiarity with the conventions of formal writing, so his education is not rudimentary, and he has access to reading materials. Fourth, he is engaged in private literary activity with a patron. What this means is that he is not writing as a spokesperson for a community of Christians.

The prologue also tells the context in which the author wrote. Much had already been written about Jesus. When scholars talk about literary sources for the Gospels, it may strike laypeople as strange given the assumption that eyewitnesses wrote them. This prologue clarifies that the author of Luke knew written sources and relied on them; he was not an eyewitness using those sources merely as supplementary material. The author clearly differentiates himself from the eyewitnesses who were there at the beginning: He is not one, and he did not talk to any. Between the eyewitnesses and the author stand time and documents. The author of Luke writes at a time when eyewitnesses are gone, and the remaining writings are texts he intends to supplant.

The author's purpose bears emphasizing. The author's explicit dissatisfaction with his predecessors' efforts is evident. He intends to set the record straight and present to his patron a Gospel with a reliability that will supersede the other texts available.

More evidence about the Evangelist appears elsewhere, but one has to skip to another book in the New Testament to find it. In reading the opening words of the Acts of the Apostles, one gets a sense of *déjà vu* for they resemble Lk 1:1–4:

> In *the first book*, *Theophilus*, I wrote about all that Jesus did and taught from the beginning [2]until the day when he was taken up to heaven, after giving instructions through the Holy Spirit to the apostles whom he had chosen. [3]After his suffering he presented himself alive to them by many convincing proofs, appearing to them during forty days and speaking about the kingdom of God. [4]While staying with them, he ordered them not to leave Jerusalem, but to wait there for the promise of the Father. "This," he said, "is what you have heard from me; [5]for John baptized with water, but you will be baptized with the Holy Spirit not many days from now." (Acts 1:1–5, NSRV, italics added)

This method of placing a preface at the beginning of a book to line it up with previous books was common practice. Here is how

Diodorus of Sicily opens the third book of *The Library of History* (3.1.1–2):

> Of the two preceding Books the First embraces the deeds in Egypt of the early kings and the accounts, as found in their myths, of the gods of the Egyptians . . . The Second Book embraces the deeds performed by the Assyrians in Asia in early times . . . In this present Book we shall add the matters which are connected with what I have already narrated, and shall describe the Ethiopians and the Libyans and the people known as the Atlantians. (trans. C. H. Oldfather, Loeb Classical Library, 2:89)

Like Diodorus, then, the author of Acts provides a preface, which alerts the reader to a previous work. The dedication to Theophilus suggests a link, specifically to the Gospel of Luke, which fits the description given. Here we realize how the author of Luke seeks to place the church into his story about Jesus: He continues into a second volume. Acts, therefore, provides another opportunity to find evidence about the author.

The connection between the Gospel of Luke and Acts undergirds the traditional identification of Luke as the Gospel's author. The evidence arises from certain passages in Acts that use the first person. That is to say, as the story in Acts unfolds, it suddenly shifts from saying "they" to "we" (note v. 10 in the following excerpt).

> [6]*They* went through the region of Phrygia and Galatia, having been forbidden by the Holy Spirit to speak the word in Asia. [7]When *they* had come opposite Mysia, *they* attempted to go into Bithynia, but the Spirit of Jesus did not allow *them*; [8]so, passing by Mysia, *they* went down to Troas. [9]During the night Paul had a vision: there stood a man of Macedonia pleading with him and saying, "Come over to Macedonia and help us." [10]When he had seen the vision, *we* immediately tried to cross over to Macedonia, being convinced that God had called *us* to proclaim the good news to them. [11]*We* set sail from Troas and took a straight course to Samothrace, the following day to Neapolis, [12]and

from there to Philippi, which is a leading city of the district of Macedonia and a Roman colony. *We* remained in this city for some days. . . . [16]One day, as *we* were going to the place of prayer, *we* met a slave-girl who had a spirit of divination and brought her owners a great deal of money by fortune-telling. [17]While she followed Paul and *us*, she would cry out, "These men are slaves of the Most High God, who proclaim to you a way of salvation." (Acts 16:6–17, NRSV, italics added)

These so-called "we-passages" occur four times in Acts: 16:10–17; 20:5–15; 21:1–18; and 27:1–28. If taken literally, they suggest the author of Acts was a travel companion of Paul's, and so the game is afoot. By comparing the we-passages with Paul's letters, people have deduced who was traveling with Paul at the times of the we-passages and who was not. This process of deduction progressively whittles down the list of companions to Paul's friend, Luke, whom tradition identifies as a physician.

A variation of this argument appears in the writings of Irenaeus. In *Against Heresies* 3.14.1, written around the year 180 CE, Irenaeus, the bishop of Lyon, uses examples of the we-passages in Acts to argue for the view that Paul's companion, Luke, wrote Acts. Irenaeus makes this argument to demonstrate the reliability of Acts—since Paul's constant companion and collaborator wrote Acts, people could trust it. Luke was present, so he could write what he saw. The example of Irenaeus is amazing. Writing within fifty to eighty years of Acts' composition, Irenaeus illustrates how early Christians were already engaging in biblical investigation to solve questions about authorship. Irenaeus' argument also indicates that there were people who denied that Paul's companion wrote Acts. In just one or two generations, the church lost the name of the person who wrote Luke and Acts. Or, more likely, few people knew it in the first place.

The problem with taking the we-passages as a guide lies precisely in the conclusion Irenaeus draws, that they make the author a companion of Paul. Comparison of Paul's letters with Acts creates too many contradictions to make it plausible that the author of Acts knew Paul. For example, Paul wrote to believers in Rome about the great opportunity to evangelize Spain, but he would stop over in Rome en route. Acts, on the other hand, says that Rome was Paul's determined goal. Acts portrays Paul as a collaborator with the church in Jerusalem, whereas he himself argued vociferously that he was not. The consequences of attributing Acts to Paul's friend lead to yet another problem, the Gospel of Luke. As Irenaeus puts it, Luke's Gospel can be trusted because he recorded Paul's preaching. This assertion lacks all credibility, because in his letters, Paul hardly ever mentions the life of Jesus. Also, the author of Luke explicitly places the time of the eyewitnesses in the past, a time he accesses through literary texts. Had the author traveled with Paul, then the author would have lived in the time of eyewitnesses. Although many interpreters continue to maintain that Paul's friend wrote Acts, the preceding considerations render this inconceivable. The we-passages are not examples of the author referring to his personal experiences as a companion of Paul.

The we-passages require a different explanation. One proposal suggests that ancient writers used the first person to add a dramatic flair to their narrative. This convention appears, particularly in Greek Romance novels, in scenes in which sea voyages are concerned. This idea holds promise, but critics want to see more ample evidence, especially parallels that sit closer to Acts chronologically

Yet another view holds that the author worked with a written source that contained the we-passages and copied them verbatim into Acts. Perhaps this document contained the written memories from one of Paul's travel companions. We know that the author of Luke-Acts used written sources for the Gospel, so it is no stretch to think he used them for Acts. Such a source would help account for the ability of Acts to do a good job of tracing Paul's missionary activity through the areas of what today are called Turkey and Greece.

Assuming the we-passages offer clues into Acts' use of written sources, Acts therefore aligns with the Gospel of Luke. We encounter an author who was a very literate person with access to a good collection of written materials, someone who investigated them carefully and created his own story. We can almost make out the author, but his name escapes us. We have to settle for calling him "the client of Theophilus."

Traditions May Be Interpretations

In arguing for anonymity, I am contradicting centuries of tradition and what appears to be airtight reasoning. Three arguments work together to make the claimed authorship of the canonical Gospels seem sound: the traditional titles, external witnesses, and internal evidence. We have already pointed out that the form of the titles indicates they became relevant only when people had more than one Gospel in their hands, at which point one had to invent titles. We have also seen that external testimony is not reliable. That leaves the final argument, internal evidence.

Nearly all discussions about authorship of the Gospels examine statements in the Gospels themselves that might help identify the author. We mentioned the argument for Luke and the value of the we-passages in Acts for drawing inferences. We also saw that Irenaeus engaged in this precise investigation, revealing that readers in the early church were just as capable as modern readers of scouring the Gospels for clues to authorship. What one considers as external testimony to authorship from the early church may originally have been an inference drawn from the text. Irenaeus exemplifies this. It is important to tread carefully elsewhere, then, because external testimony and internal evidence might just be redundant, as some scholars have asserted.

Anonymous, But Not Voiceless

Anonymity actually makes the authors of the Gospels more visible. This may sound counterintuitive, but I will explain by drawing on the examples of the Gospels of Mark and Luke.

With Mark, we return to Papias. When he thinks of Peter's interpreter, Mark, as the author, Papias defends Mark's job by arguing that Mark tried not to get in the way of what he wrote but wrote what he remembered as he remembered it. The steps in this process, then, are that Peter witnessed it and talked about it, and Mark transcribed it. This minimizes Mark's role.

When Mark and Peter are erased from the origins of the Gospel, we actually pay closer attention to what the text says. We no longer assume how the story ought to end; and we stop looking for signs of a positive attitude toward Jesus' disciples. We can see past the transitions between scenes, no longer taking them simply as the givens of memory but reading them as meaningful constructions of the anonymous author. Galilee functions symbolically and becomes a place of significance, not just a place where Jesus happened to travel. Jesus' attempts to fly under the radar look full of significance, rather than appearing as duly reported habit from his life. By jettisoning the testimony of Papias and the idea of an author really named Mark, more insightful readings can be achieved.

The same applies to the other Evangelists, but Luke will do by way of example. Assuming that the author was Luke, the companion of Paul, stirs up many guesses about the author's interactions with Paul and possible connections to other apostles as well as access to other witnesses. On the other hand, by pushing the nameless author of Luke-Acts back a number of decades, such speculation ceases. The reader must look at what the author actually wrote.

Throughout Acts, people make speeches. As many as three dozen can be counted, including more than a dozen of significant length (chapters 2, 3, 7, 10, 11, 13, 15, 17, 20, 22, 24, 25, 26) by Peter, Stephen, and Paul, among others. Speeches occupy a significant portion of the entire book of Acts. This raises the question of how the author knew what the speakers said.

The words of Thucydides help in this matter. In his landmark history of the war between Athens and Sparta, Thucydides presents many speeches. This created a problem, as he says in *History of the Peloponnesian War*:

> In this history I have made use of set speeches some of which were delivered just before and others during the war. I have found it difficult to remember the precise words used in the speeches which I listened to myself and my various informants have experienced the same difficulty; so my method has been, while keeping as closely as possible to the general sense of the words that were actually used, to make the speakers say what, in my opinion, was called for by each situation. (1.22; trans. Rex Warner, Penguin Books)

The last sentence has famously set the stage for how many people read Acts. Thucydides' views should, however, be joined with critical observations made by the historian Polybius about a rival, Timaeus.

> I must say something of the principle which Timaeus applies in composing the speeches. . . . Can any of Timaeus' readers have failed to observe that his reports of these pronouncements disregard the truth and that this is done deliberately? . . . A writer who passes over in silence the speeches which were actually made and the causes of what actually happened and introduces fictitious rhetorical exercises and discursive speeches in their place destroys the peculiar virtue of history. In this respect Timaeus is a persistent offender, and we all know that his books are full of faults of this kind. (*The Rise of the Roman Empire* 12.24–25; trans. Ian Scott-Kilvert, Penguin Books)

One can read Thucydides as providing assurances that speeches are as close as possible to transcripts and Polybius as condemning those who take broad latitude with rhetorical invention. But careful attention should be paid to the linkage between rhetorical situation and the appropriateness of speech. A commonplace is to note in Acts 17 how Paul tailored his sermon for his pagan, philosophical audience and to label this as brilliant on the apostle's part. In light of Thucydides, however, it looks like credit is misplaced. Practicing what someone should say in a specific situation was part of the standard curriculum. That the author of Luke-Acts does it, and successfully, should be expected. The debate surrounding Acts should focus on how much imagination was expended in making speeches fit the occasion, not whether the author used any.

Listening for the voice of the author when reading the speeches helps readers see the obvious. This voice advances the agenda laid out in the unique material in Lk 24, in which the risen Jesus cheers up dispirited followers by explaining how everything pertaining to his death happened in accordance with what had been written by Moses and the prophets. Frustratingly, this grand assertion receives no supporting evidence in Luke. Throughout the speeches in Acts, however, the author provides the elaboration missing in Lk 24. Two in particular—speeches by Stephen when on trial for his life before the high priest (7:2–53) and by Paul in a synagogue (13:16–41)—provide abundant detail for what was only hinted at in the Gospel of Luke. As in much ancient Greek literature, the act of people speaking provides space for authors to insert their own thoughts and ideas. The many speeches in Acts provide precisely that opportunity for its author.

The thread connecting Jesus in Lk 24 to sermons by Stephen and Paul actually begins in the opening words of Luke's Gospel when the author describes the task he has begun. He plans to follow up and improve the work of people who wrote "narratives about the matters that have been fulfilled among us." In these words, the author tips his hand about the principle he will use to organize his work. He will investigate not simply deeds or events but also a specific category of events, those that register as fulfillment of divine purposes. Although Polybius would raise an eyebrow at this, "fulfillment" provides a crucial criterion for what the author chooses to tell and how he tells it. What is seen in the speeches is not random filler but the very heart of the story the author wishes to present. This becomes much easier to see once we eliminate the view that Paul's friend wrote Luke-Acts.

As it turns out, the historical testimonies about the authorship of the Gospels provide useless information. The sense they provide that the reader knows something about the texts proves false. Setting aside these alleged witnesses forces one to read more carefully, past preconceptions. Ironically, the reader discovers authors with much to say.

Conclusion

The titles of the Gospels do not tell who wrote them. They are misleading. In fact, two Gospels make no claims whatsoever about authorship, while two make no claim but do slip in a suggestive pronoun. Readers can refer to the Gospels by their ascribed names as a matter of convenience and tradition but should recognize this as a convention only and in no way a reasonable statement of authorship. In fact, the two *I*s reveal that the origins of the Gospels are significantly more complex than the ancient titles lead one to believe.

The discussion of Mark and Luke, in particular, further demonstrates that an anonymous Gospel author actually has a clearer voice. Affixing apostolic names to Gospels sought to certify their alignment with the church's preaching. This muffled their individual voices. By removing claims of authorship, one can hear the Gospels more distinctly. It may seem that making the Gospels anonymous subtracts from our knowledge about them, but in fact, it opens a door to significant advances. Anonymity becomes insight.

Questions

1. What affect does not knowing who wrote the Gospels have on the way you read them? Conversely, how would it effect the way you read them if you did know who the authors were?

2. To think about question 1 more concretely, how might you read Mark's Gospel if you thought it recorded the memories of Peter versus if it claimed independence from Peter's influence?

3. Draw two inferences from this statement: By the year 150 CE Christians had forgotten who wrote the four Gospels.

4. Compare Jn 21:24–25 and Lk 1:1–4. Based on this comparison, which Gospel do you think was written earlier, Luke or John?

5. Luke inserts pet themes into the speeches he presents. How does this strike you?

6. The traditional authorship of Luke-Acts is commonly defended by means of internal evidence, emphasizing the "we-passages" in Acts. I presented a minority argument about the authorship of John's Gospel that used internal evidence to point to Lazarus, the beloved disciple, as its source, rather than the apostle John. Do you think the evidence for Luke is stronger than that for Lazarus? What reasons can you give for the greater popularity of the argument from internal evidence where Luke-Acts is concerned?

7. How would you factor 1 John into the discussion of authorship of the Gospel according to John?

Further Reading

Most of the specific issues in this chapter receive discussion in specialized literature, such as the article mentioned on pp. 134-35: François Bovon, "The Synoptic Gospels and the Noncanonical Acts of the Apostles," Harvard Theological Review 81 (1988): 19-36. Summaries of the arguments can be found in books that investigate the origin of each writing in the New Testament. Among the many to choose from are the following:

Brown, Raymond E. *An Introduction to the New Testament.* The Anchor Yale Bible Reference Library. New York: Doubleday, 1997.

Boring, M. Eugene. *An Introduction to the New Testament: History, Literature, Theology.* Louisville, KY: Westminster/John Knox Press, 2012.

Ehrman, Bart D. *The New Testament: A Historical Introduction to the Early Christian Writings.* New York: Oxford University Press, 1997.

Koester, Helmut. *Introduction to the New Testament.* 2 vols. Philadelphia: Fortress Press; Berlin: DeGruyter, 1982.

Kümmel, Werner Georg. *Introduction to the New Testament.* Trans. Howard Clark Kee. Nashville, TN: Abingdon Press, 1975.

Marxsen, Willi. *Introduction to the New Testament: Approach to Its Problems.* Trans. G. Buswell. Oxford: Blackwell, 1968.

White, L. Michael. *From Jesus to Christianity.* San Francisco: HarperOne, 2005

Traditional views about the authorship of the Gospels can be found in these introductions:

Carson, D. A., and Douglas J. Moo. *An Introduction to the New Testament.* Revised. Grand Rapids, MI: Zondervan, 2005.

Guthrie, Donald. *New Testament Introduction.* 4th ed. Downers Grove, IL: IVP Academic, 1990.

Searching the authorship of the Gospels online will mostly yield defenses of the traditional views.

There Are More Than Four Gospels

In view of the discussion in chapter 4 about the four Gospels, the rest of the story now must be told. In reality, there are more than four gospels, that is, more than four texts that convey the significance of Jesus through his words and/or deeds. Although there are four and only four canonical Gospels (i.e., the capital *G* four that were widely approved by bishops through centuries of common use by churches around the Mediterranean Sea and enshrined in the New Testament), many other gospels were written in the early church that did not receive similar approval.

As seen in chapter 4, differentiating the four canonical Gospels changes how one reads the New Testament and, in turn, thinks about the early church. It will come as no surprise that considering additional gospels continues to expand the picture of early Christian history and how one thinks about it. These other written gospels show a wide variety of ideas among Christians, their struggles to come to grips with faith in Christ and their many examples of creative thinking. They also affect how one reads the New Testament Gospels.

There Are Dozens of Gospels

I usually refer to the corpus of early Christian gospels as comprised of about three-dozen texts. I say "about three-dozen" because of ambiguities. Writers in the early centuries of the church refer to texts contemporary readers have never seen. Tiny fragments of papyrus mention Jesus but are not like any known text, while some well-known texts may or may not count as a gospel. The chance that there is more than one text bearing the same name or that some new text might be discovered cannot be ruled out. Stating an exact number obscures the problems and possibilities. The following survey introduces these texts.

Lost Gospels

Ancient authors mention a number of gospels that no longer exist. Were it not for these references, one would have no idea that these texts existed. Some bear the names of people the church would deem heretics, e.g., the *Gospel of Apelles, Gospel of Bardesanes, Gospel of Basilides, Gospel of Cerinthus, Gospel of Mani,* and *Gospel of Marcion.* Many scholars think the *Gospel of Marcion* is an edited and shortened version of the Gospel of Luke; similarly, the *Gospel of Cerinthus* might be a pared down version of Matthew. Apelles may have simply revised Marcion's work. Similar scant references alert readers to a *Gospel of Andrew, Gospel of Barnabas, Gospel of Bartholomew, Gospel of Eve, Gospel of Matthias,* and *Gospel of Perfection.* A little bit is known about another gospel, the Greek *Gospel of the Egyptians,* because early theologians quoted from it. The title of the *Gospel of the Encratites* takes its name from a group that emphasized sexual renunciation, so, presumably, its text incorporates this theme. These fourteen lost documents illustrate how much is unknown.

Some gospels were written among communities of Jewish followers of Christ. There are no known copies of these texts, only brief descriptions or quotations. One early group, calling themselves the Nazoreans, used, as their scripture, an Aramaic translation of the Gospel of Matthew, which today is referred to as the *Gospel of the Nazoreans.* Another group, called the Ebionites, used a Greek text that blended the Synoptic Gospels as its scripture. The Ebionites rejected the idea of the virgin birth, so these stories were excised from their text, the *Gospel of the Ebionites,* which might be the same text as the *Gospel of the Twelve.* Jewish-Christians in Egypt composed yet another text, the *Gospel of the Hebrews,* presenting Jesus as one who brings wisdom and emphasizing the authority of James. Although a saying attributed to the *Gospel of the Hebrews* also appears in the *Gospel of Thomas,* without an actual copy of the *Gospel of the Hebrews,* one cannot know how much else it shared with the *Gospel of Thomas.* These three, or four, Jewish-Christian texts hint at a fascinating but shrouded expression of Christianity and bring the running total to seventeen or eighteen noncanonical gospels.

In addition to texts mentioned by early Christian authors, there are small, unnamed fragments of ancient writings that contain material about Jesus that cannot be matched to any known texts. Two are labeled Oxyrhynchus 840 and 1224, based on the Egyptian town where they were discovered. Another is called the *Egerton Gospel,* named for the person who funded its purchase by the British Museum in 1934. This gospel is comprised of about 400 words on four scraps of papyrus. A fourth gospel has been pieced together from fragments of a codex purchased in 1961 by the Berlin Egyptian Museum. Initially designated as the *Unknown Berlin Gospel,* in 1999 editors gave it a new, more winsome title, the *Gospel of the Savior.* These accidents of discovery document a greater breadth of literary activity than we knew existed.

Infancy Gospels

Unlike the aforementioned lost gospels, two gospels remained popular and available throughout the centuries. Both focus on Jesus' birth and youth, the so-called Infancy Gospels, which pushes the running total of noncanonical gospels to twenty-three or twenty-four.

Infancy Gospel of Thomas

An entertaining text from the second century talks about Jesus as a boy, presenting a precocious child who is stubborn and vengeful. Though this text, the *Infancy Gospel of Thomas,* does not offer a flattering picture of Jesus, it does present an interesting, unvarnished consideration of how God in the flesh of a five-year-old might have behaved. Like every little child, Jesus has to grow up. At first, his powers prove dangerous to those around him, not unlike the infant Eros who works his mischief and, frankly, in line with the terror that divine appearances could inspire. But the child Jesus learns to harness his powers for good.

Comedic elements emerge with the challenge of educating Jesus, as the folly of a mortal teaching the young god makes for humorous encounters. Teachers attempt to drum lessons into the boy, while he sits in bemused silence, already fully learned in the alphabet, including the profound mysteries to which the letters point. This makes for an entertaining story.

The *Infancy Gospel of Thomas* represents a natural development in traditions about Jesus, examining his youth. What was Jesus like as a boy? As it answers this question, it does not present Jesus as a moral teacher or describe his ministry or death. Without these things, it seems too stripped-down to function as a gospel. Yet the boy-god's growth from petulance to service makes, in my opinion, for a more psychologically profound story than is typical of the New Testament.

The *Protoevangelium* of James
(aka The Infancy Gospel of James)

This short story lauds the piety of Jesus' parents and, particularly, the purity of Mary. In fact, the work is more a story about Mary and the miracles surrounding her than it is about Jesus. The first quarter of the book tells the story of Mary's birth—echoing in her old, childless parents the ancient story of Abraham and Sarah, who likewise had reached advanced age with no children. The story makes clear the tragedy in the ancient world of having no offspring, as well as the mercy and power of God to provide a child to Mary's parents, the elderly Joachim and Anna. As the plot advances toward the story of Jesus' birth, the *Protoevangelium* creatively weaves material from the Gospels of Matthew and Luke together with additional elements, adding new details and answering questions that might arise in the minds of canonical Gospel readers. For example, who was Joseph? What was his relationship with Mary? From where did Jesus' siblings come? When King Herod slaughtered the little children, how did John the Baptist survive? And, most importantly, what made Mary special? Entertaining stories emphasize and prove Mary's virtue, as well as explain why she was the one God chose. These stories led to such beliefs as Mary being born without original sin and her perpetual virginity. More broadly, the text reflects the emphasis placed by the early church on sexual abstinence.

The name of James appears in the title of this work because of the concluding sentences in which the author claims to be James writing shortly after the death of Herod. Presumably, this James was the brother of Jesus and the historical leader of the church in Jerusalem, while Herod refers to Herod the Great who died in 4 BCE. If so, James would be one of the sons that the *Protoevangelium* says Joseph already had when the pubescent Mary entered his household and, therefore, Jesus' older half-brother. The timing implies the author was an eyewitness, which is not believable because the actual author depended on Gospels that would not be written for nearly a century. This is a clearly fraudulent claim to authorship for a text written in the mid-second century.

Recovered Gospels

Since the end of the nineteenth century, fortunate circumstances have brought to light ancient manuscripts of six long-lost Christian gospels. These six provide ideas beyond the four canonical Gospels.

Gospel of Peter

Given the prominence of Peter in Christian history, it seems natural that there is a gospel bearing his name. Unfortunately, only part of the original text exists, so it is unclear where it began and where it ended. What exists offers the example of a gospel that focuses on the death, burial, and Resurrection of Jesus. Nothing of his birth and ministry appears. Perhaps these other elements existed; perhaps the passion narrative was a prelude to some special revelation from the resurrected Jesus. We do not know.

Some have proposed that the *Gospel of Peter* is "docetic." This term comes from the Greek word for "seemed," as in Christ only "seemed" human. The label suggests that this gospel plays down Jesus' physical body to conform to the docetic belief that God could not suffer; therefore, Christ did not suffer and, in Jesus' death, only appeared to do so. The clues for this type of reading are so slight that its popularity has waned.

An important question about the *Gospel of Peter* is whether or not it drew its story from the canonical Gospels. The presence of the guards at Jesus' tomb makes it look like the Gospel of Matthew lies in the background. But repeatedly in the *Gospel of Peter,* the story of Jesus reflects the ideal type of righteous sufferer one finds in Jewish traditions, suggesting an independent development of the Passion story. This has persuaded many to date the original layer of tradition in the *Gospel of Peter* as early as those in the Synoptic Gospels, to which were added secondary additions with the passage of time.

The simple fact that the *Gospel of Peter* presents the Passion makes it an important contribution to the study of early Christian traditions. While most of the other noncanonical gospels sought to present the risen Jesus providing esoteric teachings, this one asserts an important role for Jesus' death. Among the creative minds of the early church, one more—the author of the *Gospel of Peter*—placed emphasis on the climax of Jesus' ministry, which stood in line with the view of the canonical Gospels and now expands the view of how early Christian traditions about Jesus developed.

Gospel of Mary

A complete copy of the *Gospel of Mary* has not survived. There are fragments written in Greek and a larger portion in Coptic, but we still lack perhaps half of the text. What survives presents a conversation between the risen Savior and his followers. This dialogue resembles the series of questions and answers that appears in the Gospel of John. And in an echo of Matthew's Gospel, Christ charges the disciples to go preach the gospel and then leaves them. Distressed, the disciples talk among themselves until Mary speaks up, offering words of comfort. This leads Peter to ask her what the Savior had spoken to her privately. Mary conveys what Christ had taught her in a vision, only to be challenged by Andrew and Peter and defended by Levi.

This text provides theological insight into early Christianity. Christians were trying to figure out what role their new god played in the cosmos, from what their savior had rescued them, and what new destiny awaited. Some attempted to form answers by considering the makeup of humans and the order of the cosmos. A first step in this process is seen in the opening words of the Gospel of John, another in the *Gospel of Thomas*, and significantly more elaboration in the *Gospel of Mary* in which a fundamental dualism exists between what is spiritual and material. The *Gospel of Mary* brings insight into this dualism and helps people embrace the spiritual, demanding that they understand so as to pursue true humanity. Rules and laws distract from this higher enterprise. The soul must put off flesh and journey upward out of the material realm, using knowledge of truth to thwart the powers that try to prevent it. This message is not preached today, but it was widespread in the church of the second century.

The *Gospel of Mary* also exposes the politics of the early church. When Peter expresses doubt that the Savior spoke in secret to a woman and questions whether Jesus considered her more worthy than the Twelve, the bias against women is clear, as is preference for the testimony of Jesus' inner circle of male disciples. Though the views Peter expresses would prevail in the church, the *Gospel of Mary* argues against them, presenting Mary as the spokesperson for deep insight into the gospel. The cosmological mysteries that Christ solved could be comprehended only by a few. In the *Gospel of Mary*, Peter was not the person for such a job but Mary was. Mary appears to be Jesus' best student, and through her, Christ sought to reveal the nature of the cosmos and salvation.

Gospel of Judas

In the *Gospel of Judas* the reader encounters yet another view of Jesus. Scholars regained access to this text fairly recently, so its interpretation is equally young and debated. The English translation offered in 2006 presented Judas as a hero, one who understood and assisted Jesus. There is a real brilliance to this move. Who is better positioned than Judas, the traitor, the person who clearly stands apart from the other members of the Twelve, to be the one with the real insight into Jesus? Scholars Elaine Pagels and Karen King suggest that this text rejects the idea of sacrifice and physical resurrection. Being rid of the body is an improvement, so Judas actually helped Jesus. However, other scholars responded that alternative translations yield a completely different reading of the text. For example, does Judas have a great "spirit" or a "demon"? The answer to this question fundamentally changes the characterization of Judas and one's reading of the text.

In broad strokes the message of Judas resembles the *Gospel of Mary*. Readers encounter discussion about the nature of the cosmos and the many powers that the soul must overcome in its ascent to the heavenly realm. While the details differ, the need to recognize a person's true nature and overcome the powers of the material world remains constant.

Gospels Rediscovered in Nag Hammadi

One of the most fortunate manuscript finds for students of early Christianity occurred in December 1945, when shepherds from the Egyptian town of Nag Hammadi found a collection of long-lost Christian writings, a treasure of fifteen books with more than fifty texts. These increased the corpus of gospels one can actually read and brought much new information about early Christians to light.

During the second century, a number of teachers rose to prominence in the church. History branded some of these as heretics, despite their popularity and influence. An example is Valentinus, who flourished in Rome. He was one of a number of Christians who saw, in the gospel message, a revelation about God, humans, and the universe and regarded this insight as key to salvation. Because they placed the need for correct knowledge about what exists at the heart of the gospel, such people were called Gnostics, which reflects the Greek word for "knowledge," *gnosis*.

It turns out that the terms *Gnostics* and *Gnosticism* get stretched thin in an attempt to cover too much. A first problem is that one cannot assign texts to social groups that could be labeled Gnostic. Another problem is that important markers of Gnosticism fail to appear in every text that is suspected to be Gnostic. For example, one assumed trait of Gnosticism has been cosmological dualism, in which all that exists falls into two competing camps of good and evil, truth and error, spirit and body; however, this concept fails to appear in some so-called Gnostic texts. "Gnostic" texts reveal other inconsistencies as well, such as: Humans may need to be saved from ignorance or the battle may be engaged against malevolent forces; the creator may be a positive figure or ignorant and evil; and Christ may be the primary savior or one of many. These differences were unclear when the Nag Hammadi texts were discovered, so it was easy to label the texts as Gnostic; less so today. Despite these complexities, one may still encounter references to "Gnostic Gospels" that encompass the gospels found at Nag Hammadi, though what that says about the texts is no longer clear.

Gospel of Thomas

Perhaps the most significant text recovered from Nag Hammadi is the *Gospel of Thomas*. Dismissed by the early church as a heretical document, it turned out to be a collection of more than one hundred sayings by Jesus, including some short dialogues and parables. The sayings are not embedded in any kind of story, but are strung together like a compilation of favorite quotations. The find at Nag Hammadi proved that Christians did compile written collections of things Jesus said. This requires emphasis. Early Christians wrote down things Jesus said, sensing no compulsion to include anything about Jesus' birth, miracles, death, or Resurrection. Q, the text that scholars hypothesized as a source used by both Matthew and Luke, was precisely such a document. With the recovery of *Thomas*, Q gained the support of a real-life example, a twin so to speak.

The *Gospel of Thomas* offers another window into early Christian religion. On the one hand, much in *Thomas* is familiar, recording sayings that appear in the canonical Gospels. For example, "You see the sliver in your friend's eye, but you don't see the timber in your own eye" (26:1, Miller) and "No prophet is welcome on his home turf" (31:1, Miller). Moreover, *Thomas* contains two parables that appear in the New Testament, the sower and the mustard seed.

The *Gospel of Thomas* also has material that sounds familiar yet is different. For example, in Matthew's Gospel Jesus says, "For where two or three are gathered in my name, I am there among them" (18:20, Miller); the *Gospel of Thomas* says, "Where there are two or one, I am with that one" (30:2, Miller). Elsewhere, *Thomas* states, "The first will be last" (4:2–3, Miller), but follows this with the novel idea that they "will become a single one."

The *Gospel of Thomas* also has material that is unlike the canonical Gospels. Opening with the claim to present "the secret sayings" of Jesus, Thomas confesses its idiosyncrasy, as it intellectualizes the gospel, promising immortality to those who discover "the interpretation of these sayings," which involves readers knowing themselves. This self-knowledge relates to the origins of the world, when a lesser heavenly creature is posited to have caused the material world to come into being. The human who recognizes his or her true origin outside this material creation is on the path to eternal life. These ideas about salvation in Thomas are unlike the Synoptic Gospels', though their concern with cosmology and anthropology provide a family resemblance to John's Gospel.

The *Gospel of Thomas* has also become important for Christian history. Debate surrounds its date. Was it written before Mark's Gospel or not until the second century? Did it evolve over decades? While precise answers would have consequences, even the general chronology remains significant. If the later dating is correct, Thomas remained a contemporary of Luke and, if slightly earlier, approximate to Matthew and John, maybe even Mark. Broadly speaking, then, the *Gospel of Thomas* is contemporary to the canonical Gospels, showing literary and intellectual paths that the church ultimately chose to leave behind.

The *Apocryphon of James* (aka, *The Secret Book of James*)

The *Secret Book of James* is another text that can now be read because of the manuscripts discovered in Nag Hammadi. It stretches the usual concept of what constitutes a gospel, because it presents itself as a letter, recounts none of Jesus' deeds, and mostly blends dialogue and discourse, while focusing exclusively on one post-Resurrection appearance, Jesus' last, which the *Secret Book of James* places 550 days after Jesus rises from the dead and just before he ascends into heaven (which Acts places on the fortieth day).

The opening sequence of this text provides a window into how one person imagines the production of gospels to have taken place. The twelve disciples are gathered in one place recalling the Savior's teachings "to each one of them, whether secretly or openly" and writing them down (2:1, Miller). As James is busy writing down his memories—in Hebrew, we are told—Jesus appears, speaks briefly to all, and calls James and Peter aside for special, private instruction. As the three go off, Jesus tells the others to resume their writing. This story underscores what is read in other places, namely that early Christians regarded what they read in their texts as the actual memories of Jesus' immediate followers. The *Secret Book of James* stipulates that all members of the Twelve were actual authors—assuming that

they were literate and bookish—as if Jesus had checked their educational credentials before choosing them. In this, the author of the
Secret Book of James recreated the Twelve in his own image, thinking of them as literate and engaged in scribal activities. This reveals
something about the author and nothing about the Twelve.

This text also makes a political argument about authority in the
early church. In the story, on Jesus' last day on earth, he speaks privately to Peter and James, not to the others, privileging the pair with
revelatory insight. Both, being filled by Jesus, begin to follow him
up through the heavens only to be interrupted in their ascent by the
other, earthbound disciples. Yet it is James, who authors the text and
transmits Jesus' discourse, not Peter, who speaks only twice. Furthermore, the message James and Peter hear and share with the other
disciples makes the larger group angry, so James, not Peter, takes
steps to mollify them. Here James is playing a superior role to Peter
and serving as the channel of special revelation. The readers of the
Secret Book of James, a subset of Christians, would have truer knowledge of salvation than the broader church.

For this select group of Christians, what would define their faith
is what Jesus says just before he returns to heaven, much more so
than the stories of his life. In the *Secret Book of James*, a person must
seek to be "full" of knowledge, such that one should pursue spirit and
shun soul and flesh. Practically, this places great value on martyrdom
and, especially, on instruction. Simple faith, good morals, and pious
deeds are not adequate aspirations for a Christian. One must gain
self-knowledge. Yet this teaching was not for all, so James warned
the person to whom he wrote not to share it with many people. The
revelation that the risen Savior provides in this text justifies the presence, among Christians, of a special group of people who claim a
better grasp of Jesus' mission and salvation.

Dialogue of the Savior

The *Dialogue of the Savior* resembles other noncanonical gospels in its teachings but stands out because its seams are showing.
Scholars have argued that it incorporates four sources: a creation
story, heavenly vision, catalog of elemental substances, and, by far the
largest portion, a dialogue between the Lord and some disciples. The

author, therefore, pulled together a variety of sources, showing not just his own thoughts but also examples of materials in circulation. Placed together, this is a text that presents a gospel message and may be considered a gospel.

The *Dialogue's* creation story takes inspiration from Genesis but spins off in a direction no modern reader of Genesis would anticipate. When Judas asks what existed before heaven and earth, the Lord quotes Genesis 1:2 about darkness, water, and spirit but then tells Judas that what he really wants to know exists within Judas himself. In other words, a piece of the divine exists in Judas, a fragment from the godhead that predates the creation of heaven and earth. This answer seemed as obvious to many early Christians as it seems odd today.

The dialogue sections are not real conversations. A disciple—Judas, Mary, Matthew, or all of them—asks a question and Jesus answers. There is little back-and-forth exchange; the disciples rarely add substance to the give-and-take. Their role is to ask questions, which the Lord answers.

One of the questions sounds very traditional, as Judas inquires about the essence of good behavior, to which the Lord responds, "Love and goodness" (28:2, Miller). That sounds very much like a fine Sunday-school lesson but what follows takes an unexpected turn, providing a sense of the entire *Dialogue*, as the Lord adds that if the heavenly creatures that rule the world had known love or goodness, wickedness would not have come into being. A profound moral lesson quickly veers into a cosmological insight.

Salvation in the *Dialogue* is tied to one's view of the cosmos, which is the place of deception and death under the sway of archons, i.e., powerful heavenly entities that rule this world, ignorant of the greater realm beyond. Jesus enters their realm as savior and revealer, teaching that "the one who sees is also the one who reveals" (7:2; 31:2, Miller). In the *Dialogue,* when Jesus comes, it says he "opened the way and taught them, the chosen and the solitary, the passage by which they will pass," out of this world and back to the realm of the *plērōma*, the entirety of the divine being and fullness (1:5, Miller). The Lord reveals to the chosen their true origin and situation: They are from the *plērōma* but are in the mortal, material world, also known as the "deficiency." With their true origin in the divine fullness, the chosen should escape the shackles of this world. The warning is simple: "If you do not understand how the body which you bear came to be, you will perish with it. . . . Those who will not understand how they came will not understand how they will go" (16:4, 8, Miller). Their "souls have been saved from these blind limbs" to live forever (2:5, Miller); therefore, "when what is living leaves what is dead, it will be called alive" (22:4, Miller). This self-knowledge, predicated on a correct understanding of the cosmos, leads to assurance for the future, because those "who have known themselves have seen" the place of life (14:4, Miller). Ideas like these, and variations on them, were repeated throughout early Christianity.

The ideas in *Dialogue of the Savior* do not preach the atoning death of Jesus. Humans are not isolated from God because of broken laws or inappropriately offered sacrifices. Sin, burdens, and debts are not one's fundamental problems. The issue is that the material world and the physical bodies it provides blind people to their true condition. The remedy requires revelation, so Jesus talks, and his disciples ask questions that ponder the nature of the cosmos, human existence, and destiny. The *Dialogue of the Savior,* therefore, functions quite well as a sayings gospel, not a narrative one.

Survey Total: About Three Dozen

If you are keeping score, we have now run through twenty-nine or thirty gospels. I have not described all of them in detail nor mentioned the gospel harmonies, which are attempts to take the four canonical Gospels and weave them into a single story. If two harmonies are added to the total, then the four canonical Gospels and Q, we reach a total of thirty-six or thirty-seven. But given the vagaries of how most of these are known, I prefer to stick with the ballpark figure of "about three dozen."

What Is a Gospel?

Behind the question of how many gospels there are lies the more fundamental question of what a gospel is. Depending on how one defines a gospel, three dozen might expand beyond forty or shrink to four. More importantly, a definition influences how people read gospels. The preconceptions people bring to gospels shape how they read, what they notice, and the interpretations they formulate.

By analogy, three of the movies nominated in 2013 for best picture told stories from American history: *Lincoln, Argo,* and *Zero Dark Thirty*. Each raises the question of what it means to be a movie "based on historical events," which critics took turns debating, pointing out accuracy and error, and asking what standards should be applied. In *Lincoln,* the ticking of Lincoln's watch lends the film an atmosphere of immediacy and authenticity, yet also in the film two Congressmen from Connecticut vote against the Thirteenth Amendment, even though none of Connecticut's representatives really did so. The clothing and makeup in the movie suggest care was taken with history, as do the names and personality traits of historical people, yet the screenwriter obviously invented dialogue, encounters, and people. These examples raise questions about what moviegoers expect of such films and the obligations directors have to provide historical accuracy.

The Problem

Many in the early church thought that the gospels were the written memories of the earliest apostles. A Christian writer of the second century known as Justin Martyr reflected this common assumption: "For the apostles, in the *memoirs* composed by them, which are called Gospels, have thus delivered unto us what was enjoined upon them . . ." (*Apology* 1.66.3). Two other Christians, Papias, a couple decades before Justin, and Irenaeus, a couple decades after, reflect the same attitude, which can be found even in the Gospel of John and given literal expression in the *Apocryphon of James*. The previous chapter, however, argues that such traditions cannot be trusted, so identifying gospels as memoirs is false.

Once a critical eye recognizes that gospels are not memoirs, an alternative designation needs to be found. One might consider them a record of the life of Jesus, i.e., *biographies*. Although their material is at times organized thematically rather than chronologically, this fits with the methods of their day, as does presenting Jesus as an ideal type (e.g., Moses, a model of faithfulness, or a prophet). Luke's larger agenda—to write a history—was paramount, yet in so doing, he presented a good biography. Both the authors of Luke and Matthew delivered signs and omens of Jesus' birth that marked him for greatness. These satisfied ancient expectations, as did the selective vignettes John presented and Luke's story of the twelve-year-old Jesus as a great teacher. The latter previews, in his youth, the man who would come. The former forgoes comprehensiveness, providing instead the most telling stories. The Gospel of Mark, however, seems too incomplete to be a biography. That Matthew and Luke fixed Mark confirms this. In short, given the variety of ways authors wrote about people in Greco-Roman literature, it is not off base to think of the canonical Gospels as lives of Jesus. Still, the differences among them show how loosely the category fits.

This problem of classification implodes when we look outside the New Testament. The Infancy Gospels tell stories about Jesus but make no attempt to move beyond his youth. While they might loosely be called biographical, they are not biographies. Even more problematic, the *Gospel of Thomas* is no biography. Collections of an individual's teachings were common in the ancient world, so the form Thomas takes is recognizable as the "sayings of the wise." Thomas's look-alike Q shows that this form was one common way early Christians talked about and remembered Jesus. Varied editions of these texts multiply the evidence of the form's utility and persistence among early Christians. But these are not biography.

The *Gospel of Thomas* brings one to a crossroad regarding what is a written gospel. If one insists a gospel is a biography, or at minimum, a narrative about Jesus, then the *Gospel of Thomas* is not a gospel. But this is precisely the name given to the text early in church history. It seems reasonable to accept the opinions of early Christians and accept, as a gospel, what they deemed to be one. Is, then, a gospel *whatever the early church called a gospel?*

This common-sense approach also has problems. First, the identification of gospels was expanding. The *Gospel of Thomas* is called such only at the end where the title is appended, so presumably it is secondary. If there was an original title, it was more likely *The Secret Sayings of Jesus*, or some similar take on the work's opening sentence. This means that, although an early scribe labeled it a gospel, it was not always so. The *Gospel of Mary* is likewise designated such only at the end. What designation appeared at the beginning is unknown, because the opening portion of the manuscript did not survive. Perhaps it, too, originally lacked the title now given it. Combined with the originally untitled canonical Gospels, Thomas and Mary suggest that the literary designation was a growing and evolving idea. What the early church called a gospel is precisely what the church would eventually call a gospel, not what the authors labeled their writings.

The *Apocryphon of James* expands the problem. In it, the resurrected Lord appears to the disciples, and then calls James and Peter aside to provide revelation to them. This resembles the *Gospel of Mary*, in which she comforts the disciples by telling them about the instruction she received from the resurrected Savior. The two seem comparable, suggesting the *Apocryphon of James* be considered a gospel, though clearly it is not so named, nor is the *Dialogue of the Savior*.

In *The Book of Thomas the Contender*, readers encounter the secret words of the resurrected savior spoken to his twin brother, Thomas, as they walked, accompanied by Mathias who transcribed the conversation in which questions that opened up a series of teachable moments were asked. The reader learns that the height of knowledge is to know oneself, i.e., to know from where one came and to where one is going. The challenge in life is to battle the desires of the body; this is the contest referred to in the title of the work, *Thomas the Contender*. In this text, then, one reads of secret teachings that reveal the savior's vital message in a form that resembles other post-Resurrection dialogues—only the text is not called a gospel. But is it one anyway? Still other texts merit consideration, such as, *Pistis Sofia*, *Sophia of Jesus Christ*, *Epistula Apostolorum*, and *Two Books of Jeu*, but the point is made that in the emerging church the boundaries are blurry.

The *Gospel of Truth* presents the other side of the conundrum. Among the documents found at Nag Hammadi is one that opens with the words, "The gospel of truth is joy for those who have received from the Father of truth the grace of knowing him . . ." (in Robinson). From this, the document receives the title *Gospel of Truth,* and the question arises as to whether this is, in fact, the same text that the second-century bishop Irenaeus referred to as the Valentinian *Gospel of Truth*. Scholars today do interpret the text as an expression of

Valentinian teaching, tending to equate it with the text Irenaeus mentioned. Some go so far as to suggest that Valentinus wrote the *Gospel of Truth* we now read, so that today we possess one of the texts Irenaeus and subsequent defenders of the faith desired to suppress.

The *Gospel of Truth* presents a number of interesting ideas. It describes the deity as incomprehensible, inconceivable, and perfect—the one who made the totality and in whom the totality exists, the one who encircles all spaces while there is none that encircles him, the one whose name is "Father." What humans know of the world issues from error or, to be truer to the mythology of the text, from an entity named "Error." The human problem, therefore, is ignorance, and specifically ignorance of the Father, whom Jesus reveals. Through Jesus, "the word of the Father goes forth in the totality" (23.33–35). The Father summons his own people, who have knowledge: "If one has knowledge, he is from above. If he is called, he hears, he answers, and he turns to him who is calling him, and ascends to him. . . . He . . . knows where he comes from and where he is going" (22.3–7, 14–15). Reunited with the Father, such people find rest.

The *Gospel of Truth* says little about the life of Jesus. It alludes to the time in his childhood that he taught the teachers, his affirmation of children, and his sufferings and crucifixion but does not tell the actual stories. The focus lies consistently on the significance of Jesus the Christ, the enlightener, while explaining his revelation. Unlike other gospels, the speaker in the *Gospel of Truth* is the author. There is no discourse or dialogue by characters in the text. This is clearly a sermon, an essay, a treatise. But is it a gospel?

I cannot imagine anyone comparing the *Gospel of Truth* with the Synoptics and calling it a gospel, yet this is precisely the title it bears from the ancient church. Likewise, the *Coptic Gospel of the Egyptians* contains the word *gospel* in its title, but the text says nothing about the life of Jesus nor does it record his teachings from the time of his ministry. The *Gospel of Philip* appears to be a gospel in name only, for it is far removed from traditions about Jesus. In short, if one submits to the judgment of the early church, then texts qualify as gospels even though they do not appear to belong based on their content.

The variety of writings discussed suggests the difficulties. Must a gospel relate what Jesus did, or is it enough to present things he said? Must a gospel focus on the ministry of Jesus, or is it enough to focus the story before or after his ministry? To what degree must a gospel resemble others, and how unique may it be? What is the relationship between written gospel and preached gospel? The breadth of possible answers to these questions underscores the problem of defining a gospel.

At this point, the inquiry expands: Not only are we pondering expectations, we are now debating what to compare. The definition of a gospel creates a feedback loop that determines what one identifies as a gospel. Not all texts described in this chapter belong to the category of gospel but which do? The preceding survey jumped ahead of the important question, "What then is a gospel?"

Structuring a Solution

To bring some order to this deliberation, we can turn to a trio of analytical tools that have lurked in the background, namely, form, content, and function. We use these all the time and may not even notice, but they are helpful for generating analytical insight. With this trio of tools in hand, let's compare gospels in order to analyze what constitutes a gospel.

Content is the most obvious. The canonical Gospels suggest that a gospel presents things Jesus said and did during his ministry and after his Resurrection. The *Gospel of Thomas* and Q indicate satisfaction with only the teachings of Jesus. Other texts rely heavily on dialogue and look like catechetical questions and answers. Most present a Jesus speaking or acting before or after his crucifixion, sometimes focusing on Jesus' youth or, more likely, at the other extreme, his final day on earth. Within this breadth, if one stipulates that a gospel features the figure of Jesus talking or acting, then gospel is a broad category that leaves room for great variety but excludes the *Gospel of Truth*.

Tied to content is *form*, the shape or structure a text takes. Forms like biography, collected sayings of wise men, and catechetical dialogue have already been noted. Smaller forms, such as parables, healing stories, exorcisms, aphorisms, and conversational dialogue are also identifiable. These smaller forms are familiar from the canonical Gospels, so the more they appear, the more likely a text will be considered a gospel. At a more comprehensive level, however, no single, overarching form for the gospel exists. Two general types of material dominate—narrative and sayings—and provide two common categories into which one may place gospels to help determine whether or not the label *gospel* is appropriate. Once again, the *Gospel of Truth*, as an essay, is excluded.

Looking at a text's *function* is helpful. Most of these early texts attempt to express the message of Christ, i.e., the gospel. Early Christian texts are not disinterested reporting or random memories. They are serious attempts to understand Christian faith. They seek to express important points of Christian teaching and persuade readers and listeners to place trust in Christ. To this end, gospels were written with specific and often competing points of view to express the good news of Christ. This deserves emphasis. Gospels typically represent a serious attempt to express the gospel message.

Function is not without its problems. Though the Infancy Gospels express Christian theology, they do not focus on an expression of the gospel. Also, if gospel is defined as any text that presents the preached gospel, then the door is opened to Paul's letters to the Galatians and Romans, which no one has identified by the literary tag of gospel. These letters, like the *Gospel of Truth*, clearly purport to describe the gospel but are not gospels.

Summary of Solution

The point of trying to identify what constituted a gospel in the eyes of the early church is to help us compare texts and see which resemble one another and which do not. This helps us better recognize and understand what we are reading. Form, content, and function assist with this. Taking the texts the early church identified as gospels and comparing them suggests that gospels are texts that incorporate and build on traditions about Jesus, presenting the words and/or deeds of Jesus (whether as Jesus, Christ, Lord, Savior, Word, etc.) for the purpose of articulating a view of the Christian gospel. Calling something a gospel does not guarantee it will take the same form as every other gospel.

Just as important as this summary is the diversity of documents included. The use of diverse forms warns one to listen for different ideas, for the form used provides a clue about the views to be presented, which are not given facts but rhetorically shaped ideas. The life and teachings of Jesus provide the material for a text to create a view of the human condition and the remedy God provided through Jesus.

Gospels Call for More Gospels

The first written gospel compelled more to be written, and additional ones called for still others. Rhetoric is one creative driver in this process. The very act of saying something invites response, whether critical and dismissive or affirming and constructive. For example, texts including the Gospel of Mark motivated the author of Luke to compose another Gospel; Luke's Gospel in turn elicited responses such as Tatian's Gospel harmony and the Infancy Gospels.

A change in social groups also calls for revised or new material. Mark, which is very much a Gentile Gospel, became more Jewish at the hands of the author of Matthew's Gospel. Christians inside Jewish communities wanted to combat the views expressed by Christians outside those communities, so Jewish gospels were written. Early Christians also constructed identities around specific apostles, and these play out in the way texts characterize apostles negatively and positively, so while one text may champion Peter or James, others chip away at them in preference for Mary or Judas.

New perspectives also required new gospels. As Gentiles brought their own views about life to their worship of Christ, they pushed Christian ideas into new places. Some of this is visible beginning in Paul's letters to Corinth, in which he combats views about idols, the body, and resurrection that arise when Greeks tried to think about the implications of the message about Christ. When Christians tried to merge their Greek ideas about human existence and the cosmos with the gospel, ideas about the soul's ascent evolved. Ideas about God also evolved in the noncanonical gospels. Embedding these in the preached gospel motivated new gospels, e.g., those of Mary, Judas, and the *Apocryphon of James*, though the seeds of this are evident in John's Gospel as well.

That these various motivations led to creative activity is natural. That they caused people to write gospels tells us that, by the mid-second century, a gospel was a widespread, recognized, and respected text in Christian circles; it was a popular vehicle for presenting one's view of the Christian message of salvation. The success of the gospel as a genre brought imitators.

More Gospels Reframe the Canonical Gospels

The fences people place around questions determine their answers. Of course, no one consciously builds fences but they arise intrinsically from the knowledge and experience each individual brings to a problem. For example, ethnographers can provide help to product designers, information specialists to medical professionals, and geographers to business strategists but only if someone thinks to bring these adjunct specialists into the conversation. Without that invitation, a fence stands.

The presence of many gospels in the early church challenges us to consider the frameworks we apply to our reading of Christian origins. If we read and take seriously the presence of many gospels, then the framework within which early Christianity is explored expands. Three examples will illustrate this, two from the Gospels of Mark and John and a third from church history.

The Messianic Secret

In 1901, Wilhelm Wrede published a book titled, *The Messianic Secret*, in which he proposed that the attempts Jesus makes in Mark's Gospel to suppress his identity were made up to explain why people did not recognize Jesus as Messiah but crucified him. This proposal accounted for many oddities in Mark's Gospel, including: (1) Jesus tells his disciples not to tell anyone that he is Messiah; (2) Jesus commands demons not to tell anyone who he is; (3) Jesus heals someone, then asks that no one tell what he did; (4) the general inability of the disciples to understand Jesus; (5) the explanation given for the parables, namely, that they are intended to obfuscate Jesus' teaching; and (6) Jesus' attempts to avoid crowds. The bulk of such things in Mark's Gospel seems at odds with what the reader might logically expect of Jesus and the story.

Wrede proposed that Jesus did not try to hide his message or identity. The secrecy encountered in Mark's Gospel, Wrede reasoned, is a theological agenda imposed by the anonymous author to account for the disconnection between the Messianic claims about Jesus and his dismal outcome. Embarrassed by the actual historical facts, the author wove into his Gospel a secrecy motif to explain how the Son of God could achieve such little recognition and be executed.

Throughout the twentieth century, scholars responded to Wrede's proposal. Most burrowed into the details. Some pointed out that telling someone who was healed not to tell anyone was a rhetorical ploy that served to make the events all the more wondrous because, of course, no one could remain silent. Some demonstrated that elements of Wrede's secrecy motif were embedded in the traditional materials that the author of Mark's Gospel incorporated and were not the author's own creation. Such close analysis makes it difficult to embrace Wrede's solution, though the data still beg for explanation.

An alternative approach to analyzing the details of Wrede's proposal is to expand the frame of reference. At a higher level of abstraction, the question is not one of secrecy in Mark's Gospel but secrecy in gospels more generally. Here the existence of more than four gospels can affect the interpretation of the canonical Gospels.

Many gospels are self-consciously idiosyncratic and present themselves as such, offering teaching that is private. In the *Apocryphon of James*, it is James, with Peter, who receives the privileged revelation. In the *Gospel of Mary*, Mary offers the valuable teaching about the soul's ascent to the other disciples. The *Gospel of Thomas* presents its contents as the key to salvation, with the opening claim, "These are the secret sayings that the living Jesus spoke." The *Gospel of Judas* opens with similar words: "The secret account of the revelation that Jesus spoke in conversation with Judas Iscariot . . ." In light of these texts, secrecy in Mark seems natural. An author uses secrecy for clearing space to put forward his or her own ideas. Although this still does not explain secrecy in Mark, it lifts the problem to a higher level of abstraction and places the conversation in a different, larger context. One must consider secrecy in Mark in light of the larger phenomenon of secrecy in early Christian literature.

The Theology of the Gospel of John

The broader array of gospels also illuminates the ideas in the Gospel of John. The similarities and differences between John and the Synoptics have been noted for a long time, particularly the differences. Among these, John begins with a poetic introduction that situates the story of Jesus in the context of creation. John distinctively presents Jesus as a divine figure who reveals God. In connection with this, one also sees Christians begin to wrestle with the problem of God's nature and identity: John's Gospel delivers the fundamental postulate that "God is a spirit." Although God as "Father" occurs in the Synoptics, it functions differently in John. The same can be said of "eternal life." Readers also encounter a dialogue form that goes beyond simple conversation, as the disciples ask questions and Jesus answers.

After reading noncanonical gospels, many of John's differences become less idiosyncratic. The question-and-answer format occurs repeatedly and, with it, a focus on private teaching to disciples. "Eternal life" is literally "*aionic* life," and throughout noncanonical gospels, one finds Christians attempting to figure out how Christian destiny corresponds to *Aions*, which are powerful, spirit beings. How the world came to be is likewise a common theme in early Christian writings. Intense conversations were also taking place about the nature and identity of God in early Christianity. God as Father is common and takes on connotations of the incomprehensible begetter of all. The more difficult it became to know God, the more urgent was Jesus' role as revealer. Similarly, the need to understand the nature of eternal life, salvation, and the human predicament called for the presentation of Jesus as the revealer. John presents a revealer who knows from where he came and to where he is going, insights that are fundamental to salvation, which noncanonical gospels make explicit.

These similarities indicate how John stands in a line with many of the gospels that would follow. This is precisely why so-called Gnostics were among the first people to interpret John's Gospel, for they recognized John's affinity with their own ideas. This appears most clearly in another Nag Hammadi document, the *Trimorphic Protennoia*, which bears so much resemblance to John that it is hard to tell which document is using the other. The question, therefore, has been asked whether John is a Gnostic text. When put so baldly, many argue no. What matters is that, in John, questions are asked and answers formulated that go beyond the Synoptics and find continuation in subsequent gospels.

The Gospel of John illustrates the problem of comparison. If placed with the Synoptics, its ideas can be constrained and made to fit with theirs, but set next to other gospels, John's ideas find easy connection. Do similarities or differences carry greater weight? And which similarities or differences receive focus? The biblical canon creates a context for John's Gospel that determines how it will be read. With the recovery of other gospels, it is now clear that the author of John stood on the threshold of a different way of interpreting the gospel.

Church History

One approach to Christian history is to ask how Christianity got from Jesus to where it stands today. If one reads only the early authors embraced by the Western church—e.g., Luke, Irenaeus, and Eusebius—a traditional account of apostolic unity, the sure gospel, the fight against heresy, and the succession of bishops emerge.

Add the noncanonical gospels to the mix, however, and the storyline fits less comfortably. Early Christians held contradictory views. Some thought the early disciples were fools, others regarded them as heroes, and many picked a single champion from their midst. Many Jews retained their identity as Jews, while following the teachings of Jesus. At the opposite end of the spectrum, Marcion purged Christianity of Jewish history and religion. At the same time, in the second century, Christians debated the acceptability of prophetic practices with growing discomfort. Many streams of esoteric, insider knowledge developed. Both apocalyptic anticipation and the full participation of women in religious life grew objectionable; but before they did so, they were simply normal. Nor were the theologies of the noncanonical gospels fringe ideas. Teachers such as Marcion and Valentinus were well known and influential. As one reads dozens of gospels, the unity of ideas, clear transmission of teaching, and orderly transfer and succession of authority vanish from the early church.

The traditional history of the church, as it grew among speakers of Greek and Latin, tells how Providence led the church from there to here, a story of triumph. The full corpus of Christian gospels shows that the path was not inevitable and exposes the many options that might have been. Perhaps most surprising are examples of Christian religion that did not put the life of Jesus at its core. Possessing and reading these so-called "heretical" texts makes it more difficult to ignore them. The development of Christianity looks less smooth and assured and much more filled with competition and politics, while expanding with a vitality and diversity that defy a simple storyline.

Four Gospels Are Not Enough

The fact that one text sows the seeds for another demonstrates that four Gospels are not enough. But a more fundamental driver is also at work: gospels beget gospels. As Christians calibrated their teaching to varied social, cultural, and intellectual contexts, they articulated a variety of gospel messages. Writing these ideas required new gospels. This was the reality of the second century; because many gospels were preached, many gospels were written.

To say "gospels beget gospels" may sound provocative, but it is an intellectual necessity driven by people trying to understand the gospel from the constraints of their own points of view. Second-century Christians were no different. Particularly striking is how their ideas about God, the universe, and humans shaped their theology. In the same way that many today inevitably read Gen 1–2 in light of knowledge that the world is 4.5 billion years old, so the first Christians wondered how the gospel corresponded to their view of the world. They wondered who the creator was and how the creator was related to the God who is one. They wondered how Jesus was related to Christ the Savior and how the latter was related to God. They wondered what a gospel of immortality meant and how it was that one who is human could become divine. They pondered the connection between the body and spirit and their oppression by devils and other unseen, powerful beings. In thinking about these things, they raised questions not anticipated by Jesus or his inner circle, questions that, when answered, expanded the content of Christian theology. This enterprise was inevitable. It began in the first generation of Christians and, for more than a hundred years, found expression in gospels.

The Gospel of Mark launched the project of narrative gospels precisely because the author viewed the content of the gospel as related to the actions of Jesus. The experience of divine spirit and earthly sufferings are vital parts of the gospel as Mark presents it. Similarly, the Gospel of Luke presents a comprehensive view of salvation that rescues people from poverty and misery, so a narrative describes this vividly. Many of the noncanonical gospels view salvation as an antidote to the cosmic problem of the material world and physical body, a problem to which Jesus reveals the solution. He did not get around to this during his ministry because people were not ready to hear it, so he spoke in parables and other figures of speech. After his Resurrection and the putting off of mortal flesh, the time to tell the full story of the soul's journey arrived. Many additional gospels were, therefore, written to tell it.

Restraining such inquiry was the project of orthodoxy. In drawing a circle around the four Gospels that exist today in the New Testament and establishing them as the correct and authoritative four, the church recognized the insufficiency of one but tried to hold in check the problem of multiplicity. Creativity, therefore, found other outlets, the classic example being the fusion of philosophy, biblical interpretation, and politics that produced the church's great creeds.

The same creative impulse persists. It produced a popular evangelistic tool among American fundamentalists known as the "Romans Road," a series of sentences, lifted from Paul's letter to the Romans, with which one can present the gospel to sinners. The five excerpts (3:23; 6:23; 5:8; 10:9; 5:1; other verses may be added) state the human need for salvation, God's provision, and what a person must do to receive salvation. There is no "Markan Road" or "Matthaean Road." The Synoptic Gospels play no role in this kind of shorthand, because they do not provide the concise view of salvation that people traveling the Romans Road seek. This means that the Romans Road is yet another attempt to articulate the gospel, just like all of the centuries-earlier gospels, only the creativity is cloaked by quoting the apostle Paul. As Christians both ancient and modern try to focus the gospel message on the human need as they recognize it, they find themselves forced to articulate the gospel in new ways.

Conclusion

This chapter has surveyed dozens of early Christian writings that are not found in the New Testament, which may seem odd for a book introducing the New Testament. This serves to underscore the artificiality of isolating the canonical Gospels from their larger context and raises three final observations.

First, the four canonical Gospels did not exist in a vacuum. Jewish traditions influenced them, as did Greco-Roman, topics that could become separate, additional essays. This chapter seeks to place the four canonical Gospels in the larger context of Christian teaching and, specifically, within a literary tradition, in which additional writings reveal the kinds of written conversations taking place in the early church. In the *Gospel of Thomas*, the teachings of Jesus mattered most. The Synoptic Gospels countered that his life did also. John affirmed the Synoptics, though for different reasons and, in his emphasis on Jesus as the revealer, resembles noncanonical gospels. Meanwhile, the *Gospel of Peter* indicates that Jesus' death was not the exclusive preoccupation of the canonical Gospels, while the Infancy Gospels document how legends about Jesus' birth, youth, and parents continued to develop. The layers of traditions one can detect in *Dialogue of the Savior* and the *Gospel of Peter* resemble what one sees in the canonical Gospels and helps expose the evolution of Jesus traditions. The entire corpus of gospels also documents how different authors and communities asserted legitimacy for their views in the politics of the early church, whether claiming Peter or denigrating him or other figures such as James, Thomas, Judas, or Mary. In these diverse ways, noncanonical gospels help bring the canonical Gospels into better focus.

Second, the broader scope of early Christian artifacts also prevents another misconception. The miracles of Jesus, so striking in the canonical Gospels, play less of a role in later gospels. This development might lead one to think that healing people became less of a concern for Christians after the early second century; however, this is not the case. Though miracles diminish in noncanonical gospels, they thrive in noncanonical Acts. They also enter the church's visual vocabulary, appearing in early Christian art. The four canonical Gospels, therefore, are in conversation with one another, dozens of noncanonical gospels, and other types of Christian communication.

Third, consideration of noncanonical gospels underscores the artificiality of the line drawn between the New Testament and the many other documents written by early Christians. Though the New Testament helped to project a point of potential unity among these Christians and to combat the fragmentation of authority, the church's canon does not limit the historical investigation of the life of Jesus or the study of Christian origins. The church may draw a line, but history recognizes only that the church drew such lines, not that they are necessary. In the study of the early generations of Christians, no New Testament existed, only the growing variety of texts written by Christians. Even when the New Testament began to emerge, Christians continued to write new texts that furnish still more evidence about the early church. People may choose to study only the New Testament, but it is only part of the literary life of early Christians.

This essay joins the earlier one, "There Are Four Gospels," to feature two complementary ways of reading gospels. One seeks to understand a gospel on its own terms, to hear and appreciate its unique perspective and voice. The other pays attention to the much larger literary environment to recognize how individual texts interact with other texts. By uncovering the broader conversations taking place, we return to individual texts better able to understand them and their contributions.

Questions

1. Which do you think is the more natural content of a gospel: talking or doing? In the narratives of Matthew, Mark, and Luke, there is a lot of doing, as well as talking. In Q, *Thomas*, *Mary*, *Judas*, and *Dialogue of the Savior*, there is mostly talking. One may say that the sayings gospels differ from the canonical Gospels in their focus on teaching, not actions. One could also turn that statement around and say that the canonical Gospels differ from the majority of other gospels by discussing what

Jesus did. Would you privilege one group more than the other or see them as equally valid?

2. In the *Infancy Gospel of Thomas*, what changes, the behavior of Jesus or the attitude of the people around him?

3. Why do you think Christians wrote gospels?

4. What expectations do you bring to a gospel? When you begin to read one, what do you expect to encounter? What do you expect it to say, and how do you expect its message to be expressed?

5. Would you consider a gospel to be "historical fiction," "based on historical events," a "historical documentary," or a "historical investigation"?

6. Which early Christian texts would you count as a gospel?

7. Propose a definition of *gospel* and explain it.

8. If a gospel would have been written in the year 2000, what form, content, and function do you think it would present?

9. How important do you think the boundary between the New Testament and other Christian writings is?

10. The four canonical Gospels determine that Christian theology is incarnational. Explain and evaluate this statement.

Further Reading

Aune, David E. *The New Testament in Its Literary Environment.* Library of Early Christianity. Philadelphia: Westminster John Knox Press Press, 1987.

Burridge, Richard A. *What are the Gospels? A Comparison with Grae-co-Roman Biography.* Grand Rapids, MI: William B. Eerdmans Publishing Company, 2004.

Ehrman, Bart D. *Lost Christianities: The Battles for Scripture and the Faiths We Never Knew.* Oxford University Press: 2003.

King, Karen L. *What is Gnosticism?* Cambridge, MA: Belknap Press of Harvard University Press, 2003.

Kirby, Peter. *Early Christian Writings.* March 2014. *http://www.early christianwritings.com/.*

Koester, Helmut. *Introduction to the New Testament*. 2 vols. Philadelphia, PA: Fortress Press; Berlin: Walter de Gruyter, 1982.

———. *Ancient Christian Gospels: Their History and Development*. Philadelphia, PA: Trinity Press International, London: SCM Press, 1990.

Layton, Bentley. *The Gnostic Scriptures: A New Translation with Annotations and Introductions*. New York: Doubleday, 1987.

Meyer, Marvin W., ed. *The Nag Hammadi Scriptures*. The International Edition. HarperOne, 2007.

Miller, Robert J., ed. *The Complete Gospels: Annotated Scholars Edition*. San Francisco: HarperCollins, 1994.

Pagels, Elaine, and Karen L. King. *Reading Judas: The Gospel of Judas and the Shaping of Christianity*. New York: Viking, 2007.

Schneemelcher, Wilhelm, and R. Mcl. Wilson, eds. *New Testament Apocrypha, Vol. 1: Gospels and Related Writings*. Revised. Westminster John Knox Press, 1990.

Talbert, Charles H. *What is a Gospel?* Philadelphia: Fortress Press, 1977.

White, L. Michael. *From Jesus to Christianity: How Four Generations of Visionaries & Storytellers Created the New Testament and Christian Faith*. San Francisco: Harper Collins, 2004.

Paul Wrote First

The very earliest Christian writings that still exist are those composed by the persecutor-turned-missionary, Paul of Tarsus. We may wish that Jesus wrote, but like Socrates, he did not. Even worse, none of Jesus' students wrote, whereas Socrates had Plato and Xenophon. It seems odd that people who knew Jesus and spent time with him did not bother to record anything he said or did, but such is the case. It fell to an outsider to write about Christian faith and to do so largely without writing about Jesus.

This simple fact has profound consequences for understanding early Christianity. As much as one might wish to place Jesus alone at the center of Christian history, Paul stands with him. Through the apostle Paul, one sees how quickly conflict arose in the early church and how much creativity was exercised in explaining what it meant to believe in Christ. Because Paul wrote first, the exploration of Christian origins must account for the surprises this brings and the complexity it introduces.

The Accidental Author

Paul came to his role as the first Christian author accidentally. (To be more precise, he is the first Christian author of whom we are aware.) He did not aspire to be a writer; nor did he envision generations of people reading his work, as is evident in the incidental, occasional nature of what he wrote—namely, letters, real letters, not sermons masquerading as letters. For example, in First Corinthians Paul responds directly to questions raised by Christians in Corinth and problems present among the congregations there. Later, Paul wrote letters to the Corinthians to discuss a collection of money for needy Christians in Palestine and to defend the legitimacy of his ministry. Paul had to write to the Galatians in reaction to other Christian missionaries who came after him and undermined his teaching, forcing Paul to persuade the Galatians to return to his view of the gospel. Likewise, specific circumstances appear to motivate all of his letters.

To be sure, letters can rise above their circumstances, such as the letter Martin Luther King Jr. penned from a jail cell in Birmingham, Alabama. Paul's letter to the Romans approaches this most closely, as it arises for specific, transitory reasons but contains an expansiveness of thought, making it much more than a letter of self-introduction and solicitation of support. Still, these practical reasons motivated Paul to write so that even Romans reflects a specific, concrete situation.

To put Paul into perspective, he was first and foremost an evangelist and founder of communities. He came to writing secondarily, as an activity to supplement his preaching or, more precisely, to compensate for his inability to visit face-to-face. Becoming an author was not Paul's pursuit but a useful means to achieve his goals.

Perhaps other Christians were writing at the same time as Paul. Letters of introduction and recommendation likely circulated from Christians to other Christians. Paul's rivals probably used letters to extend their influence and compete with him. Some Christians may already have been writing snippets of the things Jesus taught or did. If so, none of these texts survived, nor did the names of their authors. From today's perspective, Paul was the first to write, and the only Christian author one can identify, with certainty, within sixty years of Jesus' death.

The Pauline Letters

The New Testament contains thirteen letters that appear to be written by Paul. As described in chapter 1, Paul's letters divide neatly into two sections. The first is written to churches, the second to individuals. Within each section the letters are arranged in order of length, so their arrangement provides no evidence of chronology. The collection is organized as follows:

Letters to Churches	Letters to Individuals
Romans	1 Timothy
1 Corinthians	2 Timothy
2 Corinthians	Titus
Galatians	Philemon
Ephesians	
Philippians	
Colossians	
1 Thessalonians	
2 Thessalonians	

After Philemon, the contemporary New Testament presents Hebrews, which many wrongly thought to be a letter by Paul. This misunderstanding may account for why Hebrews made it into the canon of scripture. In fact, ancient scribes typically placed Hebrews among the Pauline letters, most often after 2 Thessalonians. If Hebrews is counted as a Pauline letter, the entire collection of Paul's letters numbers fourteen, as I was taught in Sunday school.

Four problems now arise. First, we have to account for letters Paul wrote that no longer survive. For example, 1 Corinthians refers to an earlier letter that no longer exists. How many others Paul might have written cannot be known. This uncertainty adds an asterisk to whatever number is used for the final tally of Paul's letters.

Second, there is no claim within Hebrews that it was written by Paul. If compared carefully to Paul's letters, it becomes easy for the reader of Greek to see that the elegant style of Hebrews does not resemble Paul's letters. The way Hebrews argues, repeatedly turning to Jewish scripture for ideas and arguments, goes beyond Paul's normal modes of argumentation and elaboration. The author of Hebrews differentiates him or herself from and acknowledges a debt to the original witnesses to Christ, a point of view Paul would not have shared. The concern about repentance within Hebrews reflects questions that arose fifty years after Paul. And Hebrews looks much less like a real letter than do Paul's letters, which, as already stated, are actual letters. The consensus that Paul did not write Hebrews must stand so that the corpus of his letters in the New Testament cannot be counted as fourteen.

Thirteen is not correct either, though. A third and much larger problem is that some of the letters in the New Testament that claim to be written by Paul were not, which is to say that they are pseudonymous and, therefore, inauthentic. Second Thessalonians, for example, mimics the unusual structure of 1 Thessalonians and provides a different and conflicting view of the end times, suggesting that someone wrote a letter in the name of Paul and in imitation of Paul but with a message updated to address a new crisis within the church some years later. Ephesians and Colossians offer views about Christ, the cosmos, and the church that are significantly more elaborate than those found in Paul. The ethical component to these two letters is more conventional than that of Paul, who thinks his way creatively and experimentally through difficult questions and infrequently finds himself ready with canned answers.

The so-called Pastoral Epistles (1 and 2 Timothy and Titus) are even more conventional in their ideas and language. They also present a view of authority in the church that goes beyond what appears in the other Pauline letters. To read them in Greek is to encounter a writer who is decidedly not Paul. Second Timothy, in particular, appears to imitate the Jewish testamentary genre, in which a great figure from history talks about his impending death and makes predictions about what will happen afterward. This genre pretends to record the actual words of a soon-to-die historical figure; yet this genre is consistently fiction.

Once Ephesians, Colossians, 2 Thessalonians, 1 and 2 Timothy, and Titus are removed from the letters genuinely written by Paul, the list of his writings totals seven. It is, therefore, customary for scholars to refer to the seven authentic letters of the apostle Paul.

Having considered authenticity, a fourth and perhaps the most complex problem remains, that of integrity. This issue addresses the relationship between the version of Paul's writings one reads today and what Paul actually wrote. What degree of editing took place between the time Paul wrote his letters and the time they circulated throughout the early church? Some sentences were added here and there, so how broadly might the influence of editors and copyists have extended? Were entire chapters added or separate letters interwoven? Some scholars have divided Paul's letters into different, perhaps multiple, original letters; their proposals address real incongruities and discontinuities in Paul's writings. Should Paul's letters be partitioned then or their integrity taken at face value?

Second Corinthians is the clearest example of secondary editing. The tone and content of 2 Cor 10–13 are so different from the warm, conciliatory language of the preceding nine chapters, especially chapters 1, 2, and 7, that for more than a hundred years these last four chapters have been regarded as having been written at a different time than the first nine. As analysis of 2 Corinthians continued, some scholars saw it as an anthology of many letters that, at some point, a creative editor wove into a single letter. No single view has won the day, but the following suggestion sees within 2 Corinthians five distinct letters from Paul, all written in uncertain order:

2 Cor 1:1–2:13 + 7:5–16 + 13:11–13
2 Cor 2:14–6:13 + 7:2–4
2 Cor 8
2 Cor 9
2 Cor 10:1–13:10
(2 Cor 6:14–7:1 was not written by Paul.)

Similarly, some scholars have argued that Philippians is a composite of three different letters written by Paul. Romans 16, distinct from the previous fifteen chapters, has also been identified as a separate piece of correspondence from Paul. There are doubters on all these matters of partition. The strongest rebuttals come in response to Philippians and Romans. Partition theories have also been put forward for 1 Corinthians, though much less frequently and with the least traction. What is more commonly identified in the case of 1 Corinthians is the addition of non-Pauline sentences or even the first half of chapter 11.

In the end, investigations into the integrity of Paul's letters reveal that, among the seven authentic Pauline letters, more are hiding, as are the fingerprints of authors other than Paul. The seven preserve portions of at least eight letters that Paul wrote, probably more and perhaps fourteen. Fourteen? By complete accident, it would appear that my Sunday school teacher might have been right—with an asterisk, of course.

When saying that Paul wrote first, it is to the seven authentic letters that scholars refer. One must turn to these seven to hear the earliest Christian voice and gain a sense of the early church. Peter is voiceless. Jesus actually has to wait to be heard in texts. The next four sections reflect further on these consequences, as we consider the early impact of Paul's letters, and assess his biography, religion, and legacy.

Letters Influenced by Paul

The fact that Paul wrote letters set in motion a practice among other early Christians to do the same. Some imitated Paul in writing letters that arose from concrete circumstances, using the author's own name and addressing specific people. From the late first-century or early second-century, there is a letter written by Clement of Rome to Corinth and an entire corpus by Ignatius of Antioch to churches in Asia. Both knew of Paul; Clement referred explicitly to 1 Corinthians, and Ignatius held up Paul's martyrdom as an example for his own.

Both before and after Clement's and Ignatius' letters, unknown Christians wrote letters in the name of Paul. Second Thessalonians and Colossians are examples, addressing actual circumstances and imitating real letters by Paul, the former imitating 1 Thessalonians, the latter Philemon. Ephesians seems more general in its content and less tied to real events. Its author appears to have taken Colossians as his inspiration. The so-called Pastoral Epistles appear to have been written much later out of a concern to use the legacy of Paul to shore up church structure and authority. Still later, the non-canonical 3 Corinthians and the correspondence between Paul and Seneca were written. The Letter to Laodicea used Philippians as a model and source for content.

The pseudonymous Pauline letters suggest that a collection of (some of) Paul's letters was made in the first century. This collection set a precedent for the appropriate way the apostolic voice should communicate to Christian congregations at a distance. As previously mentioned, a handful of early Christians, some still in the first century, who wanted to address other Christians took up Paul's precedent, sometimes writing in Paul's name and, on other occasions, their own.

Paul's example also influenced people who wrote letters in the names of still other early Christians. Thus, there are 1 Peter, 2 Peter, and Jude. This process climaxed with 2 Peter, which refers explicitly to a previous letter by Peter, borrows much of Jude, and refers to Paul's letters. Lastly, Hebrews, which is anonymous, appears to emulate Paul in its last chapter.

This activity of letter writing was not random but reflected the habit of educated people imitating literary worthies, as discussed in chapter 3. At a general level, many pseudonymous letters were written in the names of philosophers, figures such as Plato and Diogenes. Among Christians, Paul launched the fashion of letters, so the broader Hellenistic tradition of letter writing, both authentic and pseudonymous, became part of Christian literary activity.

Therefore, a consequence of saying that Paul wrote first is that he set an example of appropriate Christian literature. In imitation of Paul, writing letters became an important component of early Christian literary activity. In many cases, the mere presence and example of Paul's letters made a deeper impression than did their content. Paul as a letter-writer was as important, or more important, as what his letters actually said.

Paul Anchors Early Christian History

Because Paul wrote first, his letters are the starting point for the investigation of early Christian history. This subverts traditional views of Christian history and Pauline biography, which depend on the second-century Acts of the Apostles and the fourth-century history by Eusebius. An easy but unsatisfactory approach to the first century is to open the New Testament and read Acts, then supplement it with information from Paul's letters. This allows for a nice narrative to guide understanding of the earliest Christians and provides slots in which one can position Paul's letters. But this is backward and results not in the discovery of Paul but in the reaffirmation of how Acts presents Paul.

Paul versus Acts

Scholars now approach Paul's letters independently of Acts to discover what they say for themselves. For example, in Acts it appears that when Paul traveled to a new city, he preached first to the Jews and then to the Gentiles but only after the Jews rejected him. No one would construct this picture of events if relying only on Paul's letters. In Galatians, Paul describes himself as the apostle to the Gentiles and thereby differentiates himself from Peter, whom he describes as the apostle to the Jews. This division of duties does not come from someone who, as Acts alleges, seeks to preach first to Jews.

The identity of Paul's opponents presents another problem. The rivals to whom Paul refers in his letters are consistently other Christian preachers, not the jealous Jews of Acts. To be sure, Paul did have run-ins with Jews, even suffering whippings at the hands of these, his kinsmen, but the apostle's biggest headaches came from other Christians. The silence in Acts about the competition among Christian preachers misses one of the major realities of Paul's ministry.

In Acts, it also appears that disagreements were resolved easily and amicably. For example, a group of disciples of John the Baptist convert quickly to Christ when Paul preaches. Even the controversy surrounding whether or not to preach the gospel to Gentiles finds smooth resolution: God intervenes to send Peter to preach to Gentiles, and later, a single meeting in Jerusalem clears the air and opens the door to Paul's continued activity. In Paul's letters, however, it is clear this issue dogs him throughout his ministry. Peter is sympathetic to Paul's position but cannot bring himself to emulate it. James, the brother of Jesus and leader of the church in Jerusalem, is probably even less agreeable.

In Acts, Christianity spreads in a controlled, orderly fashion. The gospel moves out of Jerusalem, remains connected to it, and arrives ultimately and triumphantly in Rome. To accomplish this in Acts, Paul makes repeated visits to Jerusalem and confers with the church's leaders there. This tidy picture exaggerates Paul's cooperation with the church in Jerusalem, however. In his own letters, Paul emphatically rejects any influence or control that Jerusalem might exert over him. When he talks about James and Peter, he calls them only "so-called pillars" of the church, recognizing their visibility and influence, but refusing to bow to it. Paul was not an emissary or partner with the church in Jerusalem.

Acts runs into a big problem with respect to Rome. The author of Acts wants his story to climax with the gospel's arrival in the imperial capitol. Despite knowing that the gospel reached Rome before Paul did, Acts uses Paul to introduce the gospel formally to Rome, and then uses the presence of Christians there to stage a public welcome for Paul, having them stream out of the city to meet him in an honorific gesture. More problematically, Acts presents Rome as Paul's longed-for and divinely appointed destination, whereas Paul told the Romans that he planned to travel to Spain. For Paul, Rome was but a stopover en route to reaching the Iberian Peninsula. What Paul wanted from Rome was help getting to Spain. Acts explicitly contradicts this by having the apostle claim that Rome is his objective.

The most conspicuous difference between Acts and Paul is the absence of Paul's letters. On the one hand, this can be excused, because Acts has aims that make any reference unnecessary. On the other hand, given the impact of Paul's letters on subsequent Christian authors, as described previously in the section "Letters Influenced by Paul," beginning on p. 198, the move from epistolary imitation of Paul to a narrative about Paul that is silent about his letters represents a significant change in the use of Paul's legacy. Paul is no longer the letter-writing pastor but a heroic apostle on his way to becoming a saint.

To be clear, the letters give a portrait of Paul at odds with Acts, which presents Paul as a hero of early Christian witness who exercises superior power in competition with others. God protects him and guides him along the way. Paul's own testimony, however, shows a relentless evangelist whom others feel free to mock and disparage, whose powers of the spirit fall short of other people's, whose apostolic office is disputed, and whose teachings are questioned. Moreover, he suffers dangers, deprivations, and violence. Wear and tear show on his body. Paul incorporates these difficulties into his self-description, presenting himself as an apostle and an example to Christians because of his endurance. Like Christ, Paul suffers yet continues steadfastly, proof of his apostleship. Paul's depth of suffering contrasts starkly with his spectacular powers displayed in Acts. Both portraits are heroic but in fundamentally different ways.

Paul and History

Without Acts to guide the way, the reconstruction of Paul's life becomes more difficult, with many unsolvable details. In general, his activity as a Christian missionary can be located from before the year 48 CE until his death around the year 65 CE. First Thessalonians can be identified as an early letter and Romans as late, with the Corinthian correspondence between the two. Galatians was written some time in advance of Romans, and Philippians and Philemon were in the middle to late part of Paul's career. With these general guidelines, scholars can attempt to identify how the apostle's ideas and rhetoric differed over time. In fact, doing so brings the apostle's own changes into greater focus, as shall be seen in the section "Paul's Religion," beginning on page 203.

Views of Paul shift not only in his letters, the pseudonymous letters, and Acts—but also over time. We know from where we stand, nearly two millennia later, that much was yet to come. For today's readers, Paul is not a last-minute warning about judgment but a founding figure for a global religion. He is both an actor in history and an ingredient in reconstructions of it, passing through pseudonymous letters, hagiography, iconography, Reformers, and more. Paul's legacy rests on an unexpected twist: He labored nonstop to make his mark on the soon-to-end world through his service to Christ and succeeded precisely because of the centuries that have passed. Time allowed Paul to gain a prominent place in Christian history and exceed even his own lofty ambitions.

Not only does approaching Paul's letters without reference to Acts help one see the man behind the legends, but also it clouds the picture of the mid-first century church. The development of Christianity cannot be reduced to a few key people who trace a smooth storyline. While Paul bucked the authority of key leaders such as James and Peter, his letters reveal a broad range of players in the early church who had influential roles in the growth of Christianity. Two otherwise unknown apostles, Andronicus and Junia, are encountered, as well as Apollos and the households of Stephanus, Fortunatus, and Chloe. The patroness Phoebe, who preached, supported Christians, and presided over a church is met. Unnamed preachers who rivaled Paul for influence over the churches he founded are discovered.

Paul was not unique in his practice of traveling and preaching to win converts and instruct them, neither was he uniquely gifted and successful. His letters also show that his converts were not passive receptacles for his wisdom but could be bold thinkers who ran ahead of the apostle. Other preachers contradicted Paul, argued with him, and slandered him, just as Paul did not hesitate to attack them.

In short, because Paul wrote first, the approach to early Christian history changes. Though intuitively one may want to focus on Jesus, one is forced to look at Paul. Next, one must resist the temptation to fall back on Acts and, instead, look at the evidence of the apostle's own writings. Doing so reflects a different story than the one in Acts, one that greatly complicates understanding of the development of the early church. As other early Christian writings have suggested, the ideas and people in the early church spanned a greater range than traditionally thought. Sometimes there was harmony, sometimes conflict. Never do things appear to stand still. As concerns Paul's contribution to this dynamic, one has to examine his letters to take measure of the man, as we will do in the remainder of this essay.

Paul's Religion

Since Paul wrote first, he provides the earliest look at Christian faith and practice. Whether the reader is Catholic or Pentecostal, it is easy enough to see a familiar religion in Paul's letters, but the familiarity is superficial. Upon closer examination, most Christians would find the religion Paul practiced puzzling.

With respect to Christian teaching, Paul's letters show how little established doctrine existed. He had his own favorite taglines, a baptismal confession, and a hymn or two. He had the beginnings of a confession in Christ's death, burial, and Resurrection and favorite proof-texts from Jewish scriptures. Here and there, he refers to shared or common material and references other people's words or ideas. At the same time, his letters show the early church had no articulated body of theology, received from the Twelve, that was being carefully taught and passed along. It would take a century of creative thinking to produce the New Testament and centuries more to produce the creeds that the church today can take for granted.

Paul and Jesus

A strange feature of Paul's letters is how little he refers to Jesus. While the name Jesus does appear often, it usually pairs with Christ. More substantially, Paul simply does not talk about the ministry of Jesus. For Paul, Christ is an immortal, heavenly being who rescues his people from God's impending judgment and shares immortality with them. These present and future dimensions dominate Paul's thinking.

Some have argued that, in fact, Paul does reference Jesus, if one scratches beneath the surface. These scholars have provided long lists of examples. Such maximalists have persuaded few. Their long lists only look desperate and actually work to undermine their position.

Here are a few considerations that make Paul's silence about Jesus strange. First is to compare how Paul uses scripture with possible references to Jesus. Paul certainly can be subtle in alluding to Jewish scriptures, but he is also repeatedly and frequently explicit. Since Paul is obviously comfortable referring explicitly to Jewish scriptures, why is he any less clear about referencing Jesus? Second, in his different letters, Paul generates principles of Christian conduct in a variety of ways. In this enterprise, he does not use Jesus as a fundamental strategy—rarely drawing ethical teaching from what Jesus said and did and never rooting them there. When Paul does draw on Jesus, it is through isolated examples that only underscore how inadequate traditions about Jesus were when it came to addressing the questions Paul encountered in his Gentile churches. Third, Paul draws more profound consequences for Christian conduct when he applies Christological ideas rather than instances of the historical Jesus. The example of Christ presented so beautifully in Philippians 2 coheres with its larger context, yet one sees a profoundly mythic example, not a simple reference to Jesus. Even Paul's reference to Christ's gentleness or more precisely, leniency, is a Christological insight and not a reference to Jesus' personality.

One place where Paul's silence is particularly strange is his argument about resurrection in 1 Cor 15, in which he debates with people in Corinth. His opponents see no need for a physical body to be involved in resurrection, whereas Paul argues that a body is part of resurrection. Here is the perfect place for Paul to introduce information about Jesus' condition in resurrection and thereby silence others, but he says nothing. A few years after Paul died, the Gospel of Mark was written. It, too, lacks any stories of resurrection, though the story of Jesus' transfiguration provides a clue. I infer that the well-known stories from the Gospels of Matthew, Luke, and John were unknown to Paul and the author of Mark's Gospel. Having no knowledge of these stories would provide a perfectly sound explanation for Paul's silence. The apostle said little about Jesus not because he simply did not get around to it, but because he had little to say.

To be sure, the cross does play a pivotal role in Paul's thinking. "Christ crucified" is a tagline he likes to repeat. "Christ died, Christ buried, Christ raised" is Paul's basic summary of the gospel. But these shorthand statements point to interpretations about God's chosen and anointed one, not simple memories about Jesus. Moreover, these shorthand expressions ignore anything that happened prior to the crucifixion, as does the apostle's essential confession, "Jesus Christ is Lord," which points to Christ risen, not Jesus' ministry.

The resurrection is key for Paul. It brought Jesus to his current state of heavenly existence. This immortal, spirit-existence was what Christians encountered in life and worship. Moreover, resurrection was seen as an event of the end time, Christ's Resurrection being but the first step in a sequence of events leading to the similar transformation of Christ's followers, which Paul believed would happen at any time. Motivated by this imminent change of reality, Paul had every reason to look forward, not backward. So he looked to Christ and did not go digging for Jesus.

In light of this, was Jesus relevant to Paul's Christianity? If one thinks about a church service in which a Gospel reading is a privileged part of the liturgy, wherein the assembled might hear a story about Jesus healing someone, casting out a demon, teaching, or being born, the answer is no. If the Lord's Prayer, parables, or the ethical principles of the Sermon on the Mount come to mind, the answer remains a resounding no. Even when it comes to living like a Christian, Paul infrequently references the teachings of Jesus. For the institution of the Eucharist, aka "communion," and advice about divorce, Paul does look to Jesus, but such examples are rare. Apart from death and resurrection, the life of Jesus plays an insignificant role in Paul's religion.

The surprising fact is that the earliest records of Christian faith, Paul's letters, do not show a thinker seeking insights into life and religion based on Jesus' teachings or deeds. One searches in vain for a religion that looks to the ministry of Jesus for its direction and meaning.

Paul and the Divine Spirit

In Paul's letters, one encounters a religion that focuses on the experience of the risen Christ through his spirit. Another way of characterizing this is to say that spirit possession is the hallmark and fundamental experience of faith in Christ for Paul.

The importance of spirit possession emerges in Paul's own description of his call to serve Christ. Echoing the words of ancient Hebrew prophets, Paul recalls God's decision to reveal God's son in Paul (Gal 1:16). English Bibles typically translate Paul's words as God's decision to reveal Christ *to* Paul, mistakenly trying to make Paul's testimony sound like the three stories in Acts that describe his conversion on the road to Damascus. In Acts, Christ appears to Paul and rebukes his efforts to arrest Christians. Translators have consistently read this revelation into Paul's account in Galatians and made Paul's words there conform to it, changing the obvious "revealed in me" to "revealed to me."

This evasive translation arises from a fundamental misunderstanding of Paul's religion. Paul understands Christ as a living, divine being whose spirit is sufficiently expansive to dwell among the communities of people loyal to Christ and inside individual members. Because of this, Christ's people can speak angelic languages, utter prophetic sayings, heal the sick, and experience Christ's power in other ways. This indwelling spirit also transforms the people it inhabits, energizing them, and making their very bodies more and more like their Lord's. The ultimate destiny of those loyal to Christ is full transformation from mortal flesh into immortal spirit-beings, whose bodies are just like those of Christ.

As an apostle, it was crucial to Paul that he model this experience of the divine spirit. If he could not serve as an example, he could not be an apostle. Participating in Christ's spirit qualified him to be an apostle and gave him the substance of his message. Thus, the letter to the Galatians claims that God revealed his son *in* Paul.

The experience of Christ's spirit made the final judgment seem very close, and Paul anticipated Christ's imminent return. As the years went by, Paul found himself addressing questions that the delay posed. What happens if a Christian dies? What if the possession of Christ's spirit is already the second coming? Paul even reached the point at which he wondered whether he would remain alive to witness Christ's return.

Paul also had to reconsider the implications of Christ's spirit in competition with other Christian teachers. Whereas one might expect that a religion of spirit possession would place a premium on superhuman deeds, Paul found himself lagging behind the abilities of others and needing to reposition his experiences of Christ's spirit. He embraced his hardships as evidence of his moral virtue but, even more importantly, as the imitation of Christ. Through suffering, Paul grew more like Christ and experienced, even more powerfully, Christ's spirit filling him with resurrected life. In his weaknesses, he saw proof of how profoundly the experience of Christ's spirit was transforming him into an immortal, Christ-like person. This complete experience of Christ's life being repeated in Paul filled him with confidence that his claims trumped those of any rival. Not all onlookers were persuaded.

Paul and Judaism

Christianity emerged among Jews. Over time, its membership became increasingly non-Jewish. By the middle of the second century, the demographics of Christianity were overwhelmingly Gentile and some were trying to diminish links to Christianity's Jewish roots. The first steps in this transition took place in Paul's lifetime and during his ministry within a larger debate about how Gentiles could follow Christ.

Paul was a leading agitator in this problem. As a Jew, he had been a conscientious, happy, and successful practitioner of Jewish customs, more so than most. Christians often denigrate Jewish practices as legalistic and empty, but this leads to a misunderstanding of Paul, Jews, and Judaism. When Paul turned to Christ, he viewed himself not as leaving his Jewish identity but as preaching Christ to all people.

Paul's religion encountered a problem in how it articulated what loyalty to Christ resembled. For many early Christians, living according to the Law of Moses provided a crucial ingredient for their devotion to God. Even in Matthew's Gospel, two decades after Paul, Jewish practices remained important for followers of Jesus. This Gospel defines righteousness with an eye to Jewish traditions—e.g., prayer, fasting, almsgiving, and especially mercy—and affirms the abiding relevance of the Law of Moses.

Paul took a different view, and this brought him into conflict with Peter and James, not just in a polite "we-agree-to-disagree" manner but also in vocal and theatrical confrontation. In one of the peculiarities of history, circumcision became a focal point in the debate. (Really, I wouldn't make this up.) Does a man have to be circumcised to follow Christ? To those who said, "Yes," Paul offered one of his most colorful remarks: "I hope the knife slips" (Gal 5:12; my paraphrase).

As he debated this issue, Paul learned. Many of the arguments he made early on in Galatians were easily refuted, so it is not surprising that most were not repeated. The negative tone expressed toward Jewish practices in Galatians is also softened when Paul returns to the topic in Romans. But the facts on the ground, that is, the successful evangelization of Gentiles, kept Paul resolute.

For Paul, loyalty to Christ brings righteousness, and circumcision was an unnecessary test of that loyalty. Those who proved themselves loyal to Christ would escape judgment before God, benefiting from Christ's advocacy: God would see Christ representing them and agree that they are righteous. Paul came to this conclusion because this was how he saw the divine spirit working among people who confessed Jesus as Lord. They fell into line with God's great display of power and acted out their loyalty in groups of worshippers. Evidence of God's spirit indicated God's approval and the generosity of God's loyalty in return. The spirit's presence proved that the Eschaton, "the end," had arrived; any and all whom the spirit filled would escape judgment. Thus, as Paul writes in Galatians, in Christ, "there is no longer Jew or Greek."

All of this has to be framed by the larger consideration that Paul did not convert out of Judaism and into Christianity. The latter simply did not yet exist, not even the word *Christian*. Faith in Christ remained one of many ways of practicing the religion of Jews. Paul regarded the change in his life as a call to serve as a prophet: Reevaluating his ancestral traditions in light of Christ, Paul extended the blessings of Israel to non-Jews, but he remained a Jew. Or as Pamela Eisenbaum sums it up in the title of her book, *Paul Was Not a Christian.*

Paul and Historical Thinking

For Paul, history was at its end. The course of human events was about to reach its conclusion and, literally, the end was near. Oddly, anticipating the end of history caused Paul to construct a view of it that combined the Jewish past with Christ and the apostle's personal experience.

On the surface, Paul's belief that the end was near makes him sound like Jesus, who announced the approaching kingdom of God. But Jesus anticipated God's appearance, whereas Paul anticipated Jesus' return. Jesus announced the end with prophetic authority, while Paul's view rested on Christian teachings mixed with his experience of the spirit and reflection.

There existed, in Paul's mind, a narrative that placed Jesus in a series of events leading to salvation. Resurrection was a single event with two stages: first Christ, then Christ's followers. Since stage one had happened, stage two was necessary and imminent. God was about to rescue Christ's people and judge the world. This story reflects a mixture of theological and historical thinking that is common in the Jewish scriptural tradition. Though this kind of "history" would not pass muster with modern historians, it was unremarkable for Paul.

As his theological reflections continued, Paul constructed a history that led up to Jesus and then Paul's own position poised at the end. This background story was Jewish history that involved, particularly, the promises God made to Abraham. Moreover, this history was truncated, not lengthy and detailed, but jumping from Adam to focus on Abraham and passing by Moses with occasional sideways looks at the prophets to glean useful examples and proof texts.

History plays its greatest role in Paul's final and most lengthy letter, Romans. Years of debating the Gentile mission brought Paul to address the question of God's loyalty. The relationships of Jews and Gentiles among God's people had to be described in a way that did not undermine God's earlier promises to Jews. In Romans, Paul addresses the question that had dogged his work: What about Israel? Drawing liberally on the words and ideas of Jewish scriptures, Paul defends the integrity of God's promises to Israel while, at the same time, inserting the present Gentile mission into that history, famously using the analogy of a limb grafted onto another tree. This was the history of God's saving action as it existed for Paul. From today's perspective, it could also be called Paul's history of Christianity.

For Paul, there was no such thing as church history, a claim that underscores how different Christian religion looks today. Not only was the end at hand for Paul, but also he rejected any of the constructions that might allow for incipient church history. The progression from Jesus to the Twelve, to other witnesses, to bishops, and to all was a sequence that could not exist until the Twelve, and all who knew them, were dead. But even the first handoff from Jesus to the Twelve was one Paul disputed. He gave no ground to the Twelve. The neat expansion outlined in Acts, starting with Jerusalem and circulating through Judea, then north to Samaria before spreading to the entire world, was a smooth storyline created by the author of Acts long after Paul was dead. It makes some sense geographically but still does not reflect what really happened, as the gospel spread quickly through spirit possession and social networks in a way that defied any logical progression based on centralized authority or geography. The idea that Peter and Paul played foundational roles in the church at Rome arose after both were dead and became linked into developing ideas about bishops and martyrs. Paul certainly never conceived of it. Paul's claims that God chose him and sent him, together with the opposition he encountered from other Christians, disrupt any attempt to construct a smooth progression of events in the early church.

Comparing Paul to other early Christian writers exposes where he lacks the sense of church history that was soon to emerge. In the opening words of Luke's Gospel, there is a sense of history predicated on literary research and guided by the voice of witnesses. The author of Hebrews shares a similar perspective in referring to witnesses whose testimonies guided the writer's preaching. One of the people who helped compose John's Gospel also looked retrospectively to witnesses who provided the testimony on which the Fourth Gospel rests. Elsewhere, a simple statement that the church was built on the foundation of apostles and prophets was made by someone who wrote the letter of Ephesians in Paul's name. This introduces a historical perspective that postdates Paul. In 1 Clement, readers encounter a growing sequence: God sent Christ, who sent the apostles, who appointed bishops and deacons. All these backward glances differ from the point of view seen in Paul's letters. Jesus' death lies behind Paul, but the action of apostolic witness is present and urgent. Paul, who wrote first, is involved in the game in an immediate, creative way that differs dramatically from other early Christian authors.

As the first Christian author, Paul wrote with one eye on Christ's imminent return, which colored everything Paul thought and did. As people who look back at him from almost two thousand years later, we have a perspective he never considered possible. A great deal of history followed him and can be traced through him. This requires readers to qualify what is read in his letters with one very large insight: He was wrong about one of his most fundamental beliefs. History was coming, not Christ.

Paul and the Church

The church first encountered in Paul's letters is still a teenager. What is seen of it at that age would surprise most people. For example, Paul practiced baptism but did not emphasize it. He makes no mention of infant baptism and alludes to the mysterious practice of baptism for the dead. In Paul's churches, baptism had grown beyond symbolic washing of sin and also represented the reception of the divine spirit.

The nondiscriminatory bestowal of the spirit on all believers led to important consequences for Paul. With it, he justified his evangelization of Gentiles and out of it grew the broad participation of women in Christian congregations. In Paul's congregations, women served as apostles, preachers, prophetesses, and patrons. Later Christians objected to this and redirected Christianity for centuries to come. But at Paul's time, this was not so. Women prayed, prophesied, preached, and evangelized. They helped lead the effort to spread the gospel.

How Christians in Paul's churches worshiped would strike many modern Christians as odd. Their services lacked a standard order of proceedings and their options for reading from scripture were limited. They engaged in ecstatic speech, which today is called speaking in tongues. Various individuals offered prophetic speech as moved by the spirit. No one stood behind a pulpit and read a speech written beforehand. More than one person might speak at once, though Paul frowned on this extent of hurly-burly. There was no hymnal, prayer book, or Bible, no choir or bulletin. Most disturbing to a modern person would have been the absence of a clock and the correlated ambiguity about when services would start and end.

Food was part of life within Paul's congregations. It was not provided during an extra social hour but as part of the worship. This made the Lord's Supper, aka "Eucharist," a regular and natural part of their observances not a separate feature or monthly addition. The presence of food seems normal when one remembers that church services took place in people's homes, as church buildings did not exist. This limited how large Paul's congregations could be and influenced how services were conducted. When they gathered, Christians struggled with the normal influence of social stratification, which meant food might not be shared equally and without discrimination. Imagine the person across from you eating a big cut of meat and fanciful pastries while you get a plate of boiled potatoes. This violated Paul's ideals but was completely normal to people at that time.

The modern person would also grow confused trying to figure out who was in charge. No clerical order existed in Paul's churches. Leadership arose in various ways. The first to convert might lead by virtue of precedence, or the homeowner might lead because of wealth and hospitality. Others led because of the personal initiative they took to provide service to believers. Those who best channeled the divine spirit enjoyed particularly high status. In the absence of seminary training and ordination, Christians saw speaking in tongues, healing, eloquence, and prophesying as credentials for eminence. While Paul's references to "deacons" seem to suggest the presence of church office in his churches, these passages actually refer to people who preached. Similarly, "apostles" were people preaching the gospel not holding down a job in a specific congregation. Other ad hoc roles included handling money and delivering messages.

Because Paul wrote first, he provides a window into a church whose practices were unlike those known to most Christians throughout the centuries. At the same time, he provides ways of practicing Christian worship that have provided options to dissenters and reformers.

Paul the Innovator

As the first known author, Paul is de facto an innovator, as his letters appear on the Christian stage as something new. Scholars have debated how extensive his innovations were. Given how different his religion is than that practiced by most Christians through the centuries, it is clear that many changes subsequently have taken place in Christianity. But what changes can be laid at Paul's doorstep?

Paul the Inventor

A century ago, in his important book, *Paul*, Wilhelm Wrede called Paul "the second founder of Christianity," spawning much debate about Paul's role in the creation of the Christian religion. To whom, then, is owed the religion known today as Christianity? While it seems natural to credit Jesus, not Paul, as the person responsible, important observations stand in the way of the obvious. As Wrede says, Jesus' "emphasis falls on individual piety, and its connection with future judgment. But in Paul . . . religion is nothing else but an appropriated and experienced redemption."

Wrede rests his idea that Paul invented Christianity on the simple statement that Christianity is "the religion of redemption," a summary that could not be drawn from the teachings of Jesus. One can find occasional remarks in the Synoptic Gospels that point to redemption, but they are unusual and in no way summarize the bulk of what Jesus teaches. John's Gospel offers more evidence, but Wrede thinks these examples illustrate early Christians working them into Jesus' sayings. For Wrede, the religion of redemption comes from Paul, who was "the first theologian" and whose theology "decisively transformed the incipient religion." As a theologian, Paul constructed a system of ideas based on Jesus' Incarnation, death, and Resurrection, which the apostle viewed as saving acts of God. Is Paul to be credited (or blamed) for the Christian religion?

Four problems stand in the way of giving Paul the credit. First, there is little information about the theology Paul learned from others. It seems likely, though, that what Paul had opposed is what he came to preach. What he learned about faith in Christ from those he persecuted was further supplemented in the churches he frequented after conversion. What Wrede calls Paul's religion of redemption may not have been Paul's creation but, rather, what he learned from other Christians.

Second, labeling Paul the inventor of Christianity exaggerates his role in the early church. Many people contributed to the amalgamation of ideas and practices that became Christianity. Even in the pages of the New Testament, there is ample evidence of competing ideas that should warn readers about overstating Paul's contribution and influence. With specific reference to Christ's sacrificial death, Paul's statements do not look like his own creations but, rather, ideas circulating among Christians and providing common ground with his readers.

Third, this label overemphasizes Paul the theologian as opposed to Paul the traveling preacher, founder of churches, writer of letters, and martyr. For many early Christians, the example of Paul eclipsed what he taught. Even when one reads early Christian writers talking explicitly about Paul, it is not clear how carefully they read Paul's letters. What mattered to Ignatius was the opportunity to imitate Paul in dying for Christ not quoting Paul. The author of 1 Clement waxed eloquent about Paul the martyr but hardly used Paul's letters, which is strange given how relevant Paul's letters were to the issue of church unity that Clement addressed. In the Acts of the Apostles, its author devotes significant space to Paul, yet presents a picture of Paul's activities and words that do not square easily with his letters. The letters written in Paul's name by other people further illustrate how they used him only as window-dressing and did not slavishly follow his ideas.

Fourth, the claim that Paul invented Christianity over-simplifies the definition of Christianity. Christianity in the first century was no clearer than it is today. It took decades simply to invent the word *Christian*, let alone the religion, and centuries to articulate what today are considered the fundamental elements of Christian theology. The varieties of practices and ideas in the first century further complicate identifying an essential system of beliefs and practices that can be categorized as Christian and variations of which can be judged as non-Christian. For example, was Christianity a type of Judaism? What role did the Law of Moses play in the lives of those earliest followers? Did the temple in Jerusalem have any role? How was faith defined and loyalty practiced? What did Jesus have to say to the church? While change was certainly afoot among the followers of Christ, too many options were taken up to credit any one person with responsibility for how history played out. "Paul *the* inventor" would be an exaggeration.

Paul the Outlier

While refusing to credit Paul with inventing Christianity, one certainly can appreciate his role as an innovator of lasting significance on a par with the author of Mark's Gospel. Both are innovators. Each bequeathed to Christianity a literary form that successors imitated. Paul wrote letters and inspired many others to write letters, at least eight other authors and probably more. Mark created a narrative about Jesus' life and thereby spawned imitators. The letters of Paul and the Gospel of Mark were important first steps in the creation of Christian literature, providing examples for others to follow.

These two innovators share an important trait: Both were outliers. Neither was part of Jesus' band of followers. Each found his place in the congregations of Gentile Christians apart from the Jews who formed the inner circle of Jesus' disciples.

Paul is explicit about this. He was not one of the pillars. He was not a member in one of the Jerusalem congregations. He possessed no authority delegated to him by the truly important disciples or by virtue of personal association with Jesus. This was one of the problems he faced in his ministry, as Paul tried to assert his ideas in competition with other Christian teachers with superior pedigrees and connections. Paul's authority rested on his personal experience of the risen Christ and the evidence of Christ's spirit at work through him.

Paul could offer only himself as proof of his legitimacy, not references. Paul stood outside the inner circle; he was an outlier.

An outlier likewise wrote the Gospel of Mark. Despite the erroneous tradition that links Peter to Mark, the author seems to have no personal connections to the earliest disciples. The stories Mark tells about those earliest followers undercut any claims to authority those disciples might assert. In Mark's Gospel, Jesus calls his disciples to follow; instead they flee. Jesus challenges them to stay awake; they fall asleep. They crave honor; Jesus offers humiliation. Jesus predicts suffering; Peter rebukes him. Most tragically, Peter denies Jesus—and does so three times. It is left to women to visit the tomb and discover it empty. The giants of the church are not in Mark's Gospel. Mark grounds authority for authentic Christianity not in the first disciples but in loyal imitation of the Teacher. Like Paul, one sees Mark's Gospel standing outside the inner circle, its author an outlier.

In viewing the outliers, Paul and the author of Mark's Gospel, as innovators, the degree of their accomplishments is considered next. Did they innovate incrementally or dramatically? Throughout the New Testament, one can read authors giving a new slant to baptism or the Eucharist. For example, in Rom 6, Paul discusses baptism in a new way that goes beyond the obvious metaphor of "washing" away one's sins, adding that it also signifies an identification between the believer and Christ in his death and Resurrection. In doing this, he implicitly affirms the common experience of baptism, while adding to it one more interpretation. This illustrates incremental innovation.

Paul's letters and Mark's Gospel do more than add new features to what already existed. They reframe fundamental perspectives. Paul argues that loyalty to Christ is open to people who are not Jewish and do not live like Jews. In taking this position, he tells readers he debated other Christians and even came into conflict with Peter about this matter. Paul answers an important question differently from many other early Christians and, as a result, presents a way of following Christ that creates something dramatically different from what Christians in Jerusalem imagined to be correct. While Paul joined a movement that already included Gentiles, it fell to him to explain and defend their legitimacy. Criticism for his leadership in this dramatic innovation dogged Paul.

The Gospel of Mark, likewise, reframes faith in Christ. Like Paul, the Gospel of Mark offers a way for Gentiles to follow Christ but does so by arguing for an experience that imitates Jesus. This view requires reporting the teachings and deeds of Jesus, so that one knows what to imitate. Mark, therefore, gave the church the first narrative about the life of Jesus. It was not enough to know what Jesus said; the follower needed to know what Jesus did and what action this required. In saying that lists of what Jesus taught were not enough, the author of Mark boldly reframed the way early Christians wrote about Jesus. In fact, he changed forever how the church would talk about its master.

Without the literary innovations of these two outliers—Paul and the author of Mark—early Christian literature would look vastly different, as would early Christianity. The church, today, also would differ fundamentally. But these claims are not as sweeping as saying that Christianity rests on Paul or Mark. Both were crucial innovators, and in saying this, neither can be credited as the sole agent of change, as *the* inventor.

Paul the Iterator

In the twentieth century, scholars began, in earnest, examining Paul's letters to learn how his ideas changed over time. Sometimes, statements that seem contradictory, such as Paul's negative ones about Jewish law in Galatians and positive ones in Romans, have demanded this, which leads to observations about how Paul's thinking developed or evolved.

But Paul also talks about topics in ways that are not necessarily contradictory, simply different. In Galatians, Paul's discussion about the divine spirit drives how he formulates comments about Christian moral life. This line of reasoning is not pursued with such focus in his other letters. In Philippians, the apostle draws on a Stoic line of moral guidance when he advises readers to discern the things that really matter and pursue them. An intellectual turn reappears in Romans with more elaboration.

In some cases, it is clear that circumstances have forced Paul to see something in a new light and answer a new or follow-up question. His Corinthian correspondence reflects this, because

Paul had to respond to the ideas of other people who clearly were thinking about issues of the time. Was it acceptable to eat meat from an animal slaughtered in a sacrifice to a pagan god? The Corinthians figured that since Christ was more powerful than the other gods, they were immune to any danger attached to the meat. This opinion offended Paul's scruples, and he labored to formulate an answer that refuted the Corinthians' view. As already noted, the Corinthians also thought about the nature of resurrection, compelling Paul to respond with a counter argument about the physical nature of it. Yes, there is a resurrection body, Paul responded, albeit a spiritual one.

In these cases, one sees Paul thinking and trying to invent answers. This is where it is helpful to remember that Paul wrote first. In his letters, we find ourselves in a place at which Christian thinking is still being created. Although the invention has never ceased, with Paul we are close to the beginning, where very little was in place that is now taken for granted, e.g., the doctrine of the virgin birth or the Trinity. Thus, in regard to eating meat sacrificed to an idol, Paul thinks aloud as he tries to invent arguments, which is utterly unlike how Rev 2:14 and 20 address the issue, making no effort to explain or defend but simply decreeing that such behavior is evil.

As for Paul himself, he had a handful of fundamental, nonnegotiable beliefs. For example, he believed that God was one; Christ was crucified, buried, and raised; Jesus Christ was Lord; and the Lord was a spirit. Figuring out what these mean day to day was a work in progress, carried out in conversations and fights with pagans and Jews, converts and church leaders.

In describing Paul as an innovator whose work is exploratory and probing, another label can be used to show how he went about his work: iteration. To say Paul's thinking is iterative is to say that it moves from prototype to prototype, each version, or iteration, bringing further insight and leading to new problems and questions. Like a good inventor, Paul moves from one experimental version to the next, to an initial product offering and improved versions. Sometimes earlier ideas are rejected, sometimes improved. At other times, new possibilities emerge. Iterations bring dead ends and surprises, improvements and do-overs. Sometimes, these can be charted as developments, at other times as fresh paths.

Often hard to recognize is which stage anything Paul says represents. Are his arguments about the resurrection body in 1 Cor 15 the prototype, in which he addresses the issue of the physical body in resurrection for the first time? Or are his comments practiced? If he were able to address the question again, how differently might he approach it? To me, Paul's comments appear to develop previous conversations about resurrection. They are iterations and look like neither a preliminary mock-up nor a final, polished product. Regardless, as the first Christian author, Paul presented the rhetorical prototype for many topics. His subsequent iterations sometimes led to confusion, which is precisely what proves he is thinking and makes him interesting.

Conclusion

Paul wrote first, and this innovation had a crucial legacy for Christianity. In establishing the example of letter writing, he set in motion the creation of some of the most influential documents in the Christian church, both his own letters and those by his imitators. His limited status relative to many other early preachers gave rise to much of his writing, which tells one to look for alternative views, of which there are many. Knowing of this competition and Paul's status as the first to write cautions readers that his ideas are experimental and indicates they should anticipate change and expansion. We do, indeed, discover these iterations. His preliminary and contingent ideas required subsequent writers to update Paul and align him with mainstream thinking, as happened in the early church. With these things in mind, one can evaluate further Paul's success and failure.

As the apostle to the Gentiles, Paul diverged from the views of the church's first leaders by preaching salvation to Gentiles apart from Jewish identity and practices. From this point of view, Paul won, as church membership quickly became overwhelmingly Gentile. He proved to be on the right side of this question.

Paul also built communities of believers and linked them together. These steps helped build a social organization that could transcend localities, thereby laying a foundation for the church's survival and success. Whether others imitated him consciously, the process of building socially networked communities provided a blueprint for the church's growth. Paul should receive credit for the church becoming a global enterprise, not simply because he won converts but because of the method by which he did so.

The apostle's ledger has a negative side as well. In his failure to root his preaching in the life and teaching of Jesus, Paul lost, as the church chose to focus on Jesus and root itself in the Gospels. In this sense, the documents that focused only on Jesus' teachings, e.g., Q and the *Gospel of Thomas*, also lost, though they were closer to victory than Paul.

The even larger matter Paul missed was how long Jesus would take to return. Had he anticipated the millennia to come, his views on many things—including Jesus—might have been different. Paul can hardly be faulted for this, as he lived out the implications of resurrection and Christ's spirit.

Paul's focus on the powerful activity of the divine spirit in the lives of Christ's followers is another crucial part of his legacy. Here, again, he lost out. In the developing church, the role of the spirit evolved as it merged with clerical authority and liturgy. The free-for-all of spiritual activity in Paul's congregations gave way to clerical office and liturgical order.

For centuries, religious practices typical of Paul's converts disappeared. Evidence of them remained in Paul's letters, a latent potential for reform to be exploited by restless Christians wanting to kindle faith. Paul's influence on the Reformation goes without saying, but he played an equal role in dispensationalism, charismatic renewal, and fundamentalism, which are influential on college campuses today. The mainstream church may have tamed Paul, but the apostle to the Gentiles remains a voice for change to those looking for something different—just as he was in his lifetime.

Questions

1. Among the letters attributed to Plato that survive today, Plato wrote some and not others. The same is true of letters written by the early Christian Ignatius of Antioch. Would you expect the letters of Paul to be any different in this regard? Why?

2. What motives might explain why people would write using Paul's name?

3. What are some of the advantages and disadvantages of Paul having written letters instead of other genres, say a philosophical essay, biography, or history? Why do you think Paul wrote only letters?

4. Paul tells us little about Jesus. Do you think this affects the quality of his views about Christian faith?

5. If Paul was not simply trying to relay and elaborate on Jesus' teachings, then what do you think his agenda was?

6. The New Testament refers to Christians as "filled with the Holy Spirit." We refer to people controlled by evil spirits as "demon possessed." In this essay, I refer to Paul's religion as one of "spirit possession." What do these three expressions convey to you? What do you think are the pros and cons of using the phrase "spirit possession"?

7. Should the nature of Christian experience as described by Paul be normative for all Christians? Or do you consider it just one alternative? Why?

8. Paul wasn't as good a preacher as his contemporaries. He didn't perform as many miracles. He didn't even know Jesus. He claimed that God appointed him to be an apostle. He claimed that his success in starting churches provided evidence of his apostleship. He claimed that his sufferings identified him with Christ and furnished evidence that God called him to be an apostle. Do you think that Paul's credentials are adequate to his claim to be an apostle? Does he deserve his place as one of Christianity's pillars? How relevant are his ideas about himself to his place in history?

9. What value do you place on innovation? Do you consider it a positive or negative thing that the outliers Paul and the author of Mark exerted such fundamental influence on the development of Christian literature and, therefore, ideas?

10. Paul's ideas evolved, even changed. How do you react to that?

11. Paul thought that Christ would bring God's judgment to earth any day. If a person claims that the world is about to end, are

you more inclined to lend belief or suspicion? As things turned out, of course, Paul was wrong. How does that affect your opinion of Paul?

Further Reading

Betz, Hans Dieter. "Paul." In *Anchor Bible Dictionary*, ed. David Noel Freedman, 5: 186–201. New York: Doubleday, 1992.

Eisenbaum, Pamela. *Paul was not a Christian: The Original Message of a Misunderstood Apostle*. San Francisco: HarperOne, 2009.

Furnish, Victor Paul. *Jesus According to Paul*. Understanding Jesus Today. Cambridge University Press, 1994.

Meeks, Wayne A. *The First Urban Christians: The Social World of the Apostle Paul*. 2nd ed. New Haven, CT: Yale University Press, 2003.

Murphy-O'Connor, Jerome. *Paul: His Story*. Oxford University Press, 2006.

Roetzel, Calvin J.. *The Letters of Paul: Conversations in Context*. 5th ed. Louisville, KY: Westminster John Knox Press, 2009.

Sanders, E. P. *Paul: A Very Short Introduction*. Oxford University Press, 2001.

Schnelle, Udo. *Apostle Paul: His Life and Theology*. Trans. M. Eugene Boring. Grand Rapids, MI: Baker Academic, 2005.

Wrede, Wilhelm. *Paul*. Trans. E. W. Lummis. London: Phillip Green, 1907.

CONCLUDING REMARKS

Creativity Past and Present

T he preceding essays presented seven fundamental observations about the New Testament. Six are not controversial. Some scholars would nuance the fifth thesis, i.e., that the Gospels are anonymous. While none of the four canonical Gospels explicitly names its author, making them all technically anonymous, those who trust second-century commentators would argue that the identities of the authors are known. Reasons for doubting this, however, appear in chapter 5. The other six theses would find quick assent among biblical scholars.

The New Testament provides literary evidence for the emergence of something new on the world stage, the origins of what would become a worldwide religion. One might attribute the creation of this new phenomenon to Jesus: What he said and did gave rise to the religion that followed. Even if this simple explanation was completely accurate, the line from Jesus to the religion that followed is in no way necessary. There were options to explore and actors influencing what took shape.

As the Christian religion developed, churches engaged in a widespread process of creativity that spanned centuries and involved countless and often nameless people. In writing texts, assessing their value, championing preferred texts, and putting them to use, early Christians engaged in creative activities, sometimes the result of agile minds, other times dyspeptic personalities. Similar dynamics applied to myriad ideas and practices.

Jesus, thus, was not the only creator of the Christian religion. This statement could launch an essay of its own, but at this point, the goal is to reflect on the essays already read. A thread linking them is creativity. For example, the literary innovations reflected by Paul's letters and Mark's Gospel received explicit comment, yet every Gospel reflects something new. This concluding essay will review matters touched on in the preceding essays, highlighting creativity in early Christian writings and among the scholars who study it.

By way of organization, I will highlight six ways creativity arises in connection with the New Testament: new data, methods, perspectives, social groups, circumstances, and rhetoric. As will be shown, these dynamics appear in the creative approaches taken by scholars as well.

No theoretical framework explains these six drivers of creativity. People could easily use different labels. As a generative principle, one colleague suggested "new contexts," which does indeed explain many creative insights in the creation of biblical literature and subsequent interpretation. The heading, "new contexts," could easily subsume four of my categories, and a case could be made for all six. I offer them as presented to strike a balance between being too abstract and too detailed.

The six categories are not distinct but may overlap depending on how one wishes to view them. Social groups bring a new perspective to bear, so one could consider them a specific example of perspective; however, I think that new social groups register a significant enough impact to warrant separate identification while reserving perspectives to refer specifically to ideas and theories. By circumstances, I refer mostly to historical events, be they technological, martial, political, or social. The fuzziest category is the last—rhetoric—meaning the process of communicating, which has connections to a number of previous categories. I single it out because the simple effort to communicate may result in new ways of expression or even new ideas, as anyone who has tried to write has likely experienced. Here, then, are these six sources of creativity as a list:

1. Data—access to new information.
2. Methods—new tools to analyze information.
3. Perspectives—intellectual approaches frame information in new ways.
4. Social groups—different groups see things in distinct ways.
5. Circumstances—events may compel fresh insight or bring new tools.

6. Rhetoric—an act of communicating may stimulate creativity and innovation.

Each source has made an appearance in the previous essays and in modern biblical scholarship. All will be reviewed to clarify the role of creativity in the construction of Christian scriptures but also to demonstrate that these processes remain useful ways for scholars and students to act creatively.

New Data

The expansion of traditions about Jesus added data to the knowledge base within the early church. Such a process made possible the formulation of the four Gospels, followed by additional ones. As noted, Q combined wisdom sayings with apocalyptic ones, creating a new text and a more complicated vision of Jesus. Mark's Gospels added deeds to words, creating yet another vision of Jesus. Matthew and Luke, in turn, added still more data to Mark, including stories about Jesus' birth and Resurrection and more of his teachings. John's Gospel self-consciously acknowledged new teachings and credited them to the divine spirit at work. The noncanonical gospels extended this process, some self-consciously and explicitly.

The same process of expanded data drives innovation in modern scholarship. Discovering ancient manuscripts stimulates creativity like nothing else. These have helped scholars reconstruct the biblical texts and provided fresh access to ancient Judaism and Christianity.

The careful work of finding and comparing the thousands of biblical manuscripts is a labor of love and enables all biblical scholars to carry out their work. Stories about people, like Constantin von Tischendorf, who traveled throughout Europe and the Middle East searching for manuscripts, provide a dash of romance and adventure. The existence of Codex Vaticanus, another beautiful manuscript as important as Codex Sinaiticus, maddeningly teased scholars for centuries. The Vatican Library's very first catalog of works, published in 1475, listed the manuscript. Therefore scholars knew about it for centuries; unfortunately, it remained out of reach, shielded from them by the library's staff for four hundred years. The Chester Beatty

Papyri provides a copy of Paul's letters nearly 85 percent complete. Among its notable features, it does not contain the Pastoral Epistles, adding fuel to the arguments of scholars who dispute that Paul actually wrote them. Dated to about the year 200, these papyri were unknown until 1931 and not fully published until 1958. Most of these sheets of papyrus now reside in Dublin, Ireland, and Ann Arbor, Michigan. The Bodmer Papyri were found in Egypt in 1952 and are now conserved among the treasures of the Bodmer Library outside Geneva, Switzerland. Scholars dated one of these manuscripts, Papyrus 66, to about 200 CE, making it one of the most important witnesses to the text of John. Another slightly later Bodmer papyrus contains substantial portions of the Gospels of Luke and John, allowing us to see the former at that early time and compare early copies of the latter, giving the sense that the Gospel of John already existed in different versions. Finally, a tiny fragment of John's Gospel, recovered in Egypt, has outsized importance because it dates to the early second century, perhaps 125 CE, which means the Gospel of John was written prior to that date, a helpful insight for understanding the origin of John's Gospel. Scholars can also tell that this fragment came from a codex not a scroll, added evidence of the technology of early Christian reading and writing. The roll call can go on and on, but the key observation is that much important data about the text of the New Testament is less than one hundred years old. Apart from new approaches to interpreting the text, discoveries throughout the twentieth century expanded knowledge of the text itself.

People have also discovered non-biblical manuscripts. I doubt scholars will ever tire of the often-told story of the goatherd who chanced upon a cache of two-thousand-year-old manuscripts in the Judean desert in 1947. This discovery and the flurry of successful searching it ignited over the next decade brought to light ancient writings now famous as the Dead Sea Scrolls, broadening our view of ancient Jewish society and religion. These texts made the diversity of Jewish ideas at the time of Jesus inescapable and helped make it normal to speak of first-century Judaisms, plural, in turn making it easier to classify the first Christians as another variety of Judaism.

A similar discovery in Egypt in 1945, of thirteen ancient books, brought to light dozens of long-lost Christian writings, shifting our understanding of the development of Christianity. Unearthed at Nag

Hammadi, these documents show the vitality of diverse Christian ideas and practices, which once were too easily dismissed as heretical. Such manuscripts have forced scholars to reconsider how different ideas took root in the early church. Without manuscript discoveries such as these, although we would know that more than four gospels existed in the early church, we would have much less idea what to make of the phenomenon.

Although additional documents like those from Nag Hammadi add detail and nuance to our knowledge of history, they also give a broader perspective. For example, as observed in chapter 6, multiple gospels made it possible to abstract the problem of the Messianic Secret in Mark's Gospel to a higher level, seeing it in a broader context as a problem not unique to Mark. Changing the level at which one addresses a problem offers an important method of creative thinking. Problem solvers should consider whether they are down in the mud and weeds or flying high above. The lower the level, the easier it is to innovate, but the smaller the consequences; the higher the level, the more profound the effects. Changing one's level of abstraction, or altitude, alters the conversation and allows progress on difficult problems.

Sometimes, scholars obtain new data by paying attention to what has been known for a long time but not used. In the last couple of decades of the twentieth century, translation of Greek magical papyri gave these texts widespread attention, helping break down the wall that divided religion and magic. Contemporary prejudices were exposed and greater clarity about practices in the ancient world were gained.

Even more familiar to scholars were the rhetorical writings and speeches from the ancient world. The discussion in chapter 3 of the influence of educational curricula on the New Testament could have included additional proposals about advanced studies in rhetoric. For example, the scholar Hans Dieter Betz proposed that rhetorical practices guided the apostle Paul when he wrote his letter to the Galatians. The detailed arguments Betz provided in his scholarly article and commentary focused the attention of other scholars and helped stimulate hundreds of studies exploring the intersection of Greco-Roman rhetoric and early Christianity.

As seen in both the early church and modern scholarship, then, introducing new information into a conversation pushes it in a new direction. Sometimes the new material is an obvious adjunct while, in other cases, insight needs to demonstrate relevance. By introducing new data, one can produce new ideas.

New Methods

Expanding the tools and methods one uses opens paths to creativity. For example, as biblical authors used figures of speech, they found new things to say. Paul tries an allegory in his letter to the Galatians, strangely turning the story of Hagar into a criticism and denigration of Jewish customs. In John's Gospel, irony appears frequently in many shapes: The teacher of Israel, Nicodemus, cannot understand Jesus' teachings; the recognition that nothing good can come from Galilee precisely indicates that Jesus did not come from Galilee; and Jesus' trial actually puts others on trial.

Formal structures also lead to innovation in the New Testament. Mark's construction of a narrative forces him to put story elements together that create insights such as those in the sandwiches he presents, the way he characterizes people like the underachieving disciples, and the symbolic potential of geography. John's use of dialogue represents a development in how the church taught. Luke's reading of history makes his approach to the life and history of Jesus more complete. Sorting through early Christian documents more carefully than his predecessors, he created an important study.

Educational curricula provided methods for creativity. Chapter 3 showed how school lessons taught Christians how to construct short, pithy sayings and compose anecdotes around choice sayings. Other lessons covered dramatic impersonation and parables. There were even instructions on how to formulate definitions of words. More basic lessons in the *chreiai* taught students how to put teachings together into more coherent wholes.

Just as the allegorical method aided creative interpretation throughout most of the church's history, modern methods drive contemporary scholars and provide other paths for creativity. By asking questions about sources, literary forms, and editorial activity, biblical scholars have developed a tool kit that stimulates new insights.

One question that comes to mind when reading the Bible is, "Where did the author get this information?" In the case of the four Gospels, it is easy to think that one of Jesus' followers recorded what he heard. As scholars pressed these questions, they looked for sources, and this quest generated many ideas. Some ideas gained enormous traction, such as the Priestly source for the Pentateuch, Q for Matthew and Luke, and the Signs Source for the Gospel of John. "Source criticism," then, has become a standard way for scholars to approach biblical texts and has led to many creative proposals. Knowing where information comes from stimulates insight.

Scholars have also learned to ask why things in the Bible take the shape they do. To talk about a parable is precisely to talk about one of the shapes or forms that material in the Bible may take. A genealogy is another form, as are letters and acrostic poems. These are obvious. As scholars pressed on with such questions, they found more and more forms. For example, a story about Jesus that climaxes with a pithy saying, such as, "Render to Caesar the things that are Caesar's, and to God the things that are God's" (Mk 12:17 KJV), has the same structure as stories told about other people in the ancient world, as seen in the remarks about *apophthegmata* and *chreiai* in chapter 4. Such stories about Jesus, then, follow a cultural model that guides its telling and hearing. Looking for these patterns, called "form criticism," has stimulated much creative work and continues to do so, not just in biblical studies but also in music, literature, and other arts. In fact, investigating and challenging form was an important practice across modernism.

Another way to talk about biblical texts in fresh ways involves looking for clues of editorial activity in their composition. If one observes that the three temptations Jesus faced from Satan are presented in a different order in Matthew and Luke, one can ask, "Why?" On the generally accepted view that Matthew and Luke used Mark as one of their sources, one can observe how Matthew and Luke change Mark and ask, "Why?" Such questions help scholars construct larger views about the unique interests of Matthew, Mark, and Luke and help readers hear the individual authors more clearly. Redaction is another word for editing, so this very helpful tool is called "redaction criticism," which helps scholars recognize the unique contributions of Matthew and Luke.

Source, form, and redaction criticism are methods by which biblical scholarship has advanced. One can also say that these are three tools for use in creative investigation, tools that apply more broadly than to only biblical texts.

New Perspectives

Taking a new point of view or perspective about what appears to be "normal" can result in creative thinking. Getting to that new perspective is usually the true work. Once there, consequences derive more easily.

Early Christians frequently found themselves adopting new perspectives. The earliest followers of Jesus had to rethink his death, a staggering disappointment that shook their hopes for themselves and their nation. While cultural stories of immortality helped them overcome the problem, a significant solution came through new interpretations of Jewish scriptures. Many texts could be reread in light of Jesus' death to frame a new story about the path of God's designated savior, whether prophecies of specific events related to Jesus' crucifixion or his more general rejection. What the early church knew about Jesus' fate provided a new point of view for reading scriptures.

Early Christians reexamined ideas about creation. First, they had to insert Jesus, which they accomplished by identifying him as divine wisdom, calling Jesus the firstborn of creation and identifying him as the divine *logos*. Within the context of the Gospels, adopting a cosmological perspective made John's Gospel distinct from the Synoptic Gospels and generated many creative ideas. Those who began with the premise that material creation is not a good thing had even more motive to reread Genesis—to understand the mistake that resulted in the world and remove blame from God. Other early Christians read and responded from yet another point of view. Embarrassed by the Jewish god, they reread Genesis and the rest of Jewish scriptures to assess the deity presented there and understand how this deity relates to creation and Jesus.

Problems with how to understand creation point to a significant change in perspective faced by most early Christians, monotheism. Though points of contact could be made with familiar philosophical ideas, the idea and practice of monotheism was a big departure for non-Jewish converts to Christian practices. That the shift came immediately is evidenced in 1 Corinthians, with converts thinking through the implications of their new faith. Since God is one, then idols and all other religious practices are of no consequence, so interacting with them would not matter. The seemingly valid conclusion shocked Paul, who desperately argued otherwise.

One other intellectual challenge for Christians came in regard to Rome. Paul seemed to take Rome's existence as a fact of life and regard it benignly. In Mark's Gospel, however, a fierce demon turns out to be many, who bear the name Legion. Perhaps that sounds like a fancy way to say *many*, but the word specifically denotes the large units of the Roman army, which spread Roman imperial rule. Naming demons Legion, therefore, insults Roman military might. The Revelation of St. John, in turn, reacts to Rome vehemently, offering the famous characterization of it as the "great whore," "Babylon the great" (Rev 17:1, 5). The language used by early Christians to describe their organization, namely, "kingdom" and "assembly," were political words, positioning Christians to think about their relationship to the world's power. The result was a spectrum of views about Rome.

Early Christians adopted new attitudes to various matters, reframing other familiar things in new ways. As Christian thinkers tried to anchor their faith in history, apostles became a smaller group with special authority, whereas originally they were many with a variety of callings. The Christian valuation of humility turned it from the description of an unfortunate social reality into a virtue to be pursued. Jewish social scruples about sex turned into extreme personal ideals. Christian heroes did not simply limit their sexual activity; they renounced sex altogether as an impediment to human fulfillment.

Seeing the familiar in new ways led to unanticipated ideas and behaviors. Some changes took place over time and were not likely noticed, such as the evolution of humility and sexual abstinence. Some were clear immediately, like the implications of monotheism. In these examples, the introduction of a new point of view brought about cascading consequences.

New points of view have altered biblical interpretation throughout history. The Bible could prove that Earth was the center of the universe until people discovered otherwise. People defended slavery and racism with scriptures, until it became repugnant to do so. Rationalism dampened witch hunts and downplayed miracles. Romanticism overplayed the rural and pastoral dimensions of Jesus' life. Today, in the absence of monarchs, Americans do not need to use the Bible to prop up the divine rights of kings.

In the twentieth century, a number of intellectual currents affected how people read the New Testament. Feminism compelled readers to see what long was ignored. Elisabeth Schüssler-Fiorenza's book, *In Memory of Her*, offered a devastating exposé of the blinders with which the New Testament had been read, carefully surveying the evidence provided in the New Testament about the activity of women within the early church. A year later, in 1984, Phyllis Trible published *Texts of Terror*, in which she took a sympathetic approach to four women in the Hebrew Bible who received heartless and even brutal treatment. These and other authors brought a new point of view to biblical scholarship, one that took women seriously, treated them as equals, and explored what happens when women are placed at the center of interpretation. The critique extends to biblical translation, substituting *humans* or *people* for the generic use of *men* and challenging the notion that God is only masculine. Interpreters now ask what it means to pray, "Our Father, who art in heaven." Pronouns are another problem—referring to God as "he" seems inadequate and misleading. These matters of words reflect a deep intellectual current and important change in perspective.

In *Paul and Palestinian Judaism*, E. P. Sanders revolutionized the study of the apostle Paul by reimagining the nature of first-century Judaism. Resting on the scholarly work of George F. Moore and expanding the insights of theologian Krister Stendahl, Sanders' work succeeded in forcing New Testament scholars, particularly Protestant ones, to recognize the longstanding errors made in their caricatures of Judaism and to rethink Paul's theology. This work created a "new perspective" for studying Paul. Sanders drew on underutilized data to forge an argument that resulted in a new point of view from which to examine Paul's letters.

Reframing the point of view from which one ponders an issue or biblical text leads to new insights. This has led to innovative thinking in the past and remains an elegant procedure for seeing things in new ways. Not only relevant to the scriptures or even the humanities, reframing is just as vital to corporate strategy and political discourse and can easily lead to movements, both for good and bad. It is a go-to tool in a creative person's toolbox.

New Social Groups

Reframing happens automatically when new social groups get involved. This is illustrated by the feminist critique already mentioned. In the twentieth century, women spoke, and most people learned a great deal. What women have taught has become shared knowledge, such that men also participate in feminist criticism, which is why I placed it with new perspectives rather than in social groups.

Bridging social groups played a critical role in the development of Christian practice and ideas. The transition from a Jewish sect to a Gentile religion marks one of the most important interactions in Christian history. Without that shift, Christianity would not resemble what it is today—and it may not have come into existence at all. As for the New Testament, Paul's letters would look different, assuming they still existed. Without Gentile Christianity, Paul would have lacked readers, so his letters might not have been preserved. Mark's Gospel would have been unnecessary, removing any precedent and example for the other Gospels. In chapter 7, Paul and Mark are described as outliers, representing not just the Gentile mission but also different social positions relative to the dominant leadership among Christian communities. On the positive side of the ledger, Gentile Christianity introduced new ideas about gods and humans that became integral to Christian faith, ideas without which neither Trinitarian theology nor Christian asceticism would likely have arisen.

In the twentieth century, liberation theology grew up in Latin America, reflecting the creativity inspired by new social groups and circumstances. Liberation theology seeks to construct a message of liberation from social and economic injustice, challenging readers to adopt the point of view of the poor. What do the words of scripture mean when seen as addressing poor people? Both "blessed are the poor" and "woe to the rich" sound different to someone in poverty and brokenness than they do to the comfortable and self-actuated. Not merely individualistic, the critique runs deeper and addresses the political and economic structures that place people in poverty and weakness. Once articulated, liberation theology became a new lens for reading the Bible. It, too, like feminist interpretation, could be listed as a new perspective because people outside the initial social group use it as an interpretive method.

Global Christianity has begun developing other ideas. In South Korea, an indigenous theological perspective called Minjung theology connected the particular history and experiences of Korean Christians with the gospel. Minjung theology shares a resemblance to liberation theology in its focus on social justice. In Africa, too, indigenous theologies, which seek to make the gospel resonate with lives of Africans and provide forms of expression and practice that align with African cultures, have taken root. These cultural images of Christ include Christ the healer, Christ the chief, and Christ the ancestor. New social contexts prove fertile ground for creative ideas.

New Circumstances

A shifting playing field affords opportunity for innovation. From deregulation of the airline and banking industries, to technological advances and war, fluctuating circumstances leave their mark, whether imposing change or creating opportunities for change

New circumstances affected early Christianity. Chapter 4 described how changes in social groups and circumstances created space for new Gospels, with Matthew's Gospel bringing the Jewish origins of the church into the story and the author of Luke writing to educate his patron. In 70 CE, a Roman army destroyed Jerusalem and its temple, introducing a moment of extreme crisis for worshippers of the God of the Jews. Afterward, the influence of the church in Jerusalem and its leadership seems to have waned. In 1 Thessalonians, converts to Paul's religion of immortality are startled by death. They were not supposed to die, they thought, so a believer's death called for explanation, which Paul provided in his letter. Meanwhile, as the church continued to await the return of its risen Lord—and waited and waited—it faced a crisis of delay, leading it to downplay such expectations. Big change came in the fourth century, as Christianity's relationship with Roman imperial power grew. Among key events were the Edict of Milan, which in 313 CE enacted religious tolerance, followed by the patronage of Emperor Constantine, who convened the Council of Nicea in 325 CE, which drafted the Nicean Creed.

New circumstances continue to shape biblical interpretation. One of the stains on the record of Christian history is anti-Semitism. Over the centuries, whether as a mask for general prejudice or the driver, Christians used the New Testament to justify their persecution of Jews. "Christ-killers" was an easy accusation to sling. The Holocaust changed this. The scale of the slaughter forced people to rethink anti-Semitism and racial hatred more broadly. Scholars revisited familiar texts with new sensitivities. How the stories about Jesus' death were read had profound consequences. Interpreters are now careful to identify Rome's culpability for Jesus' execution.

Current events may also stimulate speculation about the end times. When the Christian calendar rolled over to the year 1000, people thought the end was near. More recently, people who anticipate the secret rapture of Christians were excited by the renewed existence of Israel as a nation in the late 1940s. This was a sure sign of the end times, motivating many to scour current events for any inkling of Jesus' return. Many books, conferences, and sermons emerged from this excitement. More than a generation has passed since the signal event of Israel's founding, but for many, the anticipation lives on, one more example throughout Christian history of people attempting to divine the future.

New technology also affects the New Testament. Already noted was the development of the codex and its adoption by early Christians for their writings. Frescoes, reliefs, mosaics, statues, and stained glass provided additional media with which to express the New Testament. The printing press made biblical texts more accessible and played a profound role in the Reformation, a movement that also accelerated translation of the Bible into contemporary languages and helped devise new ways of reading it. Digital media presents another threshold changing the way people will interact with scripture. Whether for casual reading, liturgy, or scholarship, digitization has brought powerful tools for distribution and access, as well as searching and analyzing.

Events real and perceived shape how people think about God and read scripture. Sometimes they force one to think and act differently. Sometimes they open a window of opportunity. They compel fresh reflection and insight. Technology adds new potentials to the mix, providing physical tools that affect how people relate to scripture specifically and, even more broadly, how they work and think. These are moments of creative opportunity, whatever the realm, whether for religious insight or innovation in one's professional work.

Rhetoric

The attempt to communicate provides an opportunity for innovation. Designers like to say that making is thinking. The very act of making something changes one's understanding of a problem and brings insights. The same happens with communication. Composing a speech or writing something makes one's ideas more tangible and exposes strengths and weaknesses, while also suggesting new paths to explore.

The Gospels show how communication pushes innovation. Small collections of parables, sayings, and miracles helped inspire the author of Mark to compose a narrative about Jesus. Mark's narrative presented a platform upon which the authors of Matthew and Luke could articulate their unique ideas. Matthew and Luke saw the opportunity to write more complete lives of Jesus, bringing different structure and additional material to bear. In turn, their infancy stories stimulated further creativity, yielding the two Infancy Gospels. One text influences others. Communication creates conversations that build on one another and push ideas forward.

Discussions of form criticism throughout these essays exemplify how the simple desire to talk about Jesus forced creativity. Forms that Christians could use to structure a healing story or a clever anecdote existed. Parables, allegories, and dialogues provided ways to structure and communicate ideas, as did the *chreia*. Many more forms exist in the New Testament that were not discussed, from something as small as a definition to presenting people as moral examples to the epitome, which is a summary of a teacher's ideas. In Paul's letters, when one sees him constructing an argument for or against something, he is literally creating. The rhetorical handbooks from the Roman world label this activity *inventio*, today referred to as rhetorical invention. In all the examples enumerated, then, we witness the act of rhetoric generating creativity.

Writing and interpretation are crucial ingredients of translation, a consequential form of rhetorical creativity where the Bible is concerned. Chapter 2 provided many examples of how the move from Greek to English affected the English reader's understanding of scripture. Not only do the English words chosen affect the reader's impressions and comprehension, but also the style and formatting do so as well.

Creativity in this Book

The very fact of writing is creative. It is a form of thinking whereby ideas are tested. Each draft is a prototype in which an idea is practiced and tried, evolving with each iteration. Writing becomes a process of discovery, building momentum and bringing surprises. This happened in the writing of these essays, as the process of composition forced new ideas to come to mind. From experience, I knew this would happen. Moreover, chapter 1 purposely used the extended analogy of the Bible as a library as a device for discovery.

This discussion of creativity has sought to demystify it. Creativity does not require magic. Repeatable methods can make it happen. Diversity is one key. Socially, this implies building a diverse team of people to benefit from different social groups and varied expertise. It underscores the value of broad liberal learning and interdisciplinary cooperation.

Another essential method for innovation is to reframe a problem. This has been noted a number of times in these essays. Bringing new information to bear is an effective way of accomplishing this, as is changing the level of abstraction at which one addresses a problem. Thus, one can read Jesus' command to sell everything and give the proceeds to the poor as an ethical challenge for genuine discipleship or reframe the story economically and ask if depleting capital is an effective way to fight poverty.

The existence of such reliable approaches is good news for people who are trying to innovate and useful for those trying to understand what led to changes in the early church. Just as knowledge of historical literary forms and rhetoric help reveal how people put ideas together, so a generic knowledge of what leads to creating something new provides insight into how the early church innovated, in its thinking and in scriptures. This concluding essay, then, has one eye on history, to gain understanding about the early church, and one eye on the present, helping readers find ways and develop habits that will help them innovate as well.

Further Reading

The following reflect creative approaches within New Testament scholarship.

Betz, Hans Dieter. *Galatians: A Commentary on Paul's Letter to the Galatians*. Hermeneia. Philadelphia: Fortress Press, 1979.

Gutiérrez, Gustavo. *A Theology of Liberation: History, Politics, and Salvation*. Translated and edited by Sister Caridad Inda and John Eagleson. Maryknoll, NY: Orbis Books, 1973.

Neill, Stephen, and Tom Wright. *The Interpretation of the New Testament, 1861–1986*. 2nd ed. Oxford University Press, 1988.

Newsom, Carol A., Sharon H. Ringe, and Jacqueline E. Lapsley, eds. *Women's Bible Commentary: Revised and Updated*. 3rd ed. Louisville, KY: Westminster John Knox Press, 2012.

Sanders, E. P. *Paul and Palestinian Judaism: A Comparison of Patterns of Religion*. Philadelphia: Fortress Press, 1977.

Schüssler-Fiorenza, Elisabeth. *In Memory of Her: A Feminist Theological Reconstruction of Christian Origins*. New York: Crossroad Publishing Company, 1983.

Stinton, Diane B. *Contemporary African Christology: Voices of Contemporary Africa*. Faith and Culture Series. Orbis Books, 2004.

Trible, Phyllis. *Texts of Terror: Literary-Feminist Readings of Biblical Narratives*. Overtures to Biblical Theology. Philadelphia: Fortress Press, 1984.

The following discuss creative methods and approaches.

Dyer, Jeff, Hal Gregersen, and Clayton M. Christensen. *The Innovator's DNA: Mastering the Five Skills of Disruptive Innovators*. Boston: Harvard Business Review Press, 2011.

Erwin, Kim. *Communicating the New: Methods to Shape and Accelerate Innovation.* Hoboken, NJ: John Wiley & Sons, 2014.

Keeley, Larry, et al. *Ten Types of Innovation: The Discipline of Building Breakthroughs.* Hoboken, NJ: John Wiley & Sons, 2013.

Kumar, Vijay. *101 Design Methods: A Structured Approach for Driving Innovation in Your Organization.* Hoboken, NJ: John Wiley & Sons, 2013.

Norman, Don. *The Design of Everyday Things.* Revised and Expanded. New York: Basic Books, 2013.

Paradis, Zachary Jean, and David McGaw. *Naked Innovation.* Chicago: Institute of Design, 2007.

GLOSSARY

apocalyptse A heavenly revelation full of symbolism and concerned with God's justice.

apophthegm This Greek word refers to a terse, pointed saying, which often gave insight about life, much like a maxim. To translate it as "saying" would be too broad, so scholars use the Greek word to remain more precise about what it refers to.

apotheosis In its most common English usage, apotheosis refers to the perfect example or fulfillment of something, its apex or quintessence. As used in this book it refers specifically to divinization or deification; the elevation of a human to divine status. When a person undergoes apotheosis, he or she becomes a god or godlike.

catholic We are accustomed, today, to hearing the word *catholic* as a shorthand reference to Roman Catholicism. However, *catholic* is the transliteration of a Greek word meaning "general" or "universal"; so, in the early church, it was less a proper name—Catholic—than an actual description—the widespread communities of Christians who, together, formed a larger entity, the church.

chreia A concise report of a witty saying or action attributed to some person and suited to the person's reputation. This was a popular form at the time of the New Testament, commonly used in education.

Christ This is a transliteration of the Greek word *Christos*, which is a translation of the Hebrew word *Messiah* that, like *Christos,* means a person who is anointed. In Jewish tradition, people called to perform special service for God or country had oil poured over their heads to signify their calling, which is to say, they were anointed with oil. Christians viewed Jesus as sent by God and anointed with the divine spirit, so they gave Jesus the title of Anointed One. The Greek word became so habitually used in reference to Jesus that Anointed One became a name. In other words, *Christ* shifted from describing Jesus to serving as a second name for him.

Christology   Literally the study of Christ, this is a branch of Christian theology that investigates the person of Christ. Two common topics in Christology are the humanity and divinity of Jesus. Many different Christological views emerged throughout the early centuries of Christianity as people tried to explain how Jesus could be both human and divine. The Council of Chalcedon in 451 provided a landmark formulation of Christology. Titles that were applied to Jesus in the New Testament, e.g., Son of Man, Son of God, Son of David, Christ, or Lord, are said to be Christological titles, for they assert something about Jesus' identity and mission.

Church Fathers   Ancient and influential teachers in the church, roughly through the first six centuries. In the Orthodox traditions, important teachers have continued to be so designated. In this book, the term focuses on important figures of the ancient church whose writings still exist.

codex   The Latin word for book. It refers to folded sheets of papyrus (a stalky plant) or parchment (animal skin) that are stacked and sewn together to form a text block like a modern book. This technology was emerging during the Roman Empire when the church was coming into existence. The point of saying codex rather than book is to draw attention to the technology of the physical object, in distinction from a scroll.

Docetism   The idea that Jesus only "seemed" to be human; derived from the Greek word for "seem," *dokein*. Docetists believed, for example, that when the man Jesus suffered, the divine Christ was absent from the physical body, preserving the divinity from human sufferings. Another example of docetist belief is that Christ had no real body, only the appearance of one. The early church condemned such views as an attack on the genuine humanity of Jesus.

Eusebius   (260/265–339/340) Spent his life as a resident of Caesarea Maritima, a coastal city of Palestine, where he eventually became bishop. He wrote *Ecclesiastical History*, a narrative that presented the history of the church from the apostles to Eusebius' own day. It is hard to overestimate the importance of this work for understanding the early church. Eusebius enjoyed the good favor of the Roman emperor, Constantine, and participated in the Council of Nicaea.

form criticism Creative compositions typically use some recognizable structure, or form. Rhyme and rhythm are each examples of a form that shapes communication. A song that fits on one side of a 45 vinyl record or a symphony in four movements are additional examples of form. Scholars try to identify the forms of communication that appear in the New Testament. For example, the opening words of Paul's letters reflect the appropriate form for writing a letter in the ancient world. A short, well-expressed thought reflects the form of the maxim. Scholars try to identify forms and how and why they are used. A eulogy or a toast, for example, suggests the setting of a funeral or a celebration. Forms, likewise, can suggest what was going on in the life of the early Christians who used them. The identification and interpretation of forms is called form criticism.

Gentile Anyone who is not a Jew. The word is not a self-designation and is meaningful only in contrast to the word *Jew*, as a way of describing someone who is other than a Jew. The Greek equivalent literally refers to "the nations." Reference to Gentiles is frequent in the New Testament because the Christian faith took root in a Jewish context, which made the distinction between Jew and Gentile an important topic of discussion in the early church.

Gnosticism A view that special knowledge is necessary for salvation; it takes its name from the Greek word for knowledge, *gnōsis*. The knowledge typically involved esoteric teachings about God, the cosmos, the identity of Christ, and the true identity of one's own soul. Though what became the dominant form of Christianity regarded Gnosticism as a heresy, its practitioners probably thought of it as advanced theology. It took many forms, so scholars now talk about specific kinds of Gnosticism. In fact, many think the label Gnosticism covers too many things, creating a false impression of unity.

Irenaeus A second-century Christian who was born in Asia and moved to Gaul, where he eventually served as bishop in the city of Lugdunum (modern-day Lyon, France) and wrote many things.

Around 180 CE, he wrote a treatise in five volumes, *Against Heresies,* that attacked Christian teachers with whom he disagreed; this work provides valuable insight into the second-century church.

Jewish scriptures   See the entry under Old Testament.

Johannine   An adjective referring to four writings in the New Testament that bear the name John: the Gospel of John and three letters—I John, 2 John, and 3 John. Because of shared similarities, these four writings are referred to together as Johannine literature. The Christian group that generated these texts is referred to as the Johannine community. One could say that traditions in John's Gospel circulated among the Johannine community or that the problems reflected in 1 John tell us something about what was going on in the Johannine community (or churches). The ideas in these four writings can be referred to as Johannine theology. The Apocalypse of St. John, also known as Revelation, though attributed to a person named John, is not included in Johannine literature. Johannine applies to one Gospel and three epistles; the apocalypse is excluded.

Justin Martyr   (ca. 100–165) Born in Palestine, Justin converted to Christian faith, moved to Rome to teach, wrote a number of historically important works, and died a martyr's death. His *First Apology,* a defense of Christian faith addressed to the emperor, is particularly noteworthy.

Marcion   An important church leader of the mid-second century. Born into a wealthy family along the northern coast of modern-day Turkey, Marcion developed an extensive network of churches that respected his opinions. He believed the Old Testament taught a deficient view of God and ethics and that Christian faith had to move beyond Jewish beliefs. He used only a version of Luke's Gospel and Paul's letters. He taught these ideas in Rome, where they were opposed. He was soon rejected as a heretic and passed into church history as such, but his attempt to define what texts Christians should read are an important step in the development of the New Testament canon.

Old Testament   The first and largest portion of the Christian Bible, in contrast to the much smaller concluding section, the

New Testament. Most of the Old Testament was composed in Hebrew with a bit of Aramaic, which contrasts with the New Testament, written in Greek. The title "Old Testament" reflects a Christian point of view. For Jews, the Old Testament is simply scripture, with no prejudicial "old," and no addendum of the "new." Some people refer to the Old Testament as the "Hebrew Bible" or "Hebrew Scriptures" to avoid the Christian point of view. Contemporary Jews refer to their collection of writings as the "Tanakh," an acronym which points to its three sections: *Torah* (Teaching, the five books of Moses), *Nevi'im* (Prophets), and *Ketuvim* (Writings). The contents of the Tanakh resemble the Protestant Old Testament, but ordered and combined differently, while the Catholic Bible includes additional texts from ancient Jewish authors, some composed in Greek. The essays in this book typically refer to "Jewish scriptures" rather than "Old Testament" to avoid anachronism and reflect the broader list of Jewish texts that early Christians read.

Pentateuch The first five books of the Bible: Genesis, Exodus, Leviticus, Numbers, and Deuteronomy. These are also called the books of Moses, whom legend credits with their authorship. These five comprise the first section of the Hebrew Bible, called *Torah*, which means "teaching."

Philo A Jewish intellectual who lived in Alexandria, Egypt, and was a prolific author, writing in Greek. Alexandria was the second largest city of the Roman Empire and a significant center of learning. Philo (20 BCE–50 CE) was born before and died later than Jesus.

Q An abbreviation of the German word, *Quelle*, which means "source." Q is a document in the early church both the authors of Matthew and Luke are believed to have used when they composed their Gospels. This document no longer exists; it is only hypothetical. Scholars infer its existence because of similarities between Matthew and Luke that cannot be explained by their common knowledge of Mark's Gospel. By definition, the contents of Q are materials that appear in both Matthew and Luke but are absent from Mark. It is believed that Q contained (mostly) sayings by Jesus, so it is called a "sayings source."

redaction criticism A method of biblical study that examines the editorial history of a text. The word *redact* means "edit." When the government releases documents on national security or legal matters, for example, it may cross out sensitive information. The documents are then referred to as *redacted*. In studying the New Testament, scholars seek to understand how writers have edited the sources they use. For example, how did the author of Matthew use and change the Gospel of Mark? In answering such questions, scholars look for how Matthew edited, or redacted, Mark.

Septuagint Translations of Jewish scriptures into Greek, made in the three centuries before Jesus. *Septuagint* is the Latin word for seventy and stems from a legend that 72 (or 70) Jewish scholars worked together in Egypt to produce an official, single translation. The Roman numeral for seventy, LXX, is commonly used as shorthand for the Septuagint.

Signs Source (or **Gospel of Signs**) Scholars hypothesize that one of the sources for the Gospel of John was a written text that recounted a number of miracles performed by Jesus. This text does not exist; its ancient existence is proposed as a solution to the problems of the origins of John's Gospel and its differences from the Synoptic Gospels. Many interpreters accept this hypothesis.

Synoptic Gospels Specifically, the Gospels of Matthew, Mark, and Luke. The word *synoptic*, "to see things together," is applied to these three Gospels because of their significant similarities.

Synoptic Problem Why do the Gospels of Matthew, Mark, and Luke look so much alike, when gospels in general are often very different? This question poses the Synoptic Problem. Proposed solutions typically say that one Gospel copied from another. One theory suggests Matthew was written first, and Mark abridged it. Among the many other possible views, the most common holds that Mark came first, then Matthew and Luke independently expanded it.

Tatian (ca. 120–185) An Assyrian who converted to Christianity, studied with Justin Martyr in Rome, and eventually returned to Assyria (perhaps Iraq, though more broadly the area of the Fertile Crescent), where he led an influential school. He wrote the *Diatessaron*, in which he took what is known as the four canonical Gospels and wove them into a single story. The *Diatessaron* would become the version of the Gospel read in Syriac-speaking churches for more than two hundred years.

Torah This Hebrew word means "teaching." It specifically denotes the first five books of the Hebrew Bible. See the entries under Old Testament and Pentateuch.

transliteration Replacing the letters of a foreign word with the comparable letters of one's own language, as opposed to translating, which offers comparable meaning in one's own language. Transliteration is necessary for referencing words from a language that uses a different alphabet. Since the Bible was written in Hebrew, Aramaic, and Greek, any word borrowed (as opposed to translated) from those languages by English has to have its letters exchanged. For example, the Greek word Χριστός is transliterated into English by replacing the Greek letters with their English approximations, yielding, *Christos*, which was turned into the English word *Christ*. Similarly, ἀπόστολος is transliterated as *apostolos*, from which English invented the word *apostle*.

INDEX